Borderlands Curanderos

D1520487

Borderlands Curanderos

The Worlds of Santa Teresa Urrea and Don Pedrito Jaramillo

JENNIFER KOSHATKA SEMAN

University of Texas Press *Austin*

Requests for permission to reproduce material from this work should be sent to:
    Permissions
    University of Texas Press
    P.O. Box 7819
    Austin, TX 78713–7819
    utpress.utexas.edu/rp-form

♾ The paper used in this book meets the minimum requirements of
ANSI/NISO Z39.48–1992 (R1997) (Permanence of Paper).

Library of Congress Cataloging-in-Publication Data
Names: Seman, Jennifer Koshatka, author.
Title: Borderlands curanderos : the worlds of Santa Teresa Urrea and Don Pedrito
    Jaramillo / Jennifer Koshatka Seman.
Description: First edition. | Austin : University of Texas Press, 2021. | Includes
    bibliographical references and index.
Identifiers: LCCN 2020019513
    ISBN 978-1-4773-2191-1 (cloth)
    ISBN 978-1-4773-2192-8 (paperback)
    ISBN 978-1-4773-2193-5 (library ebook)
    ISBN 978-1-4773-2194-2 (non-library ebook)
Subjects: LCSH: Urrea, Teresa. | Jaramillo, Pedro, 1829–1907. | Healers—Mexican-
    American Border Region—Biography. | Spiritual healing—Mexican-American
    Border Region—History. | Mexican-American Border Region—History.
Classification: LCC BT732.56.U77 S46 2021 | DDC 615.8/520922721—dc23
LC record available at https://lccn.loc.gov/2020019513

doi:10.7560/321911

Contents

Borderlands Curanderos

Borderlands Curanderos: The Worlds of Santa Teresa Urrea and Don Pedrito Jaramillo

Don Pedrito Please
I come in need please
Help us get our money back from where they ripped us off
An[d] please help my boyfriend get hired at Walmart
We really need the money for our children an[d] please help us get a trailer
house
Keep my Father an[d] family in good health
An[d] keep my friend strong
FROM A NOTE FOUND AT THE DON PEDRITO JARAMILLO SHRINE IN 2014

These words, written on a torn piece of paper and tacked onto a wall in a humble shrine in rural South Texas, reveal the modest dreams of one believer in the power of deceased curandero Don Pedrito Jaramillo. In 1880, Don Pedro Jaramillo—or Don Pedrito, as he was popularly known—crossed the border from Mexico into Texas, where he practiced *curanderismo*, an earth-based healing practice that blends elements of Indigenous medicine with folk Catholicism. The shrine, located approximately 120 miles north of the international border with Mexico, houses Don Pedrito's tombstone. Inside, there is an altar, usually topped with rows of burning candles all bearing the same black and white image of his face, casting shadows on whitewashed walls decorated with crucifixes, statues of the Virgin Mary, and a banner proclaiming "We support our Troops." One of the walls is almost completely covered with notes like the one quoted above, all addressed to Don Pedrito.

The wall of notes is transfixing. Some notes are in Spanish, some in English; some are furiously scrawled on torn scraps of brown paper bags as if the writer was sinking in quicksand while on break at the grocery store. There are notes on lined paper, on notepads bearing the logos of drug companies offering scientific remedies for illnesses, and stationery declaring "America the Beautiful." These notes prayerfully ask Don Pedrito to cure cancer, restore employment, save an alcoholic spouse, reunite families, guide wayward children, or simply "take evil away." A frayed tapestry several layers deep, the wall of notes is a scrapbook of sorts that provides a glimpse into the hopes, longings, and American dreams of those who stop at the shrine with faith that Don Pedrito will answer their prayers.

On a warm summer evening in 2011—seven hundred miles west of the Don Pedrito Jaramillo Shrine, in the border city of El Paso—a local museum and community center, El Museo Urbano, is celebrating the curandera Santa Teresa Urrea. Like Don Pedrito, Santa Teresa was a curandera, a Mexican faith healer and folk saint, unsanctioned by the institution of professional medicine or the Catholic Church. As a curandera and folk saint (*santa*), she healed those in El Paso and other areas of the borderlands on the margins of power. On this night, El Museo Urbano, the former residence of Teresa when she lived in El Paso in 1896, was celebrating its grand opening. The sounds of Tejano and techno music filled the dry desert air as many of the nearly five hundred in attendance stopped to take in the murals painted on the sides of the building featuring larger than life representations of Santa Teresa, Pancho Villa, and the Mexican anarchist brothers Ricardo and Enrique Flores-Magón. Inside, it is a joyous cacophony of color and light, resounding with the voices of people speaking Spanish and English. Pictures of Santa Teresa adorn the brightly colored walls, a shrine shimmers with light from candles that illuminate statues of saints and bundles of herbs celebrating Teresa's curanderismo, and senior visitors from this community share memories with historians from the University of Texas at El Paso.[1] Although she lived in El Paso for only a year, Teresa's curanderismo made a deep impression on the historical memory of this neighborhood. Painted on the wall of El Museo on that opening night: "Her medicine is still strong."

Located in El Paso's historic Segundo Barrio neighborhood, El Museo is nestled amongst a handful of cottages, small apartment complexes, and low-slung industrial buildings now in their second and third winds of use. Segundo Barrio is a culturally vibrant neighborhood where people still celebrate Santa Teresa, and community activity mirrors the occasional splashes of brilliant orange, yellow, and purple paint giving life to walls built long ago. The neighborhood is occupied primarily by ethnic Mexicans and serves as a way station for immigrants crossing the border from Juárez. It has also been an important location for many political and cultural movements, including the Mexican Revolution.[2]

Figure 0.1. Don Pedrito Jaramillo Shrine, 1109 FM 1218, Falfurrias, Texas. On Friday, February 14, 2020, the shrine was vandalized. The statues of Don Pedrito and saints, crucifixes, and other sacred items were destroyed. This crime devastated many in the community and is still under investigation. Some members of the community have come together to help restore it, including two artists who have replastered and restored the smashed Don Pedrito statues. Photo taken by author in March 2019.

These curanderos, Teresa Urrea (1873–1906) and Pedro Jaramillo (1829–1907), crossed the border from Mexico into the United States during the late nineteenth century and practiced curanderismo in borderlands communities from the South Texas Río Grande Valley to El Paso and San Francisco. Through their practice of Mexican faith healing, they provided culturally resonant healing and spiritual sustenance to ethnic Mexicans, Indigenous peoples, Tejanos, and others in the borderlands who faced increasingly oppressive, exclusionary, and sometimes violent forms of state power deployed by both nations. The two healers attained popularity and fame for their curanderismo during their lives, and their adherents unofficially beatified them as living saints, or "folk saints." As curanderos and folk saints, unsanctioned by the Catholic Church, Santa Teresa and Don Pedrito provided, in the words of Frank Graziano, "extraordinary creative responses to deprivation and the failure of institutions."[3]

Figure 0.2. El Museo Urbano, 500 South Oregon Street, El Paso, Texas. This photo was taken by the author at the opening party in May 2011.

It was their extraordinary responses to the failure of institutions that made Santa Teresa and Don Pedrito threats—and, in some cases, assets—to state and institutional authority. Don Pedrito practiced his curanderismo on the far eastern Texas-Mexico border in the Río Grande Valley, where he healed and fed drought-stricken Tejanos at a time when the state and modern medicine could not meet their needs. Santa Teresa healed Mexican peasants as well as Yaquis, Mayos, and other Indigenous people while she spoke of a Mexico in which people did not have to obey unjust laws or confess their sins to Catholic priests. For this, she was expelled from Mexico by President Porfirio Díaz in 1890. Don Pedrito was investigated by the American Medical Association and the US Federal Post Office for fraudulent practices in 1899, yet he was also used by state authorities to distribute resources during a drought. *Borderlands Curanderos: The Worlds of Santa Teresa Urrea and Don Pedrito Jaramillo* examines how, in the US-Mexico borderlands at the turn of the twentieth century, these two popular curanderos practiced a kind of medicine that did not come from the state, the church, or professional medicine, but from below—from curanderismo, a distinct cultural practice that revitalizes sick bodies, minds, and spirits. Their biographies provide a compelling jumping-off place to examine what Mexican American curanderismo achieved not only in individual bodies, but in the social body as well.

The medicine practiced by Don Pedrito and Santa Teresa (sometimes referred to by the nickname "Teresita") was, and remains, a hybrid system of healing practiced throughout Mexico and Latin America, and in places where ethnic Mexicans have a strong presence, such as the US-Mexico borderlands.[4] While it is important to note that curanderismo is not a static cultural practice, but has changed over time and has always varied depending on where it is being practiced and who is practicing, it emerged from a history shared by Europeans, Native Americans, and Africans, and common themes originating in the colonial period to the present persist, informing the practice of curanderismo up to the present.[5]

The word *curanderismo* comes from the Spanish verb *curar*, meaning "to cure" or "to heal." Composed of a set of folk medical beliefs, Indigenous and Catholic rituals, and practices that address people's psychological, spiritual, social, and health needs, curanderismo encompasses a range of healing techniques held together with an overarching belief in the connectedness of the body, mind, and spirit, and most important, that the curandero heals through the power of God.

In the Americas, curanderismo emerged from the contact between the "Old" and "New" Worlds—that is, between European cultures and the Indigenous empires of the Americas.[6] Spanish religious beliefs and medical ideology blended many different elements, including the Christian belief in an all-powerful God who influences the actions of sinful humans and demands ritual (symbolic) sacrifice; Greek and Arabic scientific notions about the four bodily humors; and European witchcraft, with its mixture of magic, nature, and feminine healing. In the New World, Spanish conquistadors and colonizers were met with equally sophisticated, if different, systems of spirituality and healing practiced by a variety of Indigenous groups.

A story that serves as one of the likely origins of curanderismo in the borderlands is that of Álvar Núñez Cabeza de Vaca, a Spaniard who, along with three others, survived a failed expedition of New World conquest and spent six years in captivity among various Native people along the Texas-Mexico borderlands from 1528 to 1536.[7] He survived his captivity, in part, by becoming a curandero. Cabeza de Vaca wrote a *relación* (report) providing an account of this failed conquest and period of captivity. In it he describes how he and his fellow survivors—two Spaniards and one enslaved African—traveled by foot as captives across a region that today we call the

US-Mexico borderlands. However, in the sixteenth century, the map looked different than it does today. This region—like most of those in the Americas—was populated with Indigenous people and marked by their pathways. The nations of Mexico and the United States did not exist. These were lands of the Capoque, Yaqui, Han, Quevene, Mariame, Avavare, Susola, and other Indigenous people: rival groups onto which Spain projected its aspirations of empire. Along this journey, these stranded survivors of a failed conquest were passed between various tribes who kept them alive by feeding them, providing shelter, sharing resources—and demanding they become healers. As they traversed this unknown land as captives, these Spanish strangers possessed none of those instruments of power associated with conquistadors such as Hernán Cortés and Francisco Pizarro. All they had were their hands, breath, and words. They used these—at the command of their Indigenous captors—to heal.

At first, Cabeza de Vaca laughed at his captors' suggestion that they heal, telling them it was a "mockery" to make of them physicians because they "did not know how to cure."[8] Their captors refused to take no for answer. In fact, Cabeza de Vaca recounts that "they took our food until we did as they told us."[9] In their newly appointed role as healers, the castaways blended what they knew of healing from the Iberian Peninsula with careful observations of Indigenous healers. In his *relación*, Cabeza de Vaca first describes a significant aspect of the Native way of healing.

> The manner in which they perform cures is as follows: on becoming sick, they call a physician and after being cured they not only give him everything they possess, but they also seek things to give him from among their relatives.[10]

This description reveals the ritualistic exchange patterns that constituted an important part of healing in the Indigenous world.[11] Importantly, Cabeza de Vaca and his fellow castaways were integrated into this ritual exchange network by their captors.

Another distinctive feature of healing in the Indigenous world was a view of nature as sacred, alive, and filled with the power to heal.[12] Cabeza de Vaca recounts that one of his captors attempted to explain the healing power of nature to him: "the stones and other things that the fields produce have powers, and that he, by placing a hot stone on the abdomen, restored health and removed pain. . . ."[13] The sacredness and significance of nature to Native healing practices in this early encounter inform understandings of curanderismo in the nineteenth-century world of Don Pedrito (who used water as a healing agent) and Santa Teresa (who used dirt and salvia to heal), and even today in the practices of curandera Danielle López, who uses all of the elements—earth, fire, air, and water—in her *limpias* (cleansings), as the forthcoming chapters will show.[14]

Cabeza de Vaca also used Catholic ritual and symbols to heal, such as the sign of the cross and prayer. He blew on the sick body, something he had witnessed Indigenous healers do, yet something he may also have witnessed some healers do where he was from on the Iberian Peninsula. While he noted the distinctive aspects of Indigenous healing in his *relación*, he also noticed things he may have recognized from his world.

> What the physician does is to make some incisions where the sick person has pain, and then sucks all around them. They perform cauterizations with fire, which is a thing among them considered to be very effective, and I have tried it and it turned out well for me. And after this, they blow upon the area that hurts, and with this they believe that they have removed the malady.[15]

What Cabeza de Vaca describes the Native physician doing—making incisions, sucking, blowing on the body—are things he may have observed a certain kind of faith healer in Spain do, a *saludador* who would "heal with the saliva from their mouths or with their breath, saying certain words."[16] Saludadores could also heal "by means of suction," and they would travel from place to place "blessing the cattle that are presented to him gathered in a meadow and saluting them with his breath in the name of God."[17] It was understood that a saludador cured "by grace," by a gift of healing bestowed on them by the supernatural. This gift of grace was something that both Don Pedrito and Santa Teresa were said to have possessed. They called it the *don*, the gift. When Cabeza de Vaca witnessed his Native captors healing, he recognized healers, curanderos, from his homeland. He combined what he saw in this strange new world with what he already knew.

> The manner in which we performed cures was by making the sign of the cross over them and blowing on them, and praying a Pater Noster and an Ave Maria, and as best we could, beseeching our Lord God that he grant them health and move them to treat us well.[18]

In this healing, an Iberian Catholic world is mapped onto an Indigenous American one, just as an Indigenous American world is mapped onto an Iberian one. In the encounters between Native Americans, Spaniards, and Africans that took place on the American continents during the sixteenth century, new creations emerged when different peoples were forced to adapt to one another in order to survive. These adaptations led to a syncretic healing practice: curanderismo. Cabeza de Vaca's story, then, reveals important aspects of curanderismo that persist to this day: the centrality of ritual exchange to Native healing and curanderismo, the important place of Catholicism in curanderismo, and how the blending of a variety of healing strategies and techniques characterizes border medicine.

Scholars who have studied medical cultures in colonial Latin America have demonstrated how, throughout the sixteenth and seventeenth centuries, following the captivity of Cabeza de Vaca, this borderlands region and all of New Spain became a "society of hybridism and admixture, in which Europeans, Asians, Africans, and Indians mingle and compete for space and resources . . . not a place of nicely delineated borders where the spaces of indigenous inhabitants could be clearly differentiated from those of the newly arrived. Instead, it was a place of juxtaposition, of 'contacts and layering.'"[19] Even throughout the colonial period in Mexico—when curanderos were often pursued, tried, and punished by the Inquisition—the curanderos'

> knowledge and skills contributed to the health of the oppressed and led to the formation of a traditional mestizo medicine that syncretized Indian, black, and Spanish folk medicines . . . confirming the important social function of traditional medicine and its practitioners who offered a solution to the health problems of the majority of the population of colonial Mexico.[20]

Cultures merged as Spanish physicians in the colonial period (and after) appropriated maguey, cacao, and other local plants and remedies into their treatments, even as they deemed Indigenous practices inferior, dangerous, and criminal.[21]

From the Spanish colonial period through the period of the Mexican–American War (1846–1848)—when half of Mexico became the United States, and the border was drawn between them—cross-cultural contact and negotiations continued to inform the healing practices and politics of both nations and this borderlands region. However, the colonial legacy, especially the legacy of conquest and slavery, would have a lasting effect on the practice of curanderismo—how it was practiced, whom it healed, and the kinds of illnesses it treated. With the Spaniards' introduction of African slave labor to the New World, West African belief systems fused with Indigenous and European traditions, and these distinct cultures found points of common ground. For example, one belief shared across all three cultures—African, European, and Native American—is one that curanderismo attends to: that the soul can be lost.

What Western allopathic medicine today describes as depression, anxiety, and conditions such as post-traumatic stress disorder (PTSD)—psychological states that can result from emotional and physical trauma—curanderismo calls *susto*. Loosely translated, susto means "fright," but its deeper meaning is "soul loss" or "soul sickness." Symptoms might include stomach pain, loss of appetite, lethargy, anxiousness, or a feeling that something is missing— that you are not fully present in your own body.[22] Curanderos treat susto by calling the soul back to the body through rituals, prayers, and herbal remedies. As mentioned above, Danielle López is a practicing curandera in the Río Grande Valley region of Texas. She describes how she understands this condition: "In curanderismo we know the root of sickness is a broken, unbalanced, unreleased feeling separating us from connecting with the nature of our earth mother and father."[23] López uses a variety of treatments, or *remedios*, to heal her clients, to reconnect them to the earth: *limpias* (spiritual cleansings), *barridas* (sweeping the body), *pláticas* (conversations), and herbal remedies. According to Gonzo Flores, a curandero from South Texas (and the current owner of the Don Pedrito Jaramillo Shrine), curanderismo is "the medicine of the twenty-first century where no one questions the mind body separation/connection . . . no one questions the affects of PTSD on the body."[24] One influential curandera, Elena Avila, connects her healing to larger historical processes, in particular the history of colonialism, out of which curanderismo was born. She explains, "There was a need to develop a medicine that could heal the pain and immense *susto*, soul loss, that resulted from the cultural destruction, enslavement, and rape that occurred during the Spanish conquest of the Americas."[25] This book, *Borderlands Curanderos*, shows how Teresa Urrea and Pedro Jaramillo treated illnesses and sustos in individual bodies (as Danielle López and Gonzo Flores do) and also illnesses in the social body—the "immense" susto that Avila describes as originating in the colonial era but continuing into the nineteenth century through discriminatory attitudes and policies aimed at ethnic Mexicans and Indigenous people in the borderlands.

The literature on curanderismo comes from a variety of disciplines. Religious studies scholars, historians, anthropologists, and practicing curanderos have all contributed important work that has enlarged our understanding of this topic. One of the most recent works, by religious studies scholar Brett Hendrickson, emphasizes its appeal across cultures, especially to Anglo Americans.[26] Scholarship by anthropologists focuses on curanderismo as an ethnic Mexican cultural practice and its Indigenous roots.[27] Practicing curanderos—including Elena Avila, Eliseo "Cheo" Torres, and Ricardo Carrillo—use their perspectives as healers to demonstrate how this healing practice has benefitted, and continues to benefit, Mexican American, Indigenous, and even Anglo communities in the United States.[28] This book is indebted to this scholarship, as it provides the entry point into this subject and grounding in the meaning that curanderismo has for many Mexican Americans and some Indigenous people as well.

The two curanderos who are the subject of this book, Teresa Urrea and Don Pedrito Jaramillo, are represented unevenly in their own respective literatures. Teresa has been the subject of not only historical scholarship produced in Mexico and the United States, but also fiction, most famously Luis Alberto Urrea's novels that provide compelling narratives of her life in Mexico (*The Hummingbird's Daughter*) and her life after she left and lived in the United States (*The Queen of America*).[29] Mexican historians have written a great deal about Teresa and her connection to the Tomóchic Rebellion of 1891–1892. An important event in Mexican history, the rebellion arose in the small mountain pueblo of Tomóchic in the Mexican border state of Chihuahua, whose residents fought the forces of the Mexican government and the Catholic Church to defend their right to worship in their own way—in this case, a charismatic mass that focused on Teresa—and not submit to the orders of priests.[30] Less attention has been paid to Teresa's activity among the Yaqui and Mayo people, with whom she lived, or her involvement with Mexican Spiritists. The scholarship on Teresa after the period of the Tomóchic Rebellion—when she lived in the United States, from 1892 to her death in 1906—focuses mainly on the various meanings that writers and scholars have attached to her as a "borderlands saint," yet historians have overlooked her California experiences and what her transnational identities meant to her and others in the borderlands.[31] Chapters 1 and 2 attempt to fill this gap by historicizing Teresa Urrea in the Indigenous, liberal, and transnational political and spiritual milieus she moved within during this period. This analysis illuminates transatlantic political as well as medico-spiritual currents moving through Europe, Mexico, and the United States at the turn of the twentieth century through the dynamic life of a transnational curandera, *santa*, and *espiritista*.

Don Pedrito Jaramillo, on the other hand, has not received much scholarly attention at all. Except for anthropologist Octavio Romano's insightful 1964 dissertation, which contextualizes him as a folk saint occupying the top position of an ethnic Mexican "healing hierarchy," there are only a handful of book chapters, theses, and articles, which are mostly descriptive.[32] Chapters 3 and 4 flesh out Don Pedrito's history more fully by focusing on the eastern end of the US-Texas borderland, the South Texas Río Grande Valley, where the conflict between folk medicine and professional medicine was part of a larger conflict between ethnic Mexicans and the dominant Anglo culture. In this context, Don Pedrito provided an alluring alternative to costly professional medicine and a refuge from increasingly racist, anti-Mexican attitudes. Even after his death, he remained part of a larger conversation within borderlands communities about what it means to be Mexican, Mexican American, and Tejano.

In addition to the literature on curanderismo and the scholarship on individual healers, a significant body of work from Chicana scholars and Mexican American religious scholars—including Desirée A. Martin, Yolanda Chávez Leyva, Marian Perales, Gillian E. Newell, and Luis León—has examined curanderismo and folk saints in terms of what it means to community identity formation.[33] *Borderlands Curanderos* is in dialogue with this work, as well as scholarship in the fields of borderlands history, Texas history, Mexican history, and the history of medicine that touches upon medico-spiritual healing practices and state power. Scholarship that has examined the way the state and powerful institutions such as public health agencies have affected the less powerful inhabitants of the borderlands—especially the work of Mark Goldberg, Nicole Guidotti-Hernández, John Mckiernan-González, and Natalia Molina—has also been very influential.[34] Inspired by this work, *Borderlands Curanderos* engages these same themes, but from the subaltern perspectives of Santa Teresa and Don Pedrito. It shows how—through their curanderismo and their interactions with spiritual movements, professional medicine, and the state—they both provided refuge, healing, and spiritual inspiration for ethnic Mexicans and Indigenous people faced with increasingly oppressive, exclusionary, and violent state power.

Borderlands Curanderos brings together the "small worlds" of Santa Teresa and Don Pedrito, as well as the larger transnational worlds they lived in, and examines how they informed one another.[35] The chapters that follow examine how from the mid-nineteenth century to the early twentieth, three overlapping and intertwined transformations took place across the globe: the rise of scientific professional medicine; a spiritual movement heralding the progress of humanity through the "science of the spirits"; and nation-building projects that sought to expand and solidify borders while modernizing and unifying the citizenry under one national identity. These transformations influenced Santa Teresa and Don Pedrito, and they, in turn, helped shape them. Their stories demonstrate that it is not only hegemonic powers such as the state and professional institutions that support communities and build and maintain nations and national identities, but so do those less obviously powerful, including borderlands curanderos.

PART I

SANTA TERESA URREA

CHAPTER 1

The Mexican Joan of Arc: Healing and Resistance in the US-Mexico Borderlands

In the early morning hours of August 12, 1896, forty Yaquis and Mexicans crossed the border from Nogales, Arizona, to Nogales, Sonora, shouting "¡Viva la Santa de Cabora!" as they attacked the *aduana* (customs house) in an attempt to overthrow the Mexican government of Porfirio Díaz.[1] These rebels called themselves Teresistas, after the young woman who inspired their revolt: Teresa Urrea, a popular curandera known as Santa Teresa, La Santa de Cabora, by her followers. She was exiled from Mexico because she healed Yaquis (and others) while speaking out against the Díaz government's attempts to take Yaqui lands for foreign investment and development. Some of the Teresistas were found with photographs of her and letters. One fallen rebel had a picture of Santa Teresa tied up in mosquito netting and pink ribbon. He must have believed that she would protect and revitalize him, just as she did when she healed by laying on of hands or applying mud, saliva, salves, and herbs to broken and sick bodies.[2] Empowered by Santa Teresa, the Teresistas launched their attack on the Nogales *aduana* from the US, just two and a half miles from the border. Their goal was to take guns and ammunition in order to overthrow the Mexican government. Although they held the *aduana* for several hours, they were eventually overcome by the combined efforts of local, state, and national forces from Mexico and the United States.

In an impressive display of binational state power, the two countries came together to fight the Teresistas, who killed seven Mexican officials in their attack on the *aduana*. The US War Department sent two companies of the army's Twenty-fourth Infantry from Fort Huachuca to join the local Arizona militia. The Mexican government deployed the *gendermeria fiscal* (customs guard), led by Col. Emilio Kosterlitsky; the cavalry from Guaymas, Sonora; and the local police force in Nogales, Sonora. In addition,

Resultado del asalto en Nogales, sobre la línea mejicana, de los indios fanaticos de la Santa de Cabora, el 12 de Agosto de 1896.

Figure 1.1. "Resultado del Asalto en Nogales" (Result of the Attack in Nogales), August 12, 1896. The caption under this photograph of the bodies of seven dead Yaqui Teresista rebels lined up against the Nogales customs house warns: "Results of the attack on Nogales, on the Mexican line, of the fanatic Indians of the Saint of Cabora, August 12, 1896." Arizona Historical Society, #44475.

armed citizen-vigilantes from both nations joined the effort to suppress the Teresistas.[3] In the days following the insurrection, a picture of seven Yaqui Teresistas killed by these forces circulated widely in newspapers and government files on both sides of the border. The caption describes the dead Yaquis as "los indios fanáticos de la Santa de Cabora," and said they lacked all sense of civility and honor because they left "their dead scattered on all sides of the customs house."[4] Yet the agents of the state took care to gather the dead bodies and arrange them in a neat row so that they would fit within the frame of the photograph—a warning about what happens when Indigenous people challenge state power, whether Mexican or US.

The photograph of the dead Yaqui Teresistas was eerily reminiscent of one taken in the United States just six years earlier, in 1890, of the dead bodies of Lakota Indians stacked in a large ditch in Wounded Knee Creek, South Dakota. They had been massacred by the Seventh Cavalry Regiment of the US Army for engaging in the Ghost Dance resistance movement. In 1889, federal Indian policy called for redistribution of Lakota lands for Anglo homesteaders, railroads, and other business interests, as well as the removal of the Lakota from tribal encampments to single-family farms. In response, the Minneconjou and Hunkpapa Lakota joined the pan-Indian messianic Ghost Dance movement, inspired by the visions and teachings of Wovoka, a Paiute man. One of its ultimate goals was for the Great Spirit to bring back the near-extinct buffalo, but participants also believed they could destroy the white man by dancing the Ghost Dance and returning to traditional ways.[5] The photo of the dead Yaqui Teresistas, like the one of the massacred Lakotas surrounded by soldiers from the Seventh Cavalry, sent a clear message: the Mexican government, like that of the United States, would not brook resistance and was willing to exterminate Indigenous people within its borders in exchange for progress and development.[6]

Porfirio Díaz (president of Mexico from 1876 to 1880, and 1884 to 1911) wanted the Yaqui people of northwestern Mexico to open up their sacred homeland to colonization and subordinate their tribal identity and culture to economic development and Mexican state-building. Díaz wanted to colonize fertile Yaqui homelands with Mexicans and other foreigners, as well

Figure 1.2. "Burial of the Dead at the Battle of Wounded Knee, S.D.," ca. January 17, 1891, https://www.loc.gov/item/2007681010/.

as foreign capital, to assist modernization and development of the Mexican countryside. Like US president Benjamin Harrison—who demanded the "Absorption of Indians into our national life not as Indians but as American Citizens," and who stated that this would be achieved "peacefully if they will, forcibly if they must"—President Díaz wanted to make the Yaqui, who had for centuries insisted upon their own distinct identity, "Mexican."[7] He came to learn that they would not willingly give up their identity as a people nor leave their sacred homelands. As early as 1886, ten years before the Teresista Rebellion, Díaz finally grasped how important their identity and homeland were to the Yaqui. He stated that his program to coerce them would be "equivalent . . . to initiating a war of extermination, because the Indian prefers death to exile, and faced with the prospect of being driven from his home, he will fight to the death."[8]

On both sides of the border the Yaqui Teresistas faced governments that would not respect their rights and claims to sovereignty within the larger nation-states. Both the Mexican and US governments sought to take Indigenous lands for economic development as well as make Native people assimilate a national identity rather than a tribal one. In both nations, spiritual visionaries inspired and supported Indigenous resistance to this form of state power.

Santa Teresa witnessed the treatment of Yaquis by the Mexican government. She openly spoke about this to reporters when she tried to explain that Yaquis were not "indios fanáticos" acting at her behest, but people with a history of struggle against violent state power: "My father employed them on his hacienda and I knew and loved them. I have seen the many wrongs. Before my eyes children not three years old have been lynched, hanged from trees . . . by order of the military commander of the Sonora District to keep the Yaquis down."[9] She was not exaggerating. Starting in 1902 the Mexican government under Porfirio Díaz instituted a policy of punishing the Yaquis who rebelled against government policy by deporting them, including women and children, to the Yucatán—more than 1,400 miles from Sonora—to work as slaves in the henequen fields. Those who resisted deportation were killed.[10] However, state-sanctioned violence against the Yaqui had gone on long before this new phase of Yaqui policy was put into effect, as Teresa knew. Mistreatment of the Yaqui would continue to provide evidence of the unjust and corrupt Mexican government under Díaz.[11] It is in this context that Santa Teresa emerged as an advocate for Indigenous people of her region—the Yaqui, Mayo, and Tehueco—and a voice against their unjust treatment by the government: "Do you wonder why the tribe fights the forces of such a government? My poor Indians! They are the bravest and most persecuted people on earth. There are so few of them left."[12]

Who was this young woman who spoke these powerful and compassionate words? How was it that she inspired such resistance among the Indigenous peoples of northwestern Mexico? And what made Teresa—a kind and benevolent healer, a curandera—so dangerous to the Mexican government that she was expelled from the country? Even after her expulsion, when she lived on the US side of the border, Teresa was kept under surveillance by the Mexican government (often with the cooperation of US agents) to make sure she did not inspire any further rebellion in Mexico. To answer these questions, it is important, first, to note that regardless of the role she actually played in the rebellion, the 1896 Teresista Rebellion was associated with Teresa for the rest of her life. In fact, it came to be a part of her public identity, as the titles of articles about her in the press indicate. She was described as "the Joan of Arc of the Yaquis," "the Celebrated Mexican Healer Whose Powers Awe the Warlike Yaquis," and perhaps most famously, "the Mexican Joan of Arc." Second, in order to comprehend how she could at once be dangerous to the Mexican government and a *santa* for the people, one must consider the source of her healing power: the *don*.

The Gift

The conception of Niña García María Rebecca Chávez (later known as Teresa Urrea) and the way she received her *don*, the special gift to heal, reveal both the patriarchal world that she was born into and the Indigenous and political worlds she would become deeply embedded in. Niña García María Rebecca was born in 1873 in Ocoroni, Sinaloa, Mexico, to Cayetana Chávez, a fourteen-year-old Tehueco, on the dirt floor of a ramada, a kind of cabin or shack where laborers who worked on Mexican ranches and haciendas lived. Her father, Don Tomás Urrea, was the owner of the hacienda that employed Cayetana's father as a vaquero, or ranch hand. Cayetana herself may have been working as a *criada* (a house servant, or *casa chica*) for Don Tomás's uncle, Miguel Urrea, on a nearby ranch. The sources are a bit unclear on Cayetana'a exact position in relation to Don Tomás; however, what is clear is that she was a young Indigenous woman in a much less powerful position than the wealthy *hacendado* Don Tomás Urrea.[13] The relationship between Cayetana and Don Tomás reveals the patriarchal dynamic that prevailed in rural western Mexico at this time, especially in the relations be-

Figure 1.3. "Santa Teresa Urrea—healer (a Mexican girl)." This photograph of Teresa Urrea was taken when she was sixteen or seventeen, shortly after she received her *don*. It was purchased by Mr. J. B. Anderson in Nogales, Arizona, in 1890, two years before Teresa moved there, demonstrating her popularity and cross-border and cross-cultural appeal. Arizona Historical Society, Rare Portraits, #6522; original card printed by White & Lindsley, Nogales, Arizona.

tween hacendados and their Indigenous workers. Don Tomás was known to have fathered many children—both with his wife and women and girls who worked for him, including Cayetana Chávez. In fact, Don Tomás's legal wife, Loreta Esceverría, the mother of ten of his children, lived on a different ranch while Don Tomás kept a common-law wife, Gabriel Cantúa, a fifteen-year-old mestiza from a nearby ranch, in his household.[14] In interviews, Teresa described her parentage this way: "I am not a legitimate child. My mother was only fourteen when I was born. My father has eighteen children and my mother four, and not one of them is my own brother or sister."[15]

Some authors suggest the conception of María Rebecca Chávez was the result of rape.[16] Whether that was the case or not may be impossible to know. But it is certain that her father, Don Tomás, was in a position to use his power to exploit the vulnerability of Cayetana. That is to say, María Rebecca Chávez was born in a place and time where women, especially Native women working as *criadas* for Mexicans, may have felt they had little choice but to accept the sexual advances of a comparatively powerful hacendado like Don Tomás. Compliance was most likely expected behavior for young Native and mestizo girls like Cayetana.[17]

Until she was sixteen, María Rebecca Chávez lived in servant quarters near the Urrea ranch in Ocoroni, Sinaloa, with her mother and aunt, half brothers and sisters, and cousins. There she lived the traditional life of the Tehueco, a tribe in the Cahita linguistic group who, along with the Yaqui and Mayo of this region, had been farming the Fuerte River Valley since before the arrival of the Spaniards in the sixteenth century. After centuries of colonization by the Spanish and then the Mexican state, in the late nineteenth century these Indigenous people mostly worked as house servants and field workers for wealthy hacendados like Don Tomás Urrea, who came from a family drawing their lineage back to Spain as Christian Moors, or *moriscos*.[18] However, after growing up with her Tehueco family—where, some sources say, she was teased and shamed by some relatives for her light skin, which indicated her non-Indigenous father and the illicit union between her mother and Don Tomás—at sixteen María Rebecca Chávez was welcomed into her father's "legitimate" family at Rancho de Cabora.[19] Somewhere along the way she acquired the name "Teresa," but she was often called Teresista, a nickname commonly used in Sinaloan Indigenous communities.[20] Eventually she would be known only as Teresa Urrea, her father's name, discarding the name her mother gave her.

At Rancho de Cabora, Teresa was drawn to the curandera employed at the ranch, an older mestiza woman named María Sonora (in some sources referred to as "Huila").[21] From María Sonora, Teresa learned about midwifery and treating various illnesses with local herbs and poultices. It was here that she received the *don*, the gift of healing.[22] One evening in 1889, while living at Rancho de Cabora, Teresa experienced a sudden attack of violent "nervous convulsions." Witnesses described how for approximately thirteen days she alternated between short bursts of convulsions so intense that six men could not hold her down (they feared she would hurt herself) and then several hours of unconsciousness, interspersed with moments of lucidity where she talked about seeing visions and expressed her desire to eat dirt.[23]

While that desire may seem odd, it is possible that Teresa craved dirt to heal herself because she knew that certain kinds of soil could absorb and remove pathogens and toxins from the body. This knowledge was something she would have learned from her mentor, the curandera María Sonora, whose healing practice included Indigenous methods and materials. The local Yaquis would mix their saliva with dirt (or mesquite ashes) and rub it on the patient while reciting prayers and making the sign of the cross over the sick area.[24] And Teresa's mother's Tehueco family might have taught her the practice of eating dirt for its nutrients. The Mayo, another local tribe related to the Yaqui, believed that certain dirt was sacred, particularly where crosses were stationed, and therefore curative.[25] Whether Teresa's inspiration to eat dirt came from the Tehueco, Yaqui, Mayo, or María Sonora—or all of them combined—those who attended Teresa during these thirteen days remembered that she would eat only dirt mixed with her saliva—nothing else.[26]

Teresa came out of this violent episode by healing herself. On the last day of her convulsive attacks, she complained of intense pain in her back and chest. The women attending her, including María Sonora, treated the pain with a poultice of powdered mustard seed called *sinapismos*. But as soon as the pain was relieved in her chest and back, it traveled to her head. Her caretakers attempted to apply the *sinapismos* to her head, but Teresa stopped them and ordered them to apply to her temples the mixture of dirt and her saliva that was kept by her bed. Her attendants did as she asked, and when they removed the mud and saliva mixture from her temples, she claimed to finally be free of pain.[27]

Over the next three months, Teresa drifted between coherence and a kind of otherworldly daze—she seemed to be in a trance, or liminal state. She had visions. She began to heal. In one of her visions, Teresa claimed the Virgin Mary told her she had been given the gift of healing—the *don*—and that she would be a curandera.[28]

Years later, Urrea described her *don* experience to a San Francisco journalist.

> For three months and eighteen days I was in a trance. I knew nothing of what I did in that time. They tell me, those who saw, that I could move about but that they had to feed me; that I talked strange things about God and religion, and that the people came to me from all the country and around, and if they were sick and crippled and I put my hands on them they got well. . . . Then when I could remember again, after those three months and eighteen

days, I felt a change in me. I could still if I touched people or rubbed them make them well. . . . When I cured people they began to call me Santa Teresa. I didn't like it at first, but now I am used to it.[29]

Like the visionary Wovoka of the Ghost Dance movement and other Indigenous shamans, such as the Shawnee prophet Tenskwatawa (1775–1836), many curanderos undergo a kind of symbolic death and rebirth, accompanied by visions and messages from God, Jesus, the Virgin Mary, or saints and other deities.[30] Some curanderos claim the gift also gives them the power to see into the future and discern people's illnesses before they present themselves, a belief shared by the Yaqui and Mayo. Curanderos consider the ability to cure a spiritual gift, something Teresa consistently claimed.[31]

Indigenous beliefs and healing ways deeply influenced Teresa's *don*, as well as her whole life up to this point. However, the way her identity came to be connected to the Yaqui as the one directing and controlling their actions because she "held a supernatural power over the Indians, who believed she could cure them of diseases," was not only incorrect, it also hid their agency and the reasons the Yaqui fought the Mexican government.[32]

Teresa would consistently correct journalists on their interpretations of her role in Yaqui resistance. She knew that the Yaquis involved in the attack on the Nogales customs house were not simply acting at her behest, nor were they "fanatic savages . . . crazed on account of fanatical worship of Santa Teresa de Cabora," as numerous US and Mexican newspaper articles about the attack suggested.[33] Teresa defended herself against these views: "I have cured the Indians and they love me for it, but I do not tell them to make revolutions," and in a different interview she explained, "I had nothing to do with the Yaqui revolution. They were fighting always to keep their land."[34] Teresa knew that the Yaquis acted on their own initiative, as they always had, and she would not deny them their agency by taking credit. She was simply supporting them in one struggle against the Mexican government.[35] The Yaqui, many of whom worked on Rancho de Cabora, had for centuries fought to protect their homeland and identity against the forces of the Spanish and then the Mexican government. At this time of intense pressure to give up their homelands for Porfirio Díaz's program of economic development—"order and progress"—some Yaquis found a kind of political inspiration in Santa Teresa, as they came to call her. This is evident by the "Vivas" they shouted in her name as they attacked the Nogales *aduana* in 1896, as well as by the pictures of her that Mexican officials found on their murdered bodies.[36]

Map 1.1. Map of the Sonora-Arizona borderlands region, the world of Teresa Urrea. Herman Ehrenberg, Millard Fillmore, and Middleton, Strobridge & Co. *Map of the Gadsden Purchase: Sonora and Portions of New Mexico, Chihuahua & California* (Cincinnati, OH: Middleton, Strobridge & Co., 1858), https://www.loc.gov/item/98686018/.

Yaqui History of Resistance

The Yaqui (or Yoeme, as they call themselves) had their own grievances with the Mexican state that compelled them to make common cause with the Teresistas.[37] Since they first encountered the *yori*—their term for white men—the Yaqui fought to protect their homeland and maintain their distinct identity through accommodation, autonomous rebellion, and alliances with larger political parties and movements.[38] In fact, the Tehueco, Mayo, and Yaqui people had for centuries lived with the colonizing forces of Spain, Jesuit missionaries, and the Mexican government, and all three tribes resisted Spanish and then Mexican authority for most of the nineteenth century. But after the 1880s, the Mayo more fully acquiesced to Mexican encroachment into the Mayo Valley and allowed a greater degree of integration of Mexicans into their society than did the Yaqui. One reason for this may have been that the Mayo territory lacked the features conducive to guerrilla warfare that the Yaqui enjoyed. They could easily escape into the Sierra de Bacatete mountain range or cross the US-Mexico border to elude government forces, but the Mayo had neither advantage, as they were located farther south, in southern Sonora.[39] Despite cultural differences, the Mayo, Tehueco, and Yaqui spoke mutually understandable dialects of the Cahita language; they shared geography along the rivers spilling into the Gulf of California on the northwest coast of Mexico; and they all incorporated Spanish Catholicism into their spirituality.[40] Most importantly, they shared a history of resistance to Spanish and Mexican encroachment on their land.[41]

Sacred prophecy warned that the Spanish and Jesuits would come and Christianize the Yaqui. Some would become willing converts, or Yoemem, the "baptized ones," while others, the Surem, "the unbaptized ones," would forever dwell in the mountains, in the sea, and in underground caves.[42] When Alvar Núñez Cabeza de Vaca met the Yaqui on his wanderings, sometime between 1533 and 1536, he noted that they had already encountered and routed the Spanish slave raider Diego de Guzmán and were preparing for further confrontations with Spaniards. Some Yaquis had moved into the mountains, and those whom Cabeza de Vaca met gave him and his men "two thousand loads of maize," an indication that they were storing large food banks, perhaps in anticipation of more encounters—violent or otherwise—with Spaniards.[43] When the Jesuits arrived in 1617, the Yaqui observed that they had "reduced" the Mayo's scattered settlements into seven pueblos around the Mayo River. They decided it would benefit them as well, so they welcomed the Jesuits into their homeland, the *hiakem*.[44] The Jesuits assisted the Yaqui in reducing their widely scattered and loosely federated *rancherías* into eight missions, or pueblos, positioned around the Río Yaqui, unifying them more closely as a distinct people.

During the Jesuit era the Yaqui fused their Native cosmology with Catholicism.[45] For example, they believed that their ancient ancestors, the Surem, as well as Jesus and Mary (or Atom Aye, "Our Mother," as they called her) walked among them in their homeland. They also held that Christ could appear in dreams as a curer, telling the dreamer how to heal.[46] Yaqui cosmology contended that Jesus performed his miraculous healing as he wandered through the *huya ania*, the Yaqui Flower World.[47] The Yaqui also believed deeply in their own ancient and holy Surem, and that those with special powers and access to Surem, like the *moreakame* (witches), had the gift of *seatakaa* (telepathy) and could cause pain, similar to the powers attributed to Spanish *brujos* or *hechiceros*.[48] They believed that powers from Jesus, Mary, or the Surem could come to one in a vision or a dream.[49] The Yaqui also had their own doctors, or curanderos, whom they called *hitebi*: men and women who possessed the gift of *seatakaa* and were trained in the apprentice method.[50] The *hitebi* healed using a mix of Indigenous materials and techniques (herbs, saliva, dirt, dreaming) blended with Catholic symbols and rituals (the sign of the cross, recitation of the Pater Noster and Ave Maria, the sprinkling of holy water).[51]

One of the Yaqui religious beliefs explains the birth of Jesus from a flower that Mary found in the river and put in her bosom. The flower, or *seewa* in the Yaqui language, represents sacrifice, and Jesus is often referred to as a "flower person."[52] The Yaqui also tell the story of the life and death of Jesus as taking place in their homeland, the valley of the Río Yaqui. They believe that Jesus walked throughout the *huya ania*, the wilderness world where the Surem live, and when he became so distraught with humanity that he wanted to kill everyone, Mary told him he could, but only if he gave her back the breast milk she had fed him when he was a baby. When Jesus was about to be killed by soldiers, Mary left for the *huya ania* and changed herself into a tree so that Jesus would unknowingly cut her down and make her into a cross. She opened her arms, and her sacrifice made it possible for both of them to ascend to heaven. When Jesus was nailed to her, the blood that came out of his wounds bloomed into flowers (*seewam*) when it fell to the ground.[53] This story demonstrates how the Yaqui maintained elements of their pre-Hispanic cosmology while incorporating some aspects of Catholicism, creating a much more powerful and less passive Mary than traditional Catholicism allowed.

When the Jesuits were expelled from New Spain in 1767, the Yaqui and Mayo once again were the sole caretakers of their homelands.[54] Although they lost the advocacy and protection of the Jesuit priests, they were able to maintain their homeland and survive as a people by becoming an indispensable source of labor for the mining and agricultural industries, greatly stimulated by the Bourbon reforms. However, beginning in the 1820s, after Mexico gained independence from Spain in 1821, the newly formed Mexican government wanted to "pacify" the Yaqui, make them Mexican citizens, and mold them into a tractable labor pool. Although many Yaquis were willing to work in the mines and on haciendas and railroads, they wanted no part of the new Mexican nation. They wanted to live peacefully in their pueblos, according to their traditions, and relate to the outside world on their terms. The Yaqui and Mayo benefitted from economic development as wage laborers, yet they wanted Mexicans to stay out of their affairs and off their land, especially when government officials began allotting their land to Mexican agriculturalists.[55] The Mexican nation had room for Indigenous wage laborers in capitalist ventures central to the national project, and many Yaquis were willing to sell their labor to ranchers (such as Don Tomás Urrea), mining operations, railroads, and other industries in northern Sonora and across the border in Arizona, even if they always returned home to their eight pueblos along the Río Yaqui. However, the nation had no room for Indigenous people who would resist the will of the government, and violent struggles between the Yaqui and the Mexican government continued throughout the nineteenth century.[56]

In the second part of the nineteenth century, the Mexican government, along with private companies from Mexico and the United States, were making plans to colonize the Yaqui homeland. Justo Sierra, a historian, journalist, and advisor to President Porfirio Díaz, provided a justification for this. Sierra described the Mexican nation as "anemic," a condition that could only be remedied by "great quantities of iron, supplied in the form of railroads, and large doses of strong blood, supplied in the form of immigration."[57] Sierra and Díaz (among others) believed that the settlement and cultivation of what was deemed "unoccupied" land, such as Native lands and Catholic Church holdings, would create a class of small property holders, not unlike the yeoman farmers in the United States, who, it was believed, would bring "civilization" to "backward" Indian communities. Sierra also believed that privatization of Yaqui land would eventually make them part of the "mestizo family" that defined Mexican national identity.[58] The colonization efforts among the Yaqui extended beyond the Mexican government in the last decades of the nineteenth century, when venture capital from the United States financed railroad construction, farming, and irrigation projects on Yaqui land. Until the 1880s, Mexican federal and state governments had assumed responsibility for planning, funding, and supervising the colonization and irrigation projects on the Río Yaqui and Río Mayo, attracting some non-Yaqui settlers to the towns along the rivers. However, Yaqui resistance made living among them particularly unwelcoming to most settlers. To help with the colonization project, in August 1890 the Mexican secretary of development granted the first private contract to a Sonoran developer to survey, sell, and colonize the lands on the Yaqui and Mayo Rivers and to construct canals and reservoirs. The Sonoran contractor invited Americans to invest in the project, marking the beginning of large-scale and foreign private initiative in the development of land along the Río Yaqui, where both Mexico and the United States had a stake in keeping the Yaqui "pacified."[59]

The period from 1876 to 1907, roughly coinciding with the Díaz presidency, has been called the era of the Yaqui Wars because of the prolonged conflict between the Yaqui and the Mexican government, the Sonoran government, and US venture capitalists and investors.[60] It was during this period that Teresa Urrea received her *don* and became a source of healing and support for Yaquis, Mayos, Tehuecos, and Mexicans in this contested region. Also during this time some Yaquis began crossing the border into the US territory of Arizona, where they used their earnings working in mines, railroads, and other industries to buy guns and ammunition. In fact, some of the Yaquis involved in the 1896 Nogales customs house attack participated in two different labor disputes: one in Sonora and one in Arizona.

An unpublished local history of nineteenth-century Arizona suggests that it was a labor dispute between Yaquis working as adobe brick-makers and their boss—who happened to be the mayor of Nogales, Sonora—that caused the Teresita Rebellion. When Yaqui laborers refused to work for just fourteen pesos per thousand bricks and tried to press for better wages, some were killed during a "disturbance."[61] After this, authorities on both sides of the border anticipated retaliation from the Yaqui. According to a contemporary account, "Anyone who could carry a gun, and would, was issued 45–70 Springfields to keep the Indians from coming into the States, and they stood guard."[62] Soldiers stationed at Fort Huachuca, Arizona, were also brought in to defend the border. An additional source of Yaqui unrest may have been the wage disputes between Yaquis working as section hands for the Southern Pacific Railroad and their bosses in Arizona.[63] While these labor disputes may have provided the immediate sparks for the Teresista border uprisings in 1896, the long history of Spanish colonial, Mexican, and US encroachment on Yaqui land and sovereignty provided the long-burning fuse.

In Santa Teresa, the Yaqui Teresistas found not only a source of spiritual healing, but also someone who voiced an ideology that confirmed their own views on abusive state and capitalist power. The Teresistas were fighting for decent wages in these capitalist ventures, as well as their lands and their rights as a sovereign people within the Mexican nation, and Santa Teresa stood with them on these issues. Her healing touch, feminine sanctity, and radical speech inspired and affirmed the Yaqui Teresistas' rights and sovereignty within the nation. It was not only the way Teresa healed, but also those she healed—the poor, Indigenous, oppressed—that contributed to her reputation as a *santa*, a saint of the people.

Figure 1.4. Teresa Urrea's house at Rancho de Cabora. This is where Teresa retreated from healing to contemplate challenging cures in solitude. William Curry Holden Papers, SW CPC #250, Southwest Collection/Special Collections Library, Texas Tech University, Lubbock.

The Healing

The first person Santa Teresa healed after receiving her *don* (besides herself) was an *india*, a young Indigenous girl, foreshadowing Teresa's healing career among the most vulnerable: young, Indigenous, and female. The girl was brought to her for healing because she suffered from a slight impairment. One of her legs was shorter than the other, and she could not fully plant her foot on the ground, making it difficult to walk. Teresa rubbed her knee, stretched her shrunken leg, and commanded her to throw away the stick she had used to support herself—and walk. According to witnesses, the young girl did as Teresa commanded and was able to plant her foot firmly on the ground and walk well.[64]

It seems that from the moment she received her *don*, Teresa became known throughout Mexico and parts of the US Southwest for her miraculous cures, divinely sanctioned healing powers, and the multitudes of poor and oppressed people she healed at Rancho de Cabora. Her adherents (and detractors) called her La Santa de Cabora, La Niña de Cabora, or simply Santa Teresa. Various accounts from newspaper reporters, health seekers, the curious, and the skeptical, as well as concerned Mexican government agents, described the scene at Cabora, where anywhere from several hundred to more than a thousand people visited to receive the healing touch of Santa Teresa. *La Voz de México*, a major newspaper in Mexico City, reported on this remote, rural area of northwest Mexico, where "Está llamando mucho la atención en el pueblo de Cabora, cerca del Río Mayo" (Much attention is being drawn to the town of Cabora, near the Mayo River) because of the miraculous healing of "una joven de 17 años llamada Teresa Urrea" (a young girl of seventeen years called Teresa Urrea).[65] *La Voz de México* reported how the "superstitious" peoples of the *ranchos* and pueblos, and the *clase indígena* (Indigenous people, mostly Yaqui and Mayo) surrounding Cabora flocked to Santa Teresa to be healed. This article describes how Teresa healed *con tierra*, with earth. Reports claim that she healed the blind, the crippled, and those with leprosy. While the writer for *La Voz de México* was skeptical—and clearly not a believer in Teresa's miraculous healing powers—the article attests to the fact that many did believe and sought her healing.

Santa Teresa's style of healing involved touch, herbs, the client's belief in her power to heal, and the use of earth, water, and her saliva. The following cure stories reveal some of these aspects of her healing. In one case, a man was carried by his friends to Teresa because he could not walk. He had suffered a wound in a mining accident that he believed was incurable, and he came to Santa Teresa as a last hope. Her cure? She drank water, spat it out on the dirt, mixed the water and dirt into a poultice, and applied it to the man's wound. Witnesses claim he was "instantly cured."[66] Another patient brought to Teresa was a woman who had a hemorrhage in one lung. Witnesses described how Teresa said to her, "I am going to cure you with blood from my own heart." Then she took saliva, in which appeared a drop of blood, mixed it with earth, and applied it to the middle of the sufferer's back, with the result that the hemorrhage was at once controlled, and the woman cured.[67] News of such cures spread, inspiring ever more visitors to come to Cabora to be cured or to witness the amazing powers of the curandera Santa Teresa.

Sometimes, when faced with a challenging case, Teresa would escape from the throngs of people and the hot Sonoran sun and withdraw into a little adobe structure her father had made for her. Inside, she would contemplate, pray, and seek spiritual guidance. For example, one man came to her with an ulcerated sore on his leg. In her private hut, where she had retreated to contemplate how to cure this man, Teresa had a vision of a man with two pieces of bone popping out of an oozing sore on his leg. She then returned to her patient, cleaned his sore, and withdrew two small pieces of bone, as she had seen in her vision. The man was healed.[68]

One curious American physician visited in 1890, shortly after Teresa's story emerged in Mexican newspapers, and described what he witnessed at Cabora.

> On arriving at the residence of her father, Sr. Urrea, we saw what was at first, the usual dwelling houses, corrals, etc., of a Mexican hacienda, converted into a temporary town, consisting of numerous buildings hastily constructed for the convenience of the sick seeking relief through the healing power of this young girl. . . . There were three or four hundred people, patients and their friends, on the ground, and the "saint" was almost constantly moving among them. Wherever she went she was attended by a throng who sought every opportunity to express their adoration by kneeling before her and kissing her hand.[69]

This visitor described the scene at Cabora as one filled with all of kinds of people seeking healing: the blind, paralytic, consumptive, "deformed," and those hopeless cases that "try the skill and ingenuity of the most noted practitioners in the healing art."[70] This American physician went on to describe Santa Teresa herself, "a girl of seventeen or eighteen years old, of regular and handsome features, finely formed head, delicate physique, artless in manners and a very personification of candor and innocence."[71] Even as he described Teresa as possessing all of the traditional, passive, female traits that made her acceptable and nonthreatening, he also noted that she was acutely aware of her healing powers and knew exactly what she wanted to do with them: heal those "worthy and helpless." Teresa made it clear to the physician that she was aware that doctors and priests targeted her and denounced her as a fraud. He said she told him that "doctors and priests wanted to get her to an asylum or convent, as she was curing the most obstinate cases of disease and exposing the hypocrisy and fraud of priests."[72] Teresa understood her power, and that her *don*, the gift of spiritual healing—healing publicly performed by a woman—made her a threat to those in positions of institutionalized power. The medical profession deemed her insane and suggested she should be locked up in an asylum; the institution of the official Catholic Church preferred she be locked away in a convent. Teresa would do neither. While her healing practice in some ways conformed to the prescribed gender roles for women as nurturers and caregivers, she defied the rigid gender expectations that demanded women be kept sequestered in domestic spaces.

Instead, openly, in the public space of Cabora, she healed those who came to her.

La Profetisa de Cabora

In addition to the Indigenous and mestizo peasants that came to Cabora to be healed by Santa Teresa, there was another group in Mexico drawn to Urrea: *espiritistas*, or Spiritists. Mexican espiritistas followed the French metaphysical religion of Spiritism.[73] Spiritists believed that in trance sessions and séances, mediums received messages from loved ones who had died in war, babies and children whose untimely deaths left their mothers and fathers bereft with grief, and important historical figures who acted as spirit guides and would prophesy and teach the living how to create a better world. Part of the Spiritist belief system included a particular understanding of healing. Spiritism contended that gifted mediums could heal while in a trance state; Mexican espiritistas believed Teresa was one of these gifted healing mediums. They believed that espiritista mediums like Teresa prophesied, cured, and offered advice that guided their "brothers and sisters" to higher, more evolved and "scientific" ways while in trance states. Like their French counterparts, Mexican Spiritists sought to apply scientific rationale to religious faith.[74] While they were most prominent in cosmopolitan Mexico City, there were groups of espiritistas in other areas, including the Sinaloan and Sonoran groups that came to be associated with Teresa. In 1890 Mexican espiritistas from Mazatlán, Sinaloa, declared Teresa a medium. Subsequently, espiritistas from Baroyeca, Sonora, traveled to Rancho de Cabora to observe her healing. Among several miraculous healings they observed, the Sonoran espiritistas witnessed Teresa heal a deaf man in front of a hundred people simply by applying her saliva to his ears. These espiritistas came to believe that she was not a curandera or a miracle-working *santa*, but a powerful healing medium.[75]

The Spiritist ideology embraced the concept of social equality as well as a practical and Christian morality centered on charity and love for one's fellow man, reflected in Teresa's own words, published in the radical anti-Díaz newspaper *El Independiente* in 1896: "Todos somos hermanos é iguales por ser todos hijos del mismo Padre" (We are all brothers and equals because we are sons of the same Father).[76] Spiritists also espoused an egalitarian view of gender relations, purporting that because the soul was sexless, women and men deserved to be treated equally under the law. In this view, women's "lesser intelligence" was attributed to the education system that refused to admit them, not to some natural feature that made women less rational and more emotional. Yet at the same time Spiritists articulated the notion that men and women were essentially, biologically, different, and so each had different missions to fulfill on earth.[77] A major part of the ideology of Spiritism was that the privileged—whether male or female—should not forgo their obligation of charity and compassion for the less privileged.[78]

The founder of French Spiritism, Hippolyte Léon Denizard Rivail—better known as Allan Kardec, the name given to him by the spirits while he was in trance—claimed that Spiritism was compatible with Catholicism, something that would both help and potentially hinder its appeal in Latin American countries like Mexico that had deeply Catholic populations as well as anticlerical intellectuals.[79] Coincidentally, Spiritism emerged at a time when Catholic devotion in France saw a resurgence in the miraculous and increasingly frequent reports of Marian devotion, visions, miraculous cures, pilgrimages, and stigmata, revealing the possibility of compatibility between Catholic beliefs about miraculous healing and the "science of the spirits." In 1858 a lady dressed in white appeared to fourteen-year-old Bernadette Soubrious in the small village of Lourdes, France, where today thousands of pilgrims visit to bathe in the curative water. Soubrious claimed this apparition was the Blessed Virgin Mary and told the priests who questioned her, "I am the Immaculate Conception," as if she were channeling the Virgin.[80] The Virgin also revealed to Bernadette an unknown spring of fresh water in a grotto that would become famous for miraculously healing the sick. After initial skepticism and several "scientific tests," the Catholic Church accepted Soubrious's miraculous vision of the Virgin Mary and later canonized her a saint. In 1876—three years after the birth of María Rebecca Chávez in Sinaloa, Mexico—the Church officially recognized Lourdes as a place of miraculous healing and pilgrimage, installing priests and Catholic physicians.

A group of Mexican intellectuals greatly influenced by French culture and ideas championed the philosophy of Spiritism (in Latin America sometimes called Kardecismo after founder Allan Kardec).[81] Like their French counterparts, Mexican espiritistas sought to apply scientific rationale to religious faith.[82] Events and ideological currents running through Mexico in the mid-nineteenth century provided fertile ground for French Spiritism to take root. The first Mexican *espiritismo* meetings took place in Mexico City in 1857, the year Kardec's Spiritist guidebook, *Le Livre des Esprits* (The Lives of the Spirits), was first published.[83] It was also the year the Mexican nation instituted a series of liberal reforms: secularizing the state, stripping the Catholic Church of its authority, and granting Mexican citizens the freedom to participate in other religions.[84] The French occupation of Mexico from 1862 to 1867 also helped to spread the influence of Spiritism, especially among the military.[85] For example, General Refugio González—who fought for Mexican independence when he was young, for liberalism during the civil wars and Reforma, against the US invasion (1846), and then in the French occupation—became one of the founding leaders of Mexican Spiritism. General González was often referred to as the "Mexican Kardec." He founded the first official espiritista circle in Mexico in 1868, translated Kardec's books into Spanish in 1872, and helped to establish the main journal of the espiritismo movement in Mexico, *La Ilustración Espirita*.[86] Not only was General González a well-known and respected military officer, he was also a thoughtful and passionate liberal. He spoke out forcefully against the Catholic Church in *La Ilustración Espirita*, his own books (written as spiritist transmissions, like Kardec's), and in liberal Mexican newspapers such as *El Monitor Republicano* and *El Universal*.[87] González also believed in Teresa as a powerful healing medium, and he defended her often in the pages of *La Ilustración Espirita* as well as other publications.[88] In fact, González and Teresa were the only two mediums that *La Ilustración Espirita* printed images of.[89] One image of Teresa (figure 1.5) presents her as a serious, unadorned espiritista medium, dressed modestly but elegantly in black, with her long hair pulled back—a popular look among female Spiritist and Spiritualist mediums in the nineteenth century. Although there is no text accompanying the photograph, it looks as if Teresa may be in a trance state, and the book in her lap could be filled with blank pages for her to take down messages from spirits through "automatic writing," one of the practices of Spiritist mediums. The article that accompanies the picture suggests that although she was known as a *santa* in Cabora, a better name for her would be "La Profetisa."

Espiritistas explained that Teresa's Indigenous, impoverished, and (they believed) ignorant followers had been misled by Catholic priests into believing in miracles, saints, and superstitions. The educated and enlightened espiritistas knew better. They believed that her powers could be scientifically explained through magnetism and spirit channeling. She was not a religious mystic, they insisted, but a champion of the Nueva Ciencia (New Science).[90] When Teresa healed by laying on of hands, which she was known for, espiritistas did not interpret this as a miraculous, supernatural sign of God or the Virgin Mary working through her, but as proof of the vital magnetic fluid moving through her.[91] Mexican Spiritists were not alone in interpreting Teresa's healing powers in this way. American Spiritualists, who maintained contact with Latin American Spiritists through shared editorials in publications such as *La Ilustración Espirita* and the *Carrier Dove* (San Francisco),

Figure 1.5. "Teresa Urrea ó La Profetisa De Cabora," *La Ilustración Espirita*, April 1, 1891, 366–369. The globe on the table is an apt symbol of the global reach of Spiritism as interest in Teresa extended outside of Cabora to Spiritist circles in Mexico City as well as in Medellín and Bogotá, Colombia.

also became interested in Teresa's healing powers. In fact, one American Spiritualist and physician living near Cabora in 1890 judged her healing the work of the science of the spirits, not the miraculous.

"Un Problema Para La Medicina"

In an article titled "Un Problema Para La Medicina" (A Problem for Medicine), published in the Mexican Spiritist journal, *La Ilustración Espirita*, Dr. E. P. Schellhous addressed the "problem" of Teresa Urrea's power to heal through laying on of hands. Schellhous, an American, was living in the Topolobampo colony, a socialist and Spiritualist experimental community in northwestern Sinaloa on the Gulf of California. He spent days watching Teresa heal in order to "verify her extraordinary cures with only laying hands on the patient."[92] He examined Urrea and found her in *salud vigorosa* (good health) and described her character as "simple, modest, without pretension, without vanity."[93] After he witnessed approximately 1,300 cures she performed in November 1890—treating everything from blindness and paralysis to minor afflictions—Schellhous came to the same conclusion that the Mexican espiritistas did: her healing power relied on the intervention of spirits and magnetic fluid.[94] He explained that Teresa was not unique in the healing power of her laying on of hands—that throughout the ages there have been other famous *mediumidad* espiritistas who healed this way, including Jesus.[95] Her main goal, he claimed, was the same as that of the Son of God: to offer charity to "suffering mankind," the heart of Spiritist moral philosophy.

The editor of *La Ilustración Espirita* described Schellhous as "un distinguido médico Americano" (a distinguished American doctor). Indeed, he occupied a privileged position as a medical doctor, a practicing Spiritualist, and a white man whose view of Teresa was widely respected in the Mexican Spiritist and American Spiritualist communities dominated by mestizo and Anglo elites, respectively.[96] In 1890, when Schellhous went to Cabora to observe Teresa, he and several hundred Anglo American Spiritualist colonists were squatting on land that was not theirs but owned in common by several Mayo communities. The Mayo knew Teresa as Santa Teresa, La Santa de Cabora, a part-Tehueco girl, one of their living saints, prophets, and curanderos, or *hitolíos* (traditional Mayo healers). She had grown up among them, and they had seen her heal by using her hands to rub a mixture of their sacred earth and water on her patients.[97]

Schellhous did not mention the Mayo in his report, even though he and his fellow Topolobampo colonists were living in the midst of their homeland and must have interacted with them at some point or seen them attending Teresa's healings. Perhaps the colonists did not pay attention to the Mayo, as the goal of the Topolobampo colony was to create a utopian communal society and develop the agricultural potential of the valleys of the Mayo and Fuerte Rivers while paving the way for a new railroad to connect the eastern United States, Mexico, and the "Orient."[98] The Topolobampo colony was founded by Alfred Owen, who met with President Porfirio Díaz in 1879 about his plan to build a railroad connecting the eastern United States with the ports of northwestern Mexico via Texas and Chihuahua, ending in Topolobampo. Díaz granted him land for free provided he survey and develop it. Although the colony dissolved after 1894, the canals and dams that Owen and his colonists created benefited the mestizo hacendado class that took over the area. Because of colonization schemes like this, the Mayo lost their land and were reduced to poorly paid day laborers. It is likely that Schellhous was referring to the Mayo when he concluded his report by stating, "Teresa is a healing medium but the people that surround her in their ignorance insist on calling her a saint," a sentiment he would repeat in the US Spiritualist press.[99] The *Carrier Dove*, a Spiritualist newspaper published in San Francisco, reprinted Dr. Schellhous's article in the city where Teresa Urrea first performed her healing in front of an audience.[100] Schellhous explained why he believed she was such a powerful healing medium.

> In the case of Teresa Urrea, high and benevolent spirits have found a suitable medium through which to impart healing power. She is innocent, artless and unpretending; willing, obedient and faithful; with an untiring zeal and a high sense of her lofty calling. She is humble, devoted and unselfish; with a good organization and favorable temperament.[101]

In other words, Teresa fit the script for the female medium through her youth, innocence, "artlessness," and humility—in short, her idealized passive femininity. In the *Carrier Dove*, Schellhous neatly dismissed the fervent devotion to "Santa Teresa" among the Yaqui and Mayo of Mexico as a by-product of their being "almost completely dominated by the priesthood," because "Being all Catholics and very superstitious, they believed she could help them."[102]

Lauro Aguirre, a close friend of the Urrea family, was a practicing Spiritist in Guaymas, Sonora. He claimed that Teresa was a medium of the highest order, never seen before in Mexico, perhaps even one that Allan Kardec had prophesied in his *Book of the Mediums*.[103] Aguirre described the transformation of Teresa from a poor and "ignorant" girl of the countryside to a gifted Spiritist medium and claimed that before she acquired her *facultades medianímicas* (mediumship powers), she was like those who fervently believed in her as a curandera and *santa*: "vulgar and ignorant," and suffering from all of the defects of Roman Catholic fanatics.[104] Yet when she acquired her mediumship, she displayed an especially powerful *mediumnidad curativa*—the gift of spiritual healing.

The idea of the young, uneducated, and powerless female displaying the gift of mediumship was a common theme in Spiritist discourse. It demonstrated the power of the spirits to work through the most powerless and passive members of society while keeping these young women safe within the accepted social bounds.[105] However, this was mostly fabrication in the case of Teresa, who had already demonstrated sophisticated and powerful healing skills, and had taken an outspoken stance on the treatment of Indigenous people by the Catholic Church and the Mexican government before the espiritistas discovered her. Even more problematic for Mexican Spiritists was Teresa's identity as a folk saint—a *santa* and a curandera who inspired irrational and unruly behavior in "the Indians" and superstitious lower classes.

In their observations at Cabora, recorded in *La Ilustración Espirita* from 1890 to 1892, Spiritists lamented that popular national newspapers painted Teresa as a fake, a "pretended saint" who exploited the poor "superstitious" and "fanatical" Indians and peasants of the countryside who traveled to Cabora to be healed by her.[106] The Spiritists, on the other hand, claimed they had subjected Teresa to an "examen verdadero de la ciencia" (a true scientific examination), and through "la luz de la razón y la ciencia" (the light of reason and science) found that she was a true Spiritist medium. In this way they defended her from those who ridiculed her and accused her of inspiring "fanatismo religioso" in the countryside.[107] Like President Díaz's *científico* advisors, the espiritistas believed that everything could be studied scientifically, although Spiritists also believed science could be applied to things that could not be seen, such as Teresa's healing.

> In our humble judgment, young Urrea is simply a medium, an instrument that Providence has managed to make his revelations to mortals and far from ridiculing things like this, we should study them conscientiously with the purpose of deducing them as a result of natural consequences. . . .[108]

These espiritistas believed that she healed in a trance and that she could channel spirits of the dead and help them elevate Mexico to a higher plane of scientific and spiritual evolution. The Spiritist movement in Mexico typically reinforced elite, Porfirian ideas about modernization and progress, yet there was a minority of Spiritists, including Lauro Aguirre, who held more radical views about social equality and transcendence. It was this minority who embraced Teresa Urrea, and whom she embraced and influenced.[109] One of the observers at Cabora described the promise of Teresa Urrea as an espiritista regenerating agent for Mexico—as one who could return the nation to the ideals articulated in the 1857 Constitution that had been betrayed by the government of Porfirio Díaz.

> Espiritismo, we repeat, is called to bring about universal regeneration and with the help of God we will see an age not very far in the distance, the true brotherhood of man without distinction between races, nationalities; the true government of the people in order to benefit the people, without the intervention of despots or tyrants.[110]

In her own words, Teresa expressed what espiritismo meant to her:

> If for something I have affinity, and if something I try to practice, it is *espiritismo*, because *espiritismo* is based on the truth, and the truth is much greater than all the religions, and also because *espiritismo* was studied and practiced by Jesus and is the key to all the MIRACLES of Jesus and the most pure expression of the religion of the spirit. . . .
>
> I suppose, as well, that science and religion should march in perfect harmony and union, being that science should be the expression of truth and religion. . . . I think God more adores the ATHEIST that loves his brothers and works to acquire science and virtue than the Catholic monks that kill and hate men while proclaiming God.
>
> God is goodness, is love, and only for goodness and love can we elevate our soul towards him.[111]

Like many anticlerical liberals in Mexico at this time, Teresa voiced a clear disdain for the hypocrisy of institutional religion and, in particular, the Catholic Church in Mexico, which often aligned with oppressive leaders. She had no patience for "Catholic monks that kill and hate men while proclaiming God," yet she combined this with sincere Christian beliefs—particularly the belief in the centrality and goodness of Jesus—as well as the Spiritist ideals of the pursuit of God and "Truth" through science and the perfection of society.

One image of her, titled "Terecita Urrea La Sta. Niña de Cabora" (figure 1.6), from the same time as the "Profetisa de Cabora" sketch (see figure 1.5), suggests her overlapping identities as espiritista medium and folk

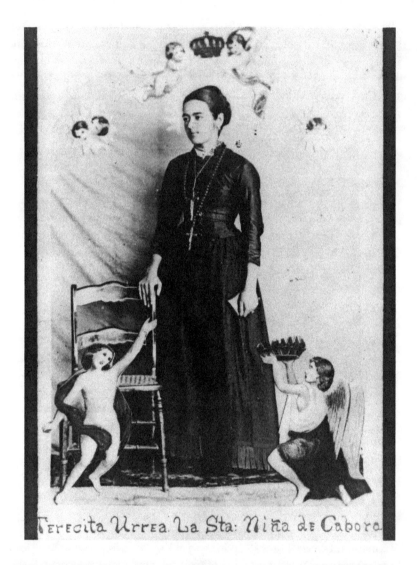

Terecita Urrea La Sta: Niña de Cabora

Figure 1.6. "Terecita Urrea La Sta. Niña de Cabora" (Terecita Urrea the Child Saint of Cabora). This image reveals Teresa's identity as both an espiritista medium (black dress, serious, unadorned) and a *santa* and curandera (rosaries and crucifixes around her neck, and the layering in of cherubs and iconography resembling La Madre de Luz). Albert Reynolds Photographic Collection, PC 107, #1671, Arizona Historical Society.

saint, revealing that Teresa was both things to different groups of people. While she healed hundreds, perhaps thousands, of people at her father's hacienda, Rancho de Cabora, through mud, saliva, herbs, laying on of hands, prayer, meditations, and visions, something that espiritistas interpreted as the manifestation of the powers of a healing medium, she was also a symbol of hope for many people, especially the Indigenous and poor mestizo peasants who suffered under the oppressive policies of the Díaz government. She spoke out against a corrupt Catholic Church and political system in Mexico, and offered hope to those oppressed by those powerful institutions. Many for whom this message resonated came to visit her at Rancho de Cabora, including villagers from Tomóchic, a mountain pueblo in the neighboring state of Chihuahua, who had their own struggles with the Mexican government.[112] But closer to home, she inspired the resistance of the Mayo and Yaqui against the Mexican government. This political stance brought her trouble in 1892.

La Santa de Cabora Crosses the Border

In 1892, the Mayo (who are closely related to the Yaqui) attacked the Mexican customs house at Navojoa, one of the seven Mayo pueblos, proclaiming "Viva la Santa de Cabora!" and "Viva la Libertad!"[113] They did so in response to the unwelcome incursions of *yori* (non-Indigenous white people) into their homelands (including Dr. Schellhous and the Topolobampo colonists) and disruption of their way of life.[114] The Mayo resented the accelerating colonization of their homelands around the Río Mayo. In addition to the railway recently built from Nogales, Sonora, to Mazatlán, Sinaloa (the state just south of Sonora), with Navojoa an important station on the line, in the last decade of the nineteenth century the government oversaw the construction of eighteen canals along the Río Mayo to irrigate the vast haciendas that had been carved out of Mayo land, reducing many Mayos to peons and wage laborers.[115] Another reason for the attack on the customs house at Navojoa was payback for the disrespect and expulsion of Mayo holy people in 1890.

In September 1890, thousands of Mayos abandoned their jobs in the mines, ranchos, and haciendas to worship and witness their holy prophets and *santos* (living saints like Santa Teresa) prophesy along the Río Mayo. One Mayo *santo*, Damian Quijano, prophesied in the name of God and La Santa de Cabora that soon a flood would come and destroy the Mexicans, and the Mayos' lands would be fully their own again, provided that after they were restored, the Mayo had right relations with God.[116] San Damian believed God gave him this message directly through Santa Teresa, who informed him which high places they must go to in order to avoid the flood. The Mayos who heard this message likely interpreted it to mean the end of laboring for Mexican hacendados on their own land. When government officials found out about the prophesy and work stoppage, they labeled the saints *sediciosos* (rebels), and after dispersing the crowds of Mayos and sending them back to work on the haciendas, the authorities forcibly deported the *santos* to work in the Santa Rosalía mine in Baja California.[117]

Even though Teresa was one of the *santos* that the insurgent Mayos took inspiration from in the Navojoa uprising, she was not deported to Baja California with them but was still forced to leave Sonora. President Díaz became convinced that the nineteen-year-old woman had incited the Mayo to rebel against him, and that her father's ranch at Cabora was the place that dissidents met to plan these uprisings. However, Teresa told a reporter in El Paso in 1896 that she had done nothing against the government to warrant her deportation and exile: "On telegraphed orders from President Díaz, the Governor and general sent me and my father out of Mexico without a trial, when I had done nothing against order."[118] However, the government claimed there was no reason for the uprising other than the "religious fanaticism" that Teresa inspired at Rancho de Cabora.[119] "Religious fanaticism" was the favorite excuse of the Mexican government for Indigenous and peasant uprisings that implicated Teresa. On the president's orders, she and her father were exiled from Mexico and sent to the United States. Díaz demanded that they go at least as far as Tucson, Arizona Territory (AT), because they were concerned about her continuing to influence the "Indios Yaquis y Mayos," who could easily cross the border. Teresa and her father defied this part of Díaz's order and stayed in Nogales, across the border from its twin city, Nogales, Sonora.[120]

To the disappointment of the Mexican government, Teresa continued to heal people and inspire resistance from the US side of the border, first in Nogales and then El Paso, Texas, where she moved in 1896. The border did not dissuade Teresa's adherents from following her. At this point in time, before the creation of the Border Patrol in 1924, it was relatively easy to cross back and forth across the border. Teresa's followers demonstrated the fluidity of this border. Some reports suggest that hundreds, even thousands, crossed the border into the United States to receive healing from Santa Teresa. In fact, the Mexican consul in Nogales, AT, wrote several letters to the secretary of foreign relations in Mexico between 1892 and 1898 expressing concern about Teresa's continuing influence in Mexico.[121] On the US side

Figure 1.7. "Nat'l Boundary Line at Nogales, 1891. Nogales, Arizona, in distance, Nogales, Sonora, in foreground, view looking NE." Albert Reynolds Photographic Collection, PC 107, #77395, Arizona Historical Society.

of the border, Santa Teresa healed hundreds of people every day from both sides of the line. John Milton Hawkins, a journalist writing for the *Los Angeles Times*, witnessed this. Hawkins visited Teresa's healing practice in El Paso in 1896 and described the way she healed both Mexicans and Americans by using her hands to massage and apply salves, and preparing and administering herbal remedies with the assistance of several older Mexicanas, healing 175 to 200 patients each day, working from 6 a.m. until 9 p.m.[122] Hawkins noted that she did not charge for her cures. He commented that she used "old woman's remedies supplied to her by wrinkled dames who flock about her," suggesting that Teresa had support from fellow Mexicanas in her large healing operation.[123]

The Mexican Joan of Arc

El Paso–based photographer Charles Rose was concerned. He had agreed to take photographs of the popular Mexican curandera Teresa Urrea and reproduce them for sale. This much was not a problem. It was what Rose did for a living. But Teresa had attracted a great deal of attention from both sides of the US-Mexico border since she arrived in El Paso in June 1896, not only because of her miraculous faith healing, but also because of her connection to the recent border rebellions involving the Yaqui.[124] And though Teresa was no stranger to being photographed (she often sat for formal portraits), Rose's photograph would be different. A Mexican gentleman told

Figure 1.8. Teresa Urrea blessing babies in El Paso, Texas, 1896. Newspapers reported that while in El Paso, Teresa treated approximately two hundred people per day. Photograph by Charles Rose, Southwest Collection/Special Collections Library, Texas Tech University, Lubbock.

Rose to print a short paragraph in Spanish and English on the back of the photographs, identifying her as "Señorita Teresa Urrea, Juana de Arco Mexicana" (Miss Teresa Urrea, Mexican Joan of Arc), explaining that she was the only one who could overthrow the government of Porfirio Díaz.[125] Although Rose claimed he could not read it because the paragraph was written in Spanish, the photographer still had reason to believe that it might contain language, as he put it, "objectionable" to the Mexican government.[126]

Rose knew the man who gave him the text for the back of the photograph. Lauro Aguirre, the author of "Señorita Teresa Urrea, Juana de Arco Mexicana," was a journalist and a friend of Teresa and her father. He was also connected to the recent uprisings in Nogales and other places on the border. Rose knew that Teresa, her father, and Aguirre had the reputation of being *revoltosos*—Mexican exiles and political insurgents who spoke out against the Mexican government from the US side of the border.[127] He knew that Aguirre, with Teresa, published an opposition newspaper, *El Independiente*, which exposed the injustices of the Díaz regime. Rather than do what Aguirre asked, Rose visited Teresa's father, Don Tomás. Through an interpreter, Rose expressed his concern about printing those words on the back of the photos of Teresa. Don Tomás suggested that Rose simply omit his name from the photographs if he was worried about it.

Rose did not take Don Tomás's advice. Instead, under the pretext of needing a "careful and correct" translation of the paragraph, Rose gave it to Francisco Mallén, the Mexican consul in El Paso.[128] Mallén had it translated and confirmed Rose's suspicions: "Señorita Teresa Urrea, Juana de Arco Mexicana" was indeed "objectionable" to the Mexican government. In fact, it was a revolutionary manifesto declaring that Teresa would overthrow the Mexican government.

> . . . her undoubted superiority has caused popular sentiment and public opinion to see in her the only person capable of changing the destiny of Mexico, shaking off the tyranny of a Government that assassinates without trial its enemies, who puts towns in flames, and exterminates, like a negro-slaver, the Yaqui and Mayo races . . . she is the only person who . . . may lead to duty and redeem a people terrorized by the cruelties of tyranny and benumbed by the fanaticism of the Roman clergy. . . . As it is believed that she will overthrow the present Government causing a change in the political situation of the Mexicans, she is looked upon as the Mexican JEANNE d' ARC.[129]

Rose must have known that the text was incendiary. Reaching out to the Mexican consul in El Paso was his way to get the manifesto to the Mexican government and warn them of another potential border insurrection—or at least to make it clear that he had no part in it if one occurred. Rose recommended himself to the Mexican consul by saying, "I have the greatest respect for your government, and from the fact of recent disturbances with which the leading papers and dispatches appear to implicate these people, I deem it best to act upon your advice."[130]

As Rose suspected, Teresa, her father, and her friend Lauro Aguirre were in El Paso not only to heal. They were also engaged in a political project that critiqued the Mexican government of Porfirio Díaz—and even sought to overthrow it and replace it with a reformed, more enlightened one. In fact, authorities on both sides of the border were coming to believe that the Teresistas' attack on the Nogales customs house on August 12, 1896, was not a singular event, but may have been only the first in a series of coordinated attacks meant to start a revolution. On August 17, rebels, some of whom were believed to have been involved in the attack in Nogales, attacked the Mexican customs house in Ojinaga, Chihuahua (across the border from Presidio, Texas). In early September, across the border from Columbus, New Mexico, fifty armed men believed to be Teresistas attacked the Mexican customs house in Palomas, Chihuahua.[131] The US consul in Paso del Norte (which is now Juárez) wrote a letter to the assistant US secretary of state on September

9, 1896, warning him of what he felt sure was the distinct possibility of an attack in the coming days by the "Mexican malcontents" Teresa Urrea and Lauro Aguirre, who were living on US soil at that moment.[132]

The combination of these three attacks launched from the US side of the border into Mexico within three months in 1896, all in the name of La Santa de Cabora, made Teresa dangerous to both the Mexican and US governments. The manifesto "Señorita Teresa Urrea, Juana de Arco Mexicana" addressed the tumultuous situation on the border, harnessed the revolutionary energy around Teresa, and made agents of the state (and those who supported them) very nervous.

The vision of Mexico presented in "Juana de Arco Mexicana" was a unique blend of liberalism and radical ideas of equality that appealed to Yaquis, Mayos, and other Mexicanos who were disillusioned with the government of Porfirio Díaz. Díaz's national project encompassed his idea of *orden y progreso*, a mantra as well as an official program whose ultimate aim was to unify and modernize Mexico by courting foreign investment in enterprises such as railroad production and mining. This development especially affected the north of the country and created an increasingly larger and discontented agrarian class, including the Yaqui, Mayo, and other *norteños*.[133] Teresa Urrea, as the Mexican Joan of Arc, threatened Díaz's *orden y progreso*. She specifically addressed—and healed—those excluded from the economic benefits of modernization or targeted by his government, like the Yaqui, who were deported from Sonora to work on henequen plantations in the Yucatán or killed for not submitting to the government's orders.[134]

The manifesto proposed that Teresa Urrea was the only one who could save Mexico from this corruption and purify it because of her moral superiority and spiritual purity. The idea of a woman as a superior moral and spiritual being reflects nineteenth-century gender ideals prominent in Mexico (and the United States) that positioned women as the protectors of moral and spiritual virtues in the domestic and private sphere, protecting their families from the corrupting influences of consumerism, urbanization, and technology in the modern world. In many ways Teresa did not conform to these nineteenth-century gender ideals as she traversed the private and public spheres with her healing—and now with her radical publications.[135] However, young, virginal, unmarried women such as Teresa (especially since she was seen as a divinely sanctioned healer) represented the pinnacle of idealized female virtues of spiritual purity and selfless caring for others. Thus the "Señorita Teresa Urrea, Juana de Arco Mexicana" manifesto juxtaposed the idealized feminine virtues of Teresa against a corrupt and violent government led by Porfirio Díaz.

Written in Spanish and translated into English, the manifesto intended to inspire support on both sides of the US-Mexico border for a rebellion against Porfirio Díaz and to return Mexico to the liberal ideals of the 1857 Constitution that had been betrayed by the Porfirian government: anticlericalism, civil liberties, individual rights, representative institutions, and constitutional guarantees against despotism.[136] Teresa's cohort and others opposed to Díaz believed these liberal ideals were more important than the collective needs of the nation to modernize.[137] Teresa and her collaborators articulated this in another document, the "Plan Restaurador de la Constitución Reformista" (Plan to Restore the Reformed Constitution). Drafted on February 5, 1896, in the Urrea home, just months before the Teresista border uprisings, this radical declaration called for restoration of the liberal Constitution of 1857.[138] It listed the evils of the Porfirian government, including their treatment of the Yaqui, and put forth a plan that would limit the powers of the government and priests so that all people in the Mexican nation would share the same rights and be treated equally: women and men, Indigenous and Mexican, rich and poor. Finally, it called for an armed revolution to overthrow the government of Porfirio Díaz. Even though Teresa, Lauro Aguirre, and Don Tomás Urrea did not sign this revolutionary manifesto, there is ample evidence to suggest they were involved. One scholar suggests that the signature of Mariana Avendano indicates that Teresa Urrea was involved. Teresa healed Mariana in Mexico, and the two became close friends when she followed Teresa to the United States and assisted in her healing practice. The signature of Tomás Esceverría may actually have been a cover for Tomás Urrea, Teresa's father. Loreta Esceverría was Tomás's legitimate wife, and it is likely he used her name to protect himself.[139] Teresa and her cohort had a distinct and radical vision of what they believed Mexico should be—a spiritual vision that eradicated race, class, and gender inequality. Lauro Aguirre and Teresa Urrea presented these views in yet another publication, a book called *¡Tomóchic!*, which was published serially in *El Independiente*—the source of the newspaper clippings found on the bodies of some of the Yaqui rebels who were killed in the rebellion.[140] In describing the Tomóchic rebellion, *El Independiente* offered a spiritual vision that proposed Teresa Urrea, a curandera and *santa* who advocated fair treatment of all races and classes of men and women, should be the savior of the nation. Although Teresa never made an appearance in Tomóchic (in fact, she was in exile in the United States when the rebellion took place), *¡Tomochic!* used the rebellion to argue the case against the corrupt government of Díaz and promote a nation led by Santa Teresa: ". . . it is the beginning of a period of true spirituality; it is the beginning of an era in which women will be emancipated, for its heroine—without intention on her part—was a young woman; it is the awakening of the poor, the illiterate, the lepers and the socially segregate."[141]

This conception of what kind of nation Mexico should be differed from that of Porfirio Díaz and his close advisors, the *científicos*. They believed that the ideals embodied in the liberal 1857 Constitution—popular sovereignty and the rights of individuals—were too abstract and metaphysical, and not based on science and material, observable reality. Justo Sierra, one of the most influential *científicos*, described the 1857 Constitution as "a generous and liberal utopia . . . destined for only slow and painful enactment."[142] Díaz and the *científicos* rejected the valorization of the individual and his rights as the most important aspect of the nation. Instead, they saw society as an evolving organic whole and proposed that an authoritarian government was sometimes needed, in the words of Justo Sierra, "to replace social disintegration and . . . the proclivity toward revolutions." Whereas liberals wanted weak government in order to protect individual rights, Sierra argued that this was an ideal that would not work in Mexico. In countries like Mexico, Sierra explained, "weak governments are the sure symptoms of death."[143] Capitalist development in Mexico was also key to their vision.

The *científicos* invoked evolutionary theory to explain their political philosophy and argued that society, like all biological life, evolved through ever higher, more complex stages according to unchanging scientific laws. The government's role was, in the words of Sierra, to "facilitate this development . . . through material improvements and education."[144] Sierra exhorted liberals to "reject dogmas and metaphysical abstractions and seek a new foundation in science."[145] Mexico was in an age of science and reason, and Sierra argued that the nation must not return to earlier, pre-scientific stages of development. Central to this was the promotion of scientific, orthodox medicine as opposed to traditional, "backward," or "superstitious" medicine. As a curandera, Teresa represented the opposite of the progressive modernity the *científicos* wanted to promote in terms of medicine and public health. In fact, the Mexican consul in El Paso claimed that she was only "a young uneducated and ignorant Mexican girl who possesses some magnetic curing power like those called faith doctors," and only "the lower classes of Mexicans consider this woman a saint."[146] One journalist writing for the Mexico City newspaper *El Monitor Republicano* dismissed Teresa as an un-evolved relic of the past: "This is certain, she (Teresa) is no saint, she is not inspired, but the result of highest ignorance. . . . Saints do not belong to these times; their age is passed, and fortunately for the honor of civilization and progress, they will not return."[147]

However, the reams of paper and ink the Mexican government (and its US counterparts) spent trying to figure out how to stymie the powerful influence of a part-Indigenous and part-Mexican *santa* betray their attempts to dismiss her and the Yaqui Teresistas as "un-evolved relics of the past." Clearly, Mexican consuls in the United States regarded "the Mexican Joan of Arc" as a serious threat to the nation, and the Mexican government took precautions to ensure that the title of the anti-Díaz manifesto, "Señorita Teresa Urrea, Juana de Arco Mexicana," was not printed on photographs of her, much less widely distributed. The ideas contained in the manifesto resonated with many in Mexico. Despite the official anticlericalism of the nation, most Mexicans were deeply religious at the turn of the twentieth century. Mexico itself was founded on a blending of Catholicism and Indigenous beliefs encapsulated in the symbol of the "brown" Virgin of Guadalupe, not unlike the folk Catholicism, Indigenous healing practices, and Spiritism that Teresa blended in her own curanderismo. She did not discount science but instead spoke of a kind of spiritual modernity as she exhorted her followers to "search for God in love and science."[148] In this, she suggested that science and spirituality were not so incompatible, and that a nation must have both to modernize, mobilize, and unify the people, like so many nations built on spiritual ideas, tapping into the deeply held beliefs and longings of citizens. As a *santa*, *revoltosa*, and mestiza *espiritista* curandera, Teresa Urrea, as both the symbol of the Mexican Joan of Arc and a real person, intentionally challenged what the government of Porfirio Díaz and his *científicos* wanted for Mexico.

The real person was no longer a girl. In 1896, Santa Teresa was twenty-three. Under the constant supervision of her father, as well as the Mexican government, she must have longed for independence. She would get that. However, like any woman in the late nineteenth century, society offered Teresa limited options: she could be a wife and mother, a nun, maybe a teacher or a nurse—but remaining single, or independent of her father or a husband, was not celebrated. The message from society for women of her age was that it was time to seriously consider marriage and starting a family—if they had not done so already. Compared to her mother, Cayetana, who gave birth to her when she was fourteen, Teresa was getting too old for marriage. In Mexico, some joked that even as young as thirty, women were old.[149] In 1900, at twenty-seven, Teresa did marry.

After the tense time in El Paso, when the Teresista uprisings and the Mexican Joan of Arc manifesto, along with the anti-Díaz publication *El Independiente*, threw more attention on her and her father, the whole Urrea family moved almost two hundred miles from the border, eventually landing in Clifton, Arizona. For three years, Teresa would continue to live with her family and use her gift of healing, becoming an important figure in the

Figure 1.9. Teresa Urrea and her father, Don Tomás Urrea. This portrait was taken in Arizona after the Urreas had left El Paso, but before Teresa left her father's home in 1900 and set out for California on her own. William Curry Holden Papers, SW CPC #58, Southwest Collection/Special Collections Library, Texas Tech University, Lubbock.

Figure 1.10. Teresa Urrea's mother, Cayetana Chávez. William Curry Holden Papers, SW CPC #100, Southwest Collection/Special Collections Library, Texas Tech University, Lubbock.

Figure 1.11. The Urrea family. William Curry Holden Papers, SW CPC #46. Southwest Collection/Special Collections Library, Texas Tech University, Lubbock.

town of Clifton and making friends with the local physician and other influential families who sought out her healing. She would also fall in love and marry. However, her marriage to Guadalupe Rodríguez would not last. In July of 1900, at the age of twenty-eight, Teresa left for California, with the support of Clifton friends, and began a healing career far from her family, on her own, in the urban cities and medical marketplaces of San Francisco, Los Angeles, St. Louis, and New York City.[150]

In these burgeoning urban centers in the United States, Teresa continued to heal those on the margins of power: Indigenous people, people of Mexican descent, and even some Anglos. Many of those she healed in these growing cities not only suffered from diseases that medical science had no cure for, but were discriminated against by US public health officials who deemed non-white "others," such as people of Mexican descent, as vectors of disease. Teresa became a source of cultural and spiritual refuge and possible revitalization for these people. She also healed those interested in her appeal as an "exotic other"—her identity as the Mexican Joan of Arc would become an intrinsic part of her public persona in US cities—and the electric thrill coming from her hands.[151]

Laying on of Hands: Espiritismo and Modernity in the Urban Borderlands of San Francisco and Los Angeles

Mr. and Mrs. Rosencrans were desperate. Their three-year-old son, Alvin, had been diagnosed with cerebrospinal meningitis. In the last two months, he had lost both speech and sight. Alvin's little body, clenched with rigidity, was almost completely paralyzed. In San Jose, California, where the Rosencrans family lived, Mrs. Rosencrans told an interviewer that five doctors had seen Alvin, and all said there was no hope for him.[1] Cerebrospinal meningitis is an illness in which the protective membranes covering the brain and spinal cord become infected and inflamed, causing severe headaches, high fever, muscle rigidity and paralysis, loss of speech, and blindness—and if not treated, leads to death.[2] At the beginning of the twentieth century, the United States witnessed a wave of meningitis cases, mostly among children under five.[3] The parents of Mrs. Rosencrans, who lived in Clifton, Arizona, where Teresa Urrea also lived, brought the famous curandera to San Jose in order to heal Alvin. They had seen her perform successful—some would say miraculous—cures in Clifton. They believed that Santa Teresa was the boy's last, and best, chance for healing.

Teresa arrived in San Jose in July 1900. She treated Alvin daily in the privacy of his bedroom. She applied a plaster to his back; she massaged him to loosen his rigid muscles and unclench his hands. During this time, Alvin's mother expressed to the interviewer that she had faith in Teresa. After six weeks of treatment, Mrs. Rosencrans claimed that Alvin was indeed healing: "He can move and talk, his is fat again, and I believe . . . that she will cure him and make him see again."[4]

The healing of Alvin Rosencrans might be understood as a miracle, yet another example of Teresa's "miraculous healing powers." Viewing Alvin's healing as miraculous would be a valid understanding, especially at this time when there were many diseases that science had no cure for, including tuberculosis, yellow fever, and the disease that afflicted Alvin—cerebrospinal meningitis.[5] However, his healing might also be considered the outcome of careful and intensive therapy by a skilled healer. As Teresa had done before in the hundreds of cures that she had administered to her Indigenous, Mexican, and Anglo patients—first in the towns of Sonora, Mexico, and then in El Paso, Clifton, and now San Jose—she employed healing knowledge that she had gained over years of training and practice, and, significantly, she used her hands to heal with electric vibrations and by applying mud, plasters, and the mustard seed poultice *sinapismos*. In both interpretations of Alvin's healing—miraculous and the outcome of successful treatment—Teresa's hands are of singular importance.

The *San Francisco Examiner* featured an interview with Teresa and the Rosencrans family suggesting that Teresa's power came through her intimate practice of "laying-on hands." During the interview Teresa demonstrated her healing techniques for the journalist, who described it like this: ". . . she took my hands in hers—hands of singular slenderness and fineness, cool, smooth, supple, firm, delicately made, charming to the touch—and placed her thumbs against mine, holding with a close, nervous grasp."[6]

While the journalist described Teresa's hands with gendered language that suggests an idealized femininity—slender, delicate, charming—other commentators described her hands as magnetic and electric, capable of sending electric currents into the bodies of patients, like an electric belt or battery, reflecting the turn-of-the-century fascination with new kinds of spiritual and scientific power, especially electricity. For example, a different journalist described how Teresa "imparts by the touch of her hands a gentle electric sensation such as might be supplied by excessive personal magnetism or a weak electric battery."[7] Like electric belts and other popular healing modalities advertised in the pages of newspapers such as the *San Francisco Examiner*, the miraculous powers coming from Teresa's hands were all part of the larger current of healing potentialities at the turn of the century. This was a time when new inventions—streetcars, telegraphs, telephones, moving pictures, electric chairs, and electric belts—challenged people's notions of the possible.[8] And electricity, which in the late nineteenth and early twentieth century was transforming the world, seemed to permeate everything, even the body, revealing its potential to heal, whether from an electric belt or Santa Teresa's hands.

The focus on Teresa's hands as the carriers of her healing power reveals this broader context of modernity and medical pluralism. It also shows how, through the intimate practice of laying hands on individual bodies, she was able to gain a following and authority as she entered a new world: the mod-

Figure 2.1. Portrait of Teresa Urrea. This photograph was taken in Clifton, Arizona, sometime between 1900 and 1905, roughly the time period that Teresa lived in California and traveled the nation demonstrating her healing. William Curry Holden Papers, SW CPC #56, Southwest Collection/Special Collections Library, Texas Tech University, Lubbock.

ern US city. After six weeks in San Jose, Teresa moved to San Francisco. There she became a part of the modern medical marketplace, using all the tools she had gained over her twenty-seven years to continue healing others and enlarging her own knowledge of medicine, spirituality, and social justice as she began the twentieth century as a woman on her own.

The Modern Medical Marketplace in San Francisco

In 1900, Teresa Urrea entered a medical landscape populated by various and diverse healing practitioners: homeopaths, Chinese herbal doctors, Spiritualists, patent medicine salespeople, Protestant faith healers, and physicians who specialized in specific disorders. At the same time, the professionalization of medicine was actively seeking to gain and maintain sovereign authority over this marketplace. An overview of this medical landscape reveals the world that Teresa, and any person living in 1900, occupied. It was a world filled with a dizzying array of healing options. To illustrate: in the Friday, September 21, 1900, issue of the *San Francisco Call*, an advertisement for the "Wonderful Mexican Girl Healer Santa Teresa" promised "successful" and "wonderful cures being made daily" for "cases given up by physicians." This ad was surrounded by others for healing devices such as "Dr. Bennett's Electric Belt," an undergarment that promised to send mild electric shocks to the genitals that would make "weak men and women strong and strong men and women stronger," and "Dr. Crossman's Specific Mixture," which promised to cure "gonorrhea . . . and analogous complaints of the Organs of Generation" for only one dollar per bottle.[9] Today, reading a newspaper from 1900 may provoke giggles as well as horror over some of the advertisements and cures offered to the public. For example, "The Electric Coronet" was advertised with a picture of a man (and sometimes a woman next to him) wearing what appears to be a crown on his head sending electric shocks into his brain that were promised to "electrify and illuminate the mind, restore lost harmony and lost vitality, and invigorate you wonderfully."[10]

Health seekers could choose from a variety of cure-all pills, oils, and nostrums advertised in the *San Francisco Call*, including "Beechman's Pills," which promised to cure insomnia; "Sloan's Liniment" to cure neuralgia (a disorder of the nervous system); "Cuticura Resolvent," a cream that promised to heal blemishes on the skin as well as disorders of the blood, kidneys, and bowels; and "Doctor DeFord's Homeopathic Remedies," which included specially formulated medicines such as "Doctor DeFord's Nerve Cure," "Doctor DeFord's Heart Cure," and "Doctor DeFord's General Debility Cure."[11] Other advertisements specifically targeted women, including "Peruna, the Great Tonic," marketed to the "many housewives that suffer from nervous depression due to . . . weaknesses peculiar to [their] sex," who could simply take this tonic and be healed.[12] If these pills, creams, nostrums, and electric devices did not do the trick, people could also consult with specific kinds of healers whose legitimacy as healers and appeal as exotic "others" holding hidden knowledge often came from their race,

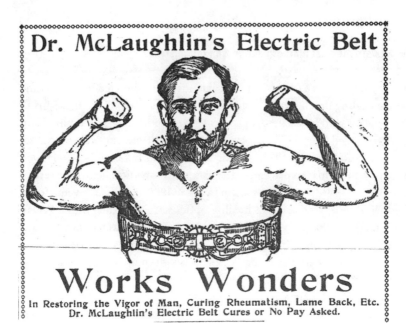

Dr. McLaughlin's Electric Belt

Works Wonders

In Restoring the Vigor of Man, Curing Rheumatism, Lame Back, Etc.
Dr. McLaughlin's Electric Belt Cures or No Pay Asked.

Dr. Bennett's Electric Belt

Figures 2.2–2.4.
Advertisements for electric belts in the *San Francisco Examiner*, September 30, 1900.

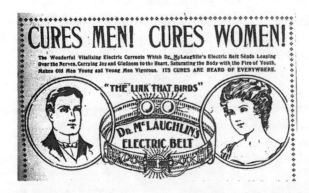

CURES MEN! CURES WOMEN!

The Wonderful Vitalizing Electric Currents Which Dr. McLaughlin's Electric Belt Sends Leaping Over the Nerves, Carrying Joy and Gladness to the Heart, Saturating the Body with the Fire of Youth, Makes Old Men Young and Young Men Vigorous. ITS CURES ARE HEARD OF EVERYWHERE.

"THE LINK THAT BINDS"

DR. McLAUGHLIN'S ELECTRIC BELT

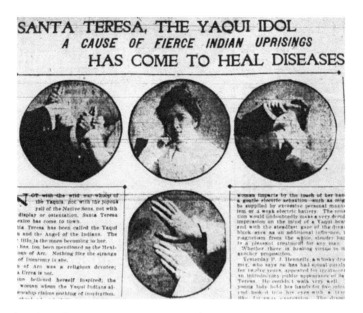

SANTA TERESA, THE YAQUI IDOL
A CAUSE OF FIERCE INDIAN UPRISINGS
HAS COME TO HEAL DISEASES

Figure 2.5. "Santa Teresa, the Yaqui Idol, a Cause of Fierce Indian Uprisings, Has Come to Heal Diseases." *San Francisco Examiner*, September 9, 1900.

ethnicity, or nationality, such as the Chinese doctors Li Wing and T. Foo Yuan of the "Foo and Wing Herb Company" and Dr. Chas Clayton, who advertised himself as a "Full Blood Indian" to sell his patented "Blood Zone" remedies for "all diseases known to medical science."[13] It is, perhaps, within this exotic "other" category that Teresa Urrea most obviously fit. In San Francisco newspapers, she was referred to as the Mexican Joan of Arc who caused Indigenous uprisings, and the "sad-eyed Mexican girl" who "comes among skeptical Anglo-Saxon civilization" to demonstrate her "wonderful cures."[14]

Part of the reason for this dizzying array of healing choices—of which Santa Teresa, the curandera, the "Mexican Girl Healer," "the Yaqui Idol," was a part—is that the late nineteenth century and early twentieth saw significant changes in medical ideology and practice. During this time, "regular" or orthodox physicians practiced alongside "irregular" healers like homeopaths, patent medicine makers, and curanderos: they all treated illnesses and diseases they often could neither clearly diagnose nor distinguish from their symptoms. The broad assumptions of humoral theory, developed by Hippocrates (c. 460–370 BCE), were shared by most healers. Humoral theory posited that the human body, like all of nature, is composed of four elements: water, air, fire, and earth.[15] Hippocrates associated

Figure 2.6. "Santa Teresa, Celebrated Mexican Healer, Whose Powers Awe Warlike Yaquis in Sonora, Comes to Restore San Jose Boy to Health," *San Francisco Examiner,* July 27, 1900.

the four elements with the four humors—phlegm, blood, yellow bile, and black bile—whose moist, dry, hot, and cold qualities coexisted in the human body in a more or less balanced way. Hippocrates stressed the importance of observing patients for signs of humoral imbalance and to "first do no harm" because he believed the body, like nature, was essentially self-balancing and self-healing. In Hippocratic medicine, the physician's first and most important job was to stimulate and support the humoral balance involved in the natural process of healing. For example, a physician might treat an illness attributed to excessive cold by heating the patient with a steam bath or warming teas. An illness attributed to the excess of yellow or black bile might be treated by an emetic (an agent that induces vomiting) to rebalance the bodily fluids. The variety of therapies used by these healers—including bloodletting, bathing, purging, sweating, electrical stimulation, and massage—sought to bring balance to sick bodies by treating general conditions such as fevers, colds, and swelling, not specific diseases.

Two therapeutic approaches based on the broad assumptions of humoral medicine, "heroic" and "botanical," were popular from the eighteenth century through the nineteenth. Most orthodox physicians practiced heroic medicine, so called because of the aggressive nature of the therapy: doctors bled, purged, and blistered their patients in order to rid their bodies of illnesses and establish humoral balance.[16] Most regular physicians accepted bloodletting well into the nineteenth century because it produced visible results. In the case of fever, when a patient was treated with bloodletting, the pulse weakened, the fevered flush of the complexion changed to pallor, and the patient began to perspire freely. At the time, these symptomatic changes provided the doctor and patient with demonstrable evidence that the cure was working.[17] Because of the popularity of bloodletting as a medical practice, and the way it demarcated professional physicians from alternative

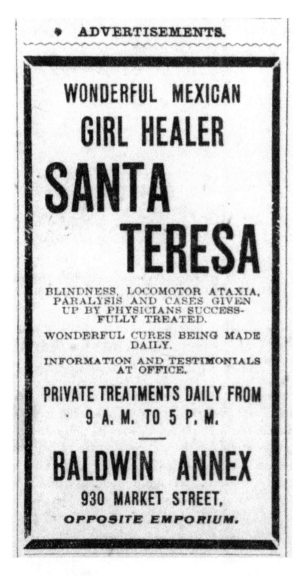

Figure 2.7. "Wonderful Mexican Girl Healer." Advertisement in *San Francisco Call*, September 21, 1900.

healers, the scalpel used to cut the skin and bleed the patient, called the lancet, became the hallmark of the medical profession.[18] However, not everyone embraced heroic medicine.[19] Skepticism of it throughout the first half of the nineteenth century was one reason that alternative, therapeutically conservative healers with less intrusive methods, broadly called "botanicals," came into prominence.

Teresa Urrea, and all curanderos, would most clearly be categorized as botanical healers because of their use of medicinal herbs and folk remedies. While botanical healers shared assumptions with heroic medicine, especially the humoral ideology of restoring the sick body to balance, their healing represents a long tradition in the American continents of relying on the medicinal use of plant material—learned from the Indigenous peoples of the Americas—to heal.[20] Consequently, botanical medicine had long been the domain of a variety of lay healers, including but not limited to midwives, Indigenous healers, and folk healers such as curanderos, as well as mothers and grandmothers producing household remedies to heal their families. Botanical medicine, broadly understood, was not considered a movement.[21] However, a botanical sect emerged in the nineteenth century that would become popular on both sides of the US-Mexico border: homeopathy.

Although Teresa did not identify as a homeopathic healer, the ideology behind it is in some ways similar to the ideology that she and other Spiritualist and *espiritista* healers subscribed to—especially in its understandings of the role of spiritual forces in healing. Homeopathy draws on the theory of vitalism, a philosophical concept that posits that all living organisms contain an invisible, spiritual, and dynamic "vital" force. Homeopaths believe this force fights agents of disease that attack the body, and the job of the physician is to manage or assist this spiritual force through the introduction of highly diluted medicines (rather than through electric currents or spirit channeling of the dead).[22] Homeopathy encompasses a theory of healing that rests on the assumption that "like is cured by like" (the Greek root *homo* means "same"), or that the curative powers of medicine come from their ability to produce in healthy persons symptoms of the disease for which they are meant to treat in sick persons. In the nineteenth century, homeopathic physicians administered "infinitesimal doses" of medicines to the sick and believed that the medicines' effectiveness came from a spiritual or dynamic power conferred on it by shaking the containers of the diluted doses.[23] Homeopathy offered a critique of prevailing "scientific" medicine as elitist and ineffectual, and offered both professional healers and lay people the opportunity to become homeopathic healers through schools, literature, and medical kits.[24]

In Mexico and the United States, homeopathy proved to be successful and highly influential, and professional doctors lashed out against homeopaths. When Mexican president Porfirio Díaz created the National School of Homeopathic Medicine in 1896, granting to its graduates the same professional status as physicians trained in orthodox medicine, Mexican physicians, angry that the state sanctioned what they considered a "superstitious" and "fanatic" healing practice populated with "charlatans," argued that homeopathy not only threatened the medical profession with its popularity but also the development of a modern, progressive, and scientific nation.[25] Mexican medical elites echoed the reigning positivistic philosophy that dominated elite intellectual thought during the Porfiriato (the period of the presidency of Porfirio Díaz: 1876–1880, 1884–1911) and discredited alternative forms of medical knowledge, especially those proposed by curanderos, midwives, and homeopaths.[26] In the United States, the American Medical Association (AMA) was formed in 1847 largely in response to the threat posed by homeopaths to the business of professional doctors. This threat can be seen in the fact that the AMA's first order of business was to discredit homeopaths by adopting a code of ethics that prohibited its members from consulting with homeopaths and, moreover, exhorted them to educate their patients about the dangerous treatments of homeopaths and other "quack" practitioners.[27]

However, even though Mexican and US members of the medical orthodoxy attempted to show how superstitious and unscientific homeopaths were, many homeopaths were trained as well as, or better, than regular doctors. Their therapeutics, judged by the scientific knowledge available at the time, were no worse or better than scientific medicine. By the 1840s, homeopaths in the United States had established medical schools and hospitals, published a wide array professional journals and medical texts, and received significant support from the professional and intellectual elite, claiming adherents such as John D. Rockefeller, President James A. Garfield, and Mexican revolutionary president Francisco Madero (1873–1913), a homeopathic healer himself who treated the workers on his large hacienda in the northern Mexican state of Coahuila.[28] Like Teresa Urrea, Madero eventually became a practicing Spiritist medium.[29]

The Healing Medium

The Mexican homeopath *hacendado* Francisco Madero and the exiled Mexican curandera Teresa Urrea represent another type of healer who vied for customers in the turn-of-the-century medical marketplace: the Spiritist and Spiritualist healing medium. Urrea's curanderismo, like Madero's homeopathy, was deeply influenced by Spiritism, or *espiritismo*, a practice connected to Spiritualism that was part of new, heterodox spiritual currents flowing through Europe, Mexico, and the United States, demonstrating how both the United States and Mexico had people within their borders like Teresa Urrea and Francisco Madero who longed to transcend the material body, evolve, and modernize the nation through a science of the spirits. These people and movements were connected across borders as well as oceans. In fact, the Spiritualist and Spiritist presses joined in 1890, forming the Federación Universal de la Prensa Espirita y Espritualista, demonstrating the trans-religious and transnational connections between these religions that Teresa Urrea's life illuminates.[30] As discussed in chapter 1, Teresa's contacts with the world of espiritistas and espiritualistas began in Mexico almost immediately after she received her *don* in 1889. Those contacts aided her when she lived and practiced her curanderismo in San Francisco. In fact, Teresa advertised herself as a Spiritualist medium in the *San Francisco Call* classifieds, demonstrating this connection between Spiritists and Spiritualists.[31]

Teresa Urrea and Francisco Madero's practice of espiritismo originated with French Spiritism (*Spiritisme*), which incorporated elements of Mesmerism and modern American Spiritualism with an overarching focus on this "spiritual science," as a way to improve and heal the individual body, as well as the social body. Mesmerism, named after its originator, Franz Anton Mesmer (1734–1815), was based on a theory of healing that suggests the transfer of energy from one body to another happens through a vital fluid that flows within and between bodies called "animal magnetism," an invisible substance similar to electricity.[32] Mesmer understood this magnetic fluid as a physical force—as scientific, not supernatural.[33] He posited that in healthy people this magnetic fluid flowed freely, but in the sick it was blocked. Mesmer believed that through the manipulation of animal magnetism by the therapeutic passing of hands or magnets over the body, he could cure the sick by rebalancing the patient's bodily energies.[34] When Mesmer moved to Paris in 1778, his theory of Mesmerism (also referred to as "magnetic healing" because of the use of magnets) became popular among amateur scientists and upper-class Parisians. In France, mesmerism came to be more strongly associated with the somnambulic trance state and the clairvoyance that often accompanied it.[35] The idea that the mesmerized patient had access to special powers and could perform wonders in this state—for example, see the insides of bodies, diagnose diseases, and communicate with distant persons or spirits of the dead—became popular.[36]

One of Mesmer's followers, Charles Poyen, crossed the Atlantic in 1836 and began to lecture to audiences in New England.[37] He told them that Mesmerism could help make the United States the "most perfect nation on earth," tapping into an already present urge in American religious life to perfect society and the self.[38] Thus, in the United States, Mesmerism moved slightly away from being the medical healing system that Franz Mesmer intended—although it always retained an element of that—and transformed into what Poyen described as "a schema demonstrating how the individual mind can establish a rapport with ever more sublime levels of reality."[39] Mesmerism caught on especially in upstate New York, a place that had witnessed religious revivals charged by the power of the Holy Spirit, a power in many ways similar to the slight electric charge felt by those in mesmeric trances.[40] In the United States, Spiritualism appealed to Quakers; Abolitionists such as Frederick Douglass, William Lloyd Garrison, and Sojourner Truth; and other reformers who sought to connect with the spirit world to make the nation more just.[41] American Spiritualism also drew less prominent women—often adolescent girls, similar to Teresa Urrea—from the private sphere into the public, offering them a voice through the privileged position of spirit medium.[42] As historian Molly McGarry has noted, Spiritualism gave young women a public voice "at the very moment when their possibilities for power, speech, and imagination were fast diminishing."[43]

Like Teresa, Francisco Madero became a Spiritist medium and would heal while in a trance state. As a "writing medium," Madero would enter into a trance and channel his younger brother Raúl, who died in a fire at age four.[44] Madero claimed Raúl sent him messages by way of automatic writing—understood by Spiritists as the dead spirit moving the hand of the medium.[45] He also blended his healing and politics through his practice of Spiritism, as did Teresa and her anti-Díaz revolutionary cohort. As Madero grew more politically active in the first decade of the twentieth century, forming *anti-reelectionismo* clubs and fomenting opposition to President Díaz, Raúl would send his brother encouraging messages, including this one: "Aspire to do good for your fellow citizens . . . working for a lofty goal that will raise the moral level of society, which will succeed in liberating it from oppression, slavery and fanaticism."[46]

Both Teresa and Madero believed they could heal bodies, humanity, and ultimately, the Mexican nation through espiritismo. Madero combined his Spiritist practice (which proposed a fluidic spiritual force linking the physical body with the spiritual realm) with homeopathy (which contained the notion that healing happened through a "vital force") and applied these practices to heal those who worked on his hacienda. According to extensive

TERESA COMES IN CAUSE OF MERCY

Mexican Girl Famed as the Joan of Arc of Yaqui Indians of Sonora Is in San Francisco.

SENORA TERESA RODERIGUEZ, KNOWN AS "SANTA TERESA."

Figure 2.8. "Teresa Comes in Cause of Mercy," *San Francisco Call*, September 9, 1900. This photo of Teresa clasping hands with a patient was probably taken at the Golden West Hotel, where she gave a demonstration of her healing to members of the San Francisco press on September 3, 1900.

notes he made of his treatments from 1901 to 1902, Madero treated his family members and workers for a wide variety of symptoms and illnesses, including fever, nervous disorders like *susto*, delusions, attacks, fainting and insomnia, menstrual disorders, alcoholism, skin rashes, herpes, dysentery, typhoid fever, consumption, flu, and pneumonia.[47] His remedies—often determined through Spiritist channeling—were mostly the homeopathic medicines he procured from special pharmacies, but he also practiced magnetism and passed his hands over a patient's body to heal, as Teresa did, and he sometimes prescribed water cures and local herbs such as belladonna.[48]

Like Teresa's cures, Madero's treatments provided efficacious healing—or at least relief from painful symptoms—to many people who had limited access to professional physicians or may simply have preferred treatment by alternative healers such as Madero and Teresa rather than the expensive and perhaps equally dubious "heroic" treatments offered by regular doctors.

Even as Teresa and Madero shared a belief in espiritismo as a source of healing for the individual body as well as the social body, there were important differences between these two revolutionary healers. Madero was a Mexican who lived up to the societal expectations of him as the head of his household and hacienda. Even as he became the figurehead of the Mexican Revolution, he did so somewhat reluctantly. He was a classic liberal who preferred to work within the system rather than overthrow it.[49] On the other hand, Teresa was a woman. This simple but important fact—as well as her connection to Indigenous rebellions and her more radical anti-Díaz stance, which demanded a more radical solution to the problems of Mexico, an overthrow of the system rather than a reformation of it—distinguished her from Madero. It also influenced interpretations and understandings of her healing. In the pages of the *San Francisco Examiner* and other US newspapers, especially in urban spaces like San Francisco, she was viewed as an exotic "other" that linked her gender, nationality, and power to inspire radical Indigenous uprisings to her healing power: she was the "Mexican Girl Healer," "Joan of Arc of Yaqui Indians," and "Santa Teresa who has been worshiped as a guide from heaven by the Indians of Mexico" to lead Indigenous rebellions.[50] In addition to her gender, connection to Indigenous peoples, and radicalism, another difference that distinguished Teresa from Madero was that she performed her healing in front of audiences in US cities.

". . . Her Hands, and the Manner in Which She Treats Her Patients"

The commentaries on Teresa Urrea's live healing performances by journalists in newspapers such as the *San Francisco Examiner* and the *San Francisco Call* provide firsthand accounts of her healing style as well as a window into the medical marketplace and the world of ideas in the late nineteenth and early twentieth centuries. Teresa's hands, as described in these articles, became conduits and signifiers of turn-of-the-century notions about gender, modernity, and race: they were lovely, slender, gentle, magnetic, electric, and white. For example, accompanied by a photo of Teresa clasping hands with a client surrounded by drawings of hands (figure 2.8), one article in the *San Francisco Call* described her healing with a focus on her hands:

Here it may be explained that the young woman imparts by the touch of her hands a gentle electric sensation such as . . . would undoubtedly make a very decided impression on the mind of a Yaqui Brave, and with the steadfast gaze of the dreamy black eyes as an additional influence, the magnetism from the white, slender hands is a pleasant treatment for any man.[51]

This journalist attended a demonstration of Teresa's healing at the Golden West Hotel, the first performance of her healing for an audience in San Francisco. The focus on the electricity in Teresa's hands in this journalist's story reflects the fascination more broadly with electricity as a symbol of modernity: it was something that existed inside the body as well as outside of it. One of the modern uses of electricity was that it could heal, as evidenced by the popularity of electric belts and coronets.[52] Indeed, it seemed to many that electricity could provide magical cures. The electricity coming from Teresa's hands could not only heal, but also make an impression on "a Yaqui Brave," reinforcing the prevailing notion of Indigenous peoples as decidedly not modern, but rather unscientific, primitive, and uncivilized: a conception of Indigenous Americans that justified the US federal policy of breaking up tribal land, allotting individual plots to Indigenous families, and assimilating them into "civilized" white society.[53] Significantly, this journalist described Teresa's hands as white, not brown. Perhaps her perceived whiteness made her an acceptable "other" for Anglos in a period defined by a racial ideology that posited their racial superiority over Indigenous people and all people of color, as well as the danger of integrating and mixing races. Finally, the description of the hypnotic "gaze of her dreamy black eyes" and the statement that Teresa's treatment would be a pleasurable experience for "any man" reinforce the notion that women's power was ultimately held in their ability to influence and control men through their sensuality and sexuality—certainly not their skills as healers.

Another description of a healing performance reveals Teresa's style as that of a medium espiritista, or Spiritualist healing medium, as well as the gendered idea that her healing was nothing if not pleasurable for men. In an article in the *San Francisco Examiner*, the writer described Teresa's healing treatment of a man named P. J. Hennelly, a whisky drummer (salesperson) who claimed to be suffering from spinal paralysis that compromised his ability to walk.

The young lady held his hands for five minutes and looked into his eyes with a trance-like, far-away expression. The drummer liked it. She placed her hands upon his cheeks, and he liked that. The back of his head she manipulated with gentle touches. The drummer smiled joyously. He was directed to sit down and take off his shoes. With no little difficulty he extracted his feet from their leather coverings; then Teresa of Sinaloa imparted to them the gentle magnetic current. That was followed by further grasping of the hands, and after fifteen minutes or so the manipulations were ended.[54]

Even though this journalist's concern was not Teresa's healing techniques, but rather its effect on her male client, continuing the trend of sexualizing her in the media, his description reveals her healing style—in a trance state, like a medium espiritista—and her "gentle touches" and "manipulations" that emitted magnetic currents and brought relief (and pleasure) to the whisky drummer. Her patient, P. J. Hennelly, described to the journalist the feeling of being treated by Teresa and the results it produced in his body.

Hennelly said after that the sensation was much like that of a strong electric battery, but without its painful twinges. Under her influence he could stand without the aid of his cane, which he had not been able to do for twelve years, and his knee joints seemed to have gained greater flexibility. "She certainly has wonderful magnetic power" Hennelly said, "but I do not think she has given me any relief that will be permanent. I will say, however, that the temporary effects of her treatment were wonderful."[55]

According to Hennelly, Teresa's treatment involved electric and magnetic power, and produced results. Even if Hennelly questioned the long-term efficacy of her treatment, his testimony reveals that she indeed made him feel better, a positive outcome even for a patient and professional physician today.

While female healers like Teresa Urrea—curanderas, nurses, midwives, Spiritualist healing mediums—used their hands to massage, soothe, manipulate muscles and energy, and transmit electric impulses, so too did medical doctors who were vying for dominance in this medical marketplace. However, the discourse that surrounded physicians' use of hands was quite different from the often sexualized and exoticized ways in which journalists described Teresa Urrea's laying on of hands. Doctors (generally characterized as male) were scientific.[56] They used their hands to "palpate," the scientific word for the use of touch to diagnose.[57] Physicians' use of "palpation" as opposed to Teresa's use of "laying on of hands" reflect what was considered proper male behavior (rational, scientific, detached) and proper female behavior (nurturing, sensual, spiritual). Yet, if the ultimate outcome of any interaction with a healer is that the patient feels better, if pain is relieved, then curanderas and professional doctors were both viable in this marketplace. Thus, even if professional physicians dismissed healers like Teresa as superstitious charlatans, lacking scientific knowledge and training, the truth is they often had just as much success in treating symptoms as professional physicians did.

These descriptions of Teresa's healing performances reveal much about her healing style as well as the medico-scientific, racial, and gender ideologies that prevailed in 1900. Yet, how did Teresa herself understand her healing? How did she describe and interpret what happened when she healed? Would she have agreed with the assessments presented above? Earlier, when she still lived in Mexico, she came to identify as an espiritista, especially a medium espiritista who could heal while in a trance. Fortunately, after she left Mexico and the borderlands, she spoke to journalists about her healing process.

One particularly insightful interview published in 1901 reveals Teresa as a woman who at age twenty-eight had been healing for fourteen years and knew her power, as well as its limitations. In this interview, Teresa explained how she would diagnose her patients: "Sometimes I can tell at a glance what ailment afflicts the patient who comes to me—just as though it were written on his face; sometimes I cannot."[58] She discussed giving botanical medicines: "Sometimes I give medicines made from herbs to my patients." The use of herbal medicine is not what Teresa was most known for—surely not what most people wrote about when they described her healing—but it is something consistently mentioned in less sensationalized accounts of her healing and reflects her training as a curandera in Mexico with María Sonora.[59]

However, Teresa went into most detail discussing the intimate moment of healing, the laying on of hands, and what transpired between the curandera and her patient.[60]

> In treating a patient, I take his hands in mine—not grasping them tightly, but only clasping the fingers and pressing each of my thumbs against each of his thumbs. Then, after awhile, I place one of my thumbs on his forehead—just over the eyes.[61]

Then she described the patient's point of view—why they come to her, what they should feel.

> It is this way: You have headaches. Sometimes your head feels heavy. Your heart does not at all times beat regularly—sometimes it palpitates too rap-

idly. Your stomach is not as good as it should be. Do you feel a little electric thrill entering your thumbs? No? Sometimes I cannot communicate the thrill to patients—and then I cannot cure them.[62]

Here, Teresa described communication between herself and her patient: the clasping of hands and touching of thumbs (shown in figures 2.5, 2.6, and 2.8) and the "little electric thrill" that the patient must feel to know that healing power is passing from her to her patient. This electricity is something P. J. Hennelly, as well as many others, described feeling when Teresa clasped their hands in this way.

In this interview, Teresa consistently spoke about her healing as powerful—as a power within her that she conveyed to sick bodies through her hands. For example, she described how she almost always used her hands to "rub" her patients "gently." However, she made a distinction between what she did and what "masseurs" do. She would only rub her patients in order to "communicate the power that I have to them," not necessarily to give pleasure, as journalists described her touch as doing.[63] In this interview, Teresa acknowledged the limitations of her power. In fact, she began her discussion of healing by admitting that she could not heal everyone. She explained the importance of belief in her healing power, that healing is a two-way street, and if some did not believe, "that power I try to send into them returns to me, and they are no better."[64] However, she said that if her patient would accept that power from her hands, "most of them get well."[65] Finally, Teresa described how she often would go into a trance when she healed, similar to the trance she was in for over three months when she received her *don*, and this was when her healing power was strongest.

I frequently go into trances, but none have lasted as long as did the first one. Then people think I am crazy. Not that I am violent: But I do not pay attention to their questions, and I say strange things. These spells do not give warning to their approach. I do not know when I am to have them except by my queer answers to their questions. In these spells my power for healing is greater than at other times.[66]

One review of another of her healing performances—this one at the Metropolitan Temple in San Francisco on September 12, 1900, for an audience of between four hundred and a thousand—reveals her healing in a style that is meditative, intimate, and quiet—similar to how she described it.[67] In fact, this article describes her healing as a "séance," reflecting the Spiritualist and Spiritist practices that Teresa and some members of her audience, as well as the reading public, would have been familiar with. On stage, she applied her

TERESA URREA, called a saint by the Yaqui Indians, an exile from Mexico who is credited with marvelous cures. This is the first photograph of her ever published.

Figure 2.9. "Teresa Urrea, called a saint by the Yaqui Indians." *St Louis Post-Dispatch*, March 3, 1901, 27. This photo accompanied the story in which Teresa described her healing.

"magnetic touch" to fifteen men, women, and children afflicted with various illnesses, including deafness, paralysis, blindness, diabetes, and a sprained ankle. They had come to have "Santa Teresa, the Mexican girl healer . . . lay hands upon them."[68] The article describes how most of the audience was "filled with doubt," yet the patients all claimed they felt better after Teresa "applied her magnetic touch," or as she called it, the "electric thrill" emanating from her thumbs.[69]

However, it seemed that Teresa's healing performance lacked the dynamism needed to entertain and hold the attention of an audience of several hundred. She was a curandera after all, not a vaudeville entertainer, like so many who graced the stage of the Metropolitan Temple.[70] In fact, her healing was so quiet that the journalist reviewing her performance described how most of the crowd left before the ninety-minute demonstration was over.[71] As the audience began leaving, Teresa's manager, a man by the name of J. H. Suits, came on stage to apologize, explaining that "her vital force had become much weakened in the treatment of fifteen cases" and invited them to come back again.[72] This free performance was the first of several that had been booked at the Metropolitan Temple on alternating nights between September 12 and September 18, and Suits must have wanted to be sure that the word spread about the miraculous cures his client, "The Wonderful Mexican Girl Healer, Santa Teresa," could perform. In addition to promoting Teresa's performances at the Metropolitan Temple, Suits had set her up in an office where she saw patients daily from 9 a.m. to 5 p.m. under his supervision. However, nine days after that first performance, Teresa, with the help of female friends, would seek legal action to get out of her contract with Suits.

Fight for Possession of Santa Teresa

As Teresa Urrea negotiated the medical marketplace, spiritual networks, and theatrical promotion in San Francisco, she did so with the help of women friends, including the three women who helped her get out of the exploitative business relationship she was in with her manager. Mrs. Beatrice Castro, accompanied by Spiritualist Madame Young and Mrs. A. Ritts, swore to a complaint before a San Francisco judge that J. H. Suits was keeping Teresa under his control and against her will in the Baldwin Annex, the office space where she healed clients under his supervision. Mrs. Castro told the judge that Teresa "had complained to her that she was virtually kept a prisoner by Suits and that she wanted to get her liberty."[73] The judge granted the arrest warrant and accompanied a detective to Suits's office. Suits called his arrest an "outrage" and argued that Teresa was under contract to him. The next morning, a judge ruled that Teresa was free to break the contract whenever she wanted, and she could not be criminally prosecuted for doing so.[74]

Teresa did indeed break her contract. A few days after Suits's arrest she took out an advertisement in the *San Francisco Call* classifieds under "Spiritualism," announcing herself as "Santa Teresa, the Mexican healer, removed to 2630 California Street." [75] While she kept the title of *santa* bestowed on her by her Indigenous and mestizo adherents, as well as her identification as a "Mexican healer," she took "girl" out, perhaps signifying a new, mature identity, one that was independent from the oversight of a man and the patriarchal relationships that in many ways had dominated her life: with her father, Don Tomás Urrea, for so many years; with her husband during their short-lived marriage; and then with Suits. Now she had independence, gained with the help of Madame Young, a visible part of the Spiritualist community in San Francisco who advertised in the pages of the *San Francisco Call* as a Spiritualist medium and held meetings of the Mediums Protective Association at her home; Beatrice Castro, a friend of her family; and Mrs. Ritts, about whom less is known. All three must have been women Teresa knew and trusted enough to share her experiences with.[76] They must have cared about her and recognized the exploitative relationship she had with Suits given that they used their names and reputations to publicly file a complaint and help Teresa gain independence. With their support, Teresa liberated herself from the contract with Suits and opened her own healing practice.[77]

Shortly after Teresa set up her own practice in San Francisco, she embarked on a world tour without a manager or promoter, only a friend to help her translate Spanish to English.[78] The purpose of this tour, according to an interview Teresa gave in St. Louis (the first stop), was to "learn the source of her power to heal."[79] While she had expressed that she believed her power was from God, that she understood how the power moved through her hands, and that in a trance state she had greater power, at this point in her life she sought an even deeper understanding. In this interview, Teresa described how she was considering various interpretations of her healing power, revealing the different spiritual and healing traditions she had come in contact with.

> Theosophists say that some astral body is making itself manifest through me; Spiritualists say the spirit of some great and good person, who has lived before me, is the source. Some doctors say my powers are derived from purely physical or nervous peculiarities. I do not know what it is. It came to me without my knowledge, and when I was in a trance. It has remained with me. I have cured thousands, and I expect to cure thousands more.[80]

Teresa's voice here is confident. She does not question that she has power to heal and that this power remains with her.

> But I seek to find out whence the power is derived. I shall go to Paris, to Oberammergau, to Jerusalem, to India, and thence to Egypt; perhaps some-

where I may find someone, wise in such matters, who can and will tell me the secret.[81]

One researcher has demonstrated that Teresa's itinerary reveals a "veritable roadmap for Theosophical travel."[82] In later interviews, Teresa's interest in Theosophy—an occultic spiritual movement that shares some things in common with Spiritualism but is more focused on Asian religious traditions, including Buddhism—becomes more evident.[83] At the turn of the twentieth century, Theosophy was gaining in popularity while Spiritualism was in decline. It is quite possible that Teresa's interest in Theosophy began when she lived in Mexico or directly thereafter, as indicated in the anti-Díaz newspaper she co-edited. *El Independiente* featured stories about Theosophy alongside news of espiritismo and Teresa Urrea's spirit transmissions.[84]

In interviews, Teresa continued to speak of her plans to travel the world.[85] However, she never made it to any of those places. It seems that, as is the case for so many women, domestic concerns intervened and cut short her dreams. Teresa lived in New York City for a year with her translator, a family friend from Clifton named Jon Van Order with whom she had two children.[86] She gave birth to her first child, Laura, in February 1902. Then, in September 1902, she received news that her father, Don Tomás, had passed away. The sources are silent on her reasons for abandoning the world tour and returning to California, but it seems possible that Teresa wanted to raise her children somewhat closer to family and friends.[87] Whatever her reasons, by December 1902 she had settled in an East Los Angeles neighborhood near Sonoratown, named for miners from Sonora, Mexico, who came to southern California during the Gold Rush. In Los Angeles, Teresa continued to heal and attract the attention of the popular press. She also became involved in the politics of the city and the Mexican community that she was a part of.

An Unattended Death

In December 1902, Tomás García spent the last of his money to travel more than a hundred miles from his home in Escondido, California, to be healed by Santa Teresa Urrea, the famous "Mexican Joan of Arc," now living in Los Angeles.[88] García was suffering through the last stages of tuberculosis—the leading cause of death in the United States during the nineteenth century and into the twentieth—and it was slowly killing him.[89] Unfortunately, by the time he reached Los Angeles, García was too exhausted from the journey to make it to Teresa's cottage, which was only a few miles from where he had taken a bed.[90] Instead of experiencing the electric, healing touch of Santa Teresa, García ended up dying in a cheap downtown lodging house, coughing up blood, surrounded by fellow Mexicans who refused to let a doctor attend him.[91]

The death of Tomás García—a Mexican man known today only through a brief article in the *Los Angeles Times*—raises two questions. First, why did he seek the healing of the curandera Santa Teresa? And second, why did his fellow countrymen refuse to let doctors attend him? The *Los Angeles Times* article offers a simple answer to the first question that echoes the racist sentiments prevalent in Mexican papers as well as newspapers across the United States: only "ignorant" Mexicans believed Teresa possessed "superhuman powers in curing diseases."[92] The real reason was, of course, far more complex and had to do with Teresa's curanderismo as well as the state of medical knowledge at the turn of the century.

Tomás García knew that Teresa was a curandera and *santa*, a popular saint unsanctioned by the Catholic Church but embraced by the people. He would have heard, from the family members and neighbors who persuaded him to make the pilgrimage to Los Angeles, about her powerful hands that could transmit the healing power of God. He might have read in newspapers from both sides of the US-Mexico border how some believed she transferred magnetic currents and electricity to her patients through her hands, and how she "used water and earth and laid on her hands and cured."[93] Even her simple touch, many believed, could heal. García might have heard or read countless testimonials of her healing hands, like that of one man who witnessed her healing in El Paso: "I have seen nervous women become unconscious in the hands of Teresa, and recover free from the headaches which sent them to her."[94] After observing a healing performance in San Francisco, one journalist described how "A boy who could barely distinguish objects with his right eye said he could see more clearly after it had been rubbed by Santa Teresa."[95] Four days before the article "Dies Unattended" announced García's death, a journalist described the scene at Teresa's home in Los Angeles and commented on the pull of her powerful healing hands: "none go there without the belief that by the laying on of her magic hands they will be cured."[96] This journalist described her special appeal to Mexicans: "Santa Teresa, the famous Mexican girl . . . who is implicitly believed in by the majority of Mexicans of the Southwest as a healer, who exercises supernatural powers, her followers say . . . is daily besieged by a pitiful throng of Mexican enfermos. . . . The halt, the blind, the inwardly diseased, paralytics almost helpless," and some like Tomás García, "with bodies ravaged by consumption."[97]

According to the *Los Angeles Times*, García was in the last stages of tuberculosis. Because it takes years to develop in the body and kill its victims, he likely had been suffering for a long time.[98] In 1902, modern medicine had no cure for tuberculosis—or consumption, as it was known then—and there were very few effective therapies available.[99] If García had sought out professional medicine, it very likely would have failed him, as it did many people who suffered from tuberculosis in the early twentieth century.[100] García was not "ignorant," as the article quoted above suggests. He was dying, and he believed, or must have desperately hoped, that Teresa could lay her hands on him and cure him, as she had done for so many others.

The *Los Angeles Times* answered the second question raised by García's death—why his fellow countrymen refused to let doctors attend him—by implying that it was due to the "ignorance" and irrationality of Mexicans who did not understand that his body had to be taken to the morgue.[101] Again, the real answer belies such a simple, racist explanation. Ethnic Mexicans who lived in Los Angeles (whether Mexican nationals, migrant laborers, or US citizens) were seen in a certain light by the city's health officials: as racially inferior disease carriers, dangerous to the health of the city—and thus the American nation. So when García's countrymen surrounded him in his final hours, they did so to protect him, for they knew that any interest a doctor might have in the body of a sick, consumptive, and dying ethnic Mexican man in a downtown lodging house would likely not have been motivated by benevolence, but a belief that he was a danger to the city, contaminating it with deadly germs.[102] In turn-of-the-century Los Angeles and across the United States, ideas about race, ethnicity, and national belonging were becoming ever more exclusionary. Those with non-white bodies were segregated in public spaces in both the Jim Crow South and the "Juan Crow" Southwest.[103] In this environment, Teresa's curanderismo was a source of comfort for the many ethnic Mexicans she healed who experienced an increasingly hostile environment in Los Angeles because of their race.

For Tomás García, Santa Teresa offered the hope of a culturally familiar form of miraculous healing that transgressed the boundaries of culture, race, and nation. What the *Los Angeles Times* article describes as Santa Teresa's "superhuman healing powers," ethnic Mexicans like García knew as the traditional healing practice of curanderismo.

Los Angeles, Public Health, and Curanderismo

Santa Teresa was indeed Tomás García's last and best hope for treatment because in 1902, tuberculosis was the leading cause of death in the United States. There was no known cure and very few effective therapies to treat it.[104] The free, miraculous, culturally resonant healing that Teresa Urrea represented must have held great appeal to García. Public health officials linked his disease with his race, portraying him and ethnic Mexicans generally as a threat to public health and a drain on state resources.[105] In 1902, Los Angeles was not a welcoming place for a poor, tubercular Mexican man. The outward signs of a person in the last stages of tuberculosis—a diminished body, unrelenting cough, pale complexion, and overall lack of vitality and vigor—all signaled to those around him that not only could he no longer be of productive use to society, but he posed a danger to it as well.[106]

In Los Angeles, physicians, health reformers, civic boosters, and city officials associated tuberculosis with immigrants and "foreigners" living in crowded tenements.[107] Robert Koch's discovery of the tubercle bacillus in 1882 proved that tuberculosis was not inherited (as previously believed) but communicable through sputum, the blood-tinged mucous coughed up from a sufferer's lungs. Despite the scientific proof of tuberculosis as a communicable disease, ideas about the inheritability and essential nature of racial characteristics in connection with tuberculosis were slow to change. In medical literature, explanations for causes of the disease shifted from racially inherited traits to a focus on racial "predispositions" and environmental conditions that made some races and nationalities more likely to become infected than others. One physician, Dr. Sherman J. Bonney, wrote an eight-hundred-page book on treating tuberculosis that reflected this ideology, *Pulmonary Tuberculosis and Its Complications, With Special References to Diagnosis and Treatment For General Practitioners and Students* (1908).[108] Bonney contended that "One-seventh of all deaths in civilized countries are reported to result from this disease," but he did not clarify what he meant by "civilized."[109] The influence of Social Darwinism and burgeoning eugenics theory can be detected in Bonney's work through his use of words such as "race" and "civilized."[110] Much of the medical and popular literature at this time constructed the tuberculosis sufferer as a racial inferior, and this contributed to an environment in the Southwest, particularly in California, that was hostile to non-white people (Mexicans, but also African Americans and Asians) who appeared to be sick with tuberculosis.[111] Bonney expressed a commonly held belief when he wrote about "essential differences among various races in the degree of resistance to pulmonary tuberculosis."[112] Even though Bonney left Mexicans out of his racial analysis, he included a group often associated with Mexicans: American Indians, who Bonney asserted were second only to "the negro race" in their inherent vulnerability to tuberculosis.[113] One US Public Health Service physician, however, suggested that "Mexicans are possessed of an extremely low racial immunity, which is probably due to the large admixture of Indian blood."[114]

Charles Dwight Willard, a Los Angeles civic leader and public health re-former, linked Mexicans with communicable diseases and initiated housing reforms in the 1900s that reflected this. Willard echoed Bonney's ideas when he explained why closing down Mexican housing courts was actually good for them: "Fortunately the weather is pleasant, and they are accustomed to out-of-door life and the worse that can happen to them will scarcely be as bad as the conditions under which they have been living."[115] Although these housing courts provided seasonal workers with the only affordable housing available, Willard believed that by removing Mexicans from their homes, he would lift them "from conditions of helpless misery and wretchedness" and eliminate them as "disseminators of disease and crime to the entire city."[116] Willard was himself suffering from tuberculosis and had moved to Los An-geles to seek a cure, but he died there after a twenty-eight-year struggle.[117]

Unlike the public health reformer Willard, Tomás García died in a bed at the Los Angeles Lodging House on 418 North Main Street, a cheap place downtown next to Sonoratown.[118] In 1902, it was a somewhat danger-ous place where other "consumptives," as well as predominantly Mexican migrant laborers, stayed.[119] But, like the city itself, the lodging house had changed over time. Just a few decades earlier, it had been the opulent Pico Hotel, in the center of the plaza of the Pueblo de Los Angeles, named after Pio Pico, the last governor of Mexican California before it became part of the United States in 1848.[120] From 1848 to the early twentieth century, the Pueblo de Los Angeles grew rapidly into a city and witnessed massive pop-ulation growth: from 1890 to 1930 the population increased from 50,000 to 1.2 million.[121] During this time Los Angeles evolved from a predominantly Mexican pueblo to an ethnically diverse urban center. In 1872, half of the city's population was Spanish or Mexican, but by 1900 only 15 percent iden-tified as Mexican, and most of these were labeled "immigrants" and lived in the downtown district, in Sonoratown, or in the slightly nicer and more ethnically diverse neighborhood of Boyle Heights, where Teresa owned a cottage.[122]

However, in 1900, the Mexicans of Sonoratown were viewed differently from the Californios who had held extensive land grants and thought of themselves as *gente de razón*—civilized descendants of Europeans like Gov-ernor Pico and those he entertained in his luxurious hotel.[123] Anglo new-comers viewed mixed blood (or mestizo) Mexican immigrants like Tomás García and Teresa Urrea as racial inferiors who carried dangerous germs that threatened the health of more "civilized" Anglo Americans.

Tomás García's fellow countrymen who surrounded him on his death-bed at the lodging house, and refused to let his body be moved until the cor-oner came, understood the racial politics of the city. It is no wonder they guarded his body. They likely feared that it would be disrespected by city health officials, as it was not uncommon for the bodies of dead "consumptives" to be dumped somewhere and burned.[124] Perhaps they wanted to take him back to his family in Escondido, where his body could be dressed and given a proper burial. It is also no wonder that García desired the healing power that Teresa represented. Her curanderismo encompassed attending to both sick bodies and to those oppressed by governments, state power, and corporations.

Ironically, at the same time that Garcia's racialized, sick body was understood as dangerous to public health and possibly disease-laden because it was Mexican, the hands of Teresa Urrea, also Mexican, were believed by many to contain the power to transmit healing, magnetism, and electricity to sick bodies—white and brown. How can we understand this contradiction, where one Mexican body delivers sickness and another healing? A possible explanation might be that one is a view from outside the community, imposed on Mexicans by Anglo public health officials, among others; the other view comes from inside the community, from Mexicans who understand curanderismo as a valid and efficacious form of healing.[125]

Still, one might ask how Teresa escaped the virulent anti-Mexican attitudes that others faced. Perhaps it was her appeal as an exotic "other" in the United States, and her ability to bridge her various identities through her healing performances and relationships with Anglo Americans. However, even as she enjoyed a privileged position in comparison to Tomás García, Teresa did not abandon her identity as a Mexican, nor her tendency to support those who were treated unfairly by the government and capitalism. In Los Angeles—as she had done in Sonora, Texas, and Arizona—Teresa supported her fellow Mexicans. She also used her position as a famous curandera to draw attention and support to a local strike by Mexican workers.

Santa Teresa Takes Hand in the Strike

On April 27, 1903, Teresa Urrea led twenty-eight Mexican women in a procession down Main Street in downtown Los Angeles. They marched past the lodging house where Tomás García had died four months previously, and past the Pacific Electric construction site where over fifty Mexican railroad track workers, or *traqueros*, dropped their tools, walked off the job, and followed the women to join the strike for higher wages. These *traqueros* followed Santa Teresa and her fellow Mexicanas into La Unión Federal Mexicana (UFM) headquarters in Sonoratown, the Mexican barrio adjacent to where the men were laying track.[126] At the UFM headquarters, where a Mexican flag had been raised, Teresa gave a speech that, according to one source, "exhorted the virtues of working class and ethnic solidarity."[127] Afterward, she sat with the Mexicanas who had joined her in procession and listened to other speeches. Then, "followed by her band of women friends," she left the room when the negotiations began.[128]

In March and April of 1903, several hundred Mexican *traqueros* organized themselves into La Unión Federal Mexicana to press for better wages. They demanded an increase from fifteen to twenty cents per hour for day work, thirty cents for night work and overtime, and forty cents per hour for work on Sunday. They had timed the April 27 strike to interfere with plans to have the track ready for Fiesta, a yearly parade and celebration in Los Angeles that took place from 1894 to 1916 to boost tourism and the profile of the city. In 1903, President Theodore Roosevelt was scheduled to attend, so the city was especially concerned that everything go smoothly. Ironically, even as the Spanish name of this celebration nodded to the Mexican history and culture that defined the city, the *traqueros* and their allies were characterized as "foreign meddlers" who posed a threat to the "Americans" in Los Angeles.[129] However, many in the Sonoratown community, including women, assisted the strikers. A group of Mexicanas from Sonoratown (perhaps some of the same women who marched with Teresa down Main Street) helped the cause of the UFM when, according to the *Los Angeles Times*, "more than thirty of the Amazons" attempted to seize shovels, picks, and tamping irons from the *esquiroles* (scabs) who had been imported from El Paso by Pacific Electric to replace the striking workers.[130]

Despite the efforts of the UFM, track was laid in time for the Fiesta celebration, and the Pacific Electric street cars, decorated in flowers, chugged along the lines during the annual parade, impressing President Roosevelt as a symbol of the progress and modernization of Los Angeles.[131]

Santa Teresa demonstrated her solidarity with fellow Mexicans by using her influence to help the cause of struggling *traqueros* and their families. One journalist, while exaggerating Teresa's power, still revealed her genuine influence: "Mexicans will obey her. They fear, worship, and bow in humble submission to this strange little woman. . . . The laborers asked no questions but simply followed."[132] Her presence during the Pacific Electric strike inspired many to remain loyal to the union, despite pressure from Pacific Electric, the threat of violence from the police, and the possibility of losing their jobs.[133] The support that Santa Teresa lent to the strike was similar to the support Tomás García's fellow countrymen showed him by surrounding his bed and protecting him from racist Anglo city health officials. Teresa used her fame to inspire and draw attention to a cause that affected her community.

Teresa Urrea's extraordinary life was cut short in 1906. In Clifton, Arizona, at the age of thirty-three, she died of tuberculosis, the same disease that took the life of Tomás García.

Teresa had left Los Angeles in 1904 and moved her family, including her daughter Laura and partner John Van Order, to Clifton. This move was likely inspired by the fact that in August 1903, her Los Angeles home burned down while she was in Ventura filing for a divorce from Guadalupe Rodriguez, which was granted to her by a Ventura judge on January 24, 1904.[134] The choice to move back to Clifton must have been influenced by the fact that both Teresa's and John's extended families lived there, as well as the fact that their own family was growing: it was in Clifton that Teresa would give birth do her second daughter, Magdalena. She may also have known she was sick and wanted to be close to family and friends for support. Whatever combination of these factors and others inspired this move, it seemed like it was meant to be permanent, as Teresa bought a plot of land in a new subdivision in Clifton and built a home, where she gave birth to Magdalena.[135] This was where she spent her final days.

At the end of her life, Teresa was surrounded by women, as she was in other crucial moments, including the three months in Sonora when she was reborn as a curandera and received her *don*; in San Francisco when she emancipated herself from the exploitative contract with J. H. Suits; and when she visibly showed her support of the Mexican union in Los Angeles.[136] Before her death, she summoned her mother, Cayetana Chavez, her deceased father's common-law wife, Gabriela Cantúa, and her close friend Mariana Avendano to her home for support and to decide guardianship for her two daughters. She ended up giving legal guardianship of Laura and Magdalena to Mariana.[137]

It might seem that Teresa Urrea's life was filled with failure: the failure to overthrow the government of Porfirio Díaz and bring justice to the Yaquis, the failure to make it to Europe and Asia to discover the source of her powers, the failure of the Pacific Electric strike of 1903, and, finally, her failure to heal herself. Perhaps the ultimate failure, as much of the literature on her suggests, was her failure to maintain the sanctity and traditional virtues of a curandera and *santa* when she abandoned the US-Mexico borderlands for the secular trappings of modernity in American cities, where she likely caught the disease that killed her.[138] The novelist Luis Alberto Urrea, a

Figure 2.10. "Teresa Urrea (1873–1906)." Photograph taken in Clifton, Arizona, 1905, shortly before she died of tuberculosis. William Curry Holden Papers, SW CPC #57, Southwest Collection/Special Collections Library, Texas Tech University, Lubbock.

distant relative of Teresa, wrote of her wearing American modernity as if it were a heavy, oppressive garment.

> The dress fell like heavy crepe to the floor and she stepped out of it and let it lie. It formed a small battlement—looked like a one-woman prison. She undid her under-things and set herself free and dropped a loose nightdress over her head and slipped her feet into sheepskin moccasins and twirled her hair into a braid.[139]

In the modern magic of the city, had she lost the Indigenous magic of the desert? To many, it seemed as if she was a different person in San Francisco, Los Angeles, and other American cities where journalists splashed images across the entertainment sections showing her conducting healings in fashionable shirtwaists and upswept hairdos. Where was the Mexican Joan of Arc, the part-Tehueco girl who spoke to the masses of Yaquis, Mayos, and other oppressed people of northern Mexico wrapped in a rebozo, baptizing babies and healing the sick with mud and saliva? By leaving her traditional culture in rural Mexico and embracing modernity in big American cities, had she contaminated her *don*?

The answer to these questions is that Teresa Urrea had never been only a curandera. She had also been an espiritista medium from her earliest days in Cabora, and although she surely changed and matured during her time in US cities, the overall trajectory of her life represents more continuity than disjuncture.[140] This longing for Teresa to have remained a "pure" borderlands *santa* reflects a larger theme prevalent at the turn of the century. Modernity did not exclusively belong in American cities, nor did tradition belong only in the rural US-Mexico borderlands. Teresa explored the spiritual science of espiritismo in the rural environment of Rancho de Cabora in Sonora, Mexico, even as she was a practicing curandera and *santa* to Mayos, Yaquis, and Mexicans. In San Francisco and Los Angeles, she practiced curanderismo for the ethnic Mexican communities as well as for Anglos, even as she moved among the world of spiritualist mediums.

Teresa Urrea and her hybrid practice of curanderismo/espiritismo were a part of this transnational movement and moment when secularizing modernity overlapped with the science of the spirits. She encountered a different kind of modernity in American cities—a plethora of spiritualties, ideas, and healing practices. She continued to be a *santa* and a curandera in her own way, sometimes performing her healing in front of audiences, sometimes advertising her curanderismo alongside Spiritualist mediums and clairvoyants in newspapers, and sometimes healing people in her home, in an office, or on the stage. Teresa's time in American cities reveals the ways in which an enchanted modernity produced a traditional and modern curandera espiritista.

On the opposite end of the border, in the Río Grande Valley of South Texas, another curandero was gaining popularity. Like Teresa, Don Pedrito Jaramillo healed among a community of Tejanos and Mexicanos, and gained a reputation as a powerful and compassionate healer throughout this borderlands region. And like Teresa's followers, his adherents sought him out to heal diseases that science had not yet found a cure for. However, Don Pedrito's successful cures would draw the attention and ire of the newly professionalizing medical establishment, which was trying to secure dominance in communities that might have preferred a curandero to a physician.

PART II

DON PEDRITO JARAMILLO

All Roads Lead to Don Pedrito Jaramillo: Healing the Individual and the Social Body in the South Texas Río Grande Valley

Doña Tomasita Canales could not recognize her sons. Albino and Andrés had come from Matamoros, Mexico, where they were attending school, to comfort their mother, who was sick with a dangerously high fever. She did not know them. Soon after this, Doña Tomasita lost consciousness. Don Andrés Canales, her husband, told the two physicians he had hired to heal her to take his wife to the hospital in San Antonio to be treated.[1] The doctors told him that she would not survive the 25-mile journey to the nearest train station, let alone the 125 miles to San Antonio. The physicians apologized to Don Andrés, explaining that they had done "all that science prescribed," but they could not cure her.[2]

Doña Tomasita's mother, Eulalia Tijerina, who was also at her bedside, would not accept the doctors' diagnosis. She demanded that Don Andrés send someone to Don Pedrito Jaramillo, the curandero at Rancho de Los Olmos, for a remedy. Even though Don Andrés did not have faith in the curandero and the power of his cures taken "en el nombre de Dios y don Pedrito," as so many Tejanos (Texans of Mexican descent) from South Texas did, he was desperate. So he obeyed his mother-in-law and sent one of his vaqueros to Los Olmos for a *receta* (prescription) from the curandero.[3] Don Pedrito's *receta* instructed Doña Tomasita to bathe in "natural" or cold water three times, once every two hours. One of the physicians was still at the Canales residence when the vaquero returned, and he said Don Pedrito's remedy was "estupidez" (stupidity) and Doña Tomasita would surely die if she bathed in cold water.[4] Despite this, the family followed Don Pedrito's *receta*, and after the baths she regained consciousness and once again recognized her sons.

Based on the description of her symptoms and the year she became ill (1889), Doña Tomasita might have been experiencing the first stages of yellow fever, an epidemic disease for which there was no cure that had ravaged South Texas in 1882.[5] In fact, the place she lived, Rancho de Las Cabras, had been enclosed in the Corpus Christi–Laredo Cordon, an area quarantined during the 1882 epidemic. Surely the memories of that devastating time were still fresh. A viral disease transmitted by a particular mosquito (*Aedes aegypti*) found in humid tropical climates, doctors often described yellow fever as a "malignant fever," as did the two physicians who attended Doña Tomasita.[6]

The first sign of yellow fever is a high fever that lasts for three or four days, during which the afflicted suffer from a continuous headache and severe body aches, muscle and joint pain, chills, nausea, and delirium. In most cases the fever subsides, and a slow recovery ensues. If Doña Tomasita had been suffering from yellow fever and had not recovered, her agony would have been appalling. The disease would have attacked her internal organs, causing liver failure that makes the skin and eyes turn yellow, followed by bleeding from the eyes, nose, mouth, and stomach. Finally, before dying, she would have vomited a black liquid consisting of digested blood, the symptom that gave the disease its Spanish name: *vómito negro*.[7] Fortunately, this was not her fate. Doña Tomasita Canales lived for thirty-eight more years, until her death in 1928 at age seventy.[8]

The story of Don Pedrito healing Doña Tomasita when two physicians could not reveals several overlapping historical contexts that inform this time and place. During the late nineteenth century and early twentieth, there were many diseases for which scientific medicine had no cure, including yellow fever and tuberculosis, which took the life of Tomás García and Teresa Urrea (discussed in chapter 2). Accordingly, in the United States and Mexico a medical marketplace existed that offered patients a variety of different therapies. Alternative healers such as homeopaths and curanderos vied for patients alongside regular doctors like those who attended Doña Tomasita.[9] This period also saw the rise of tropical medicine, which combined pseudo-scientific ideas about race with new scientific advances in parasitology, bacteriology, and epidemiology, in efforts to contain and eradicate diseases associated with hot and humid climates, such as yellow fever, which had invaded Cuba, the US South, and South Texas.[10]

Most importantly, the healing of Doña Tomasita Canales reveals the significance of Don Pedrito's curanderismo to this borderlands region. He healed ethnic Mexicans and Tejanos during a period that saw widespread, often violent efforts of Anglos to displace Tejanos from their land; the cultural and racial exclusion of Tejanos from political activity and education; extra-legal violence against Mexicanos by Anglos and Texas Rangers; and the transition from a subsistence to a capitalist economy.[11] Don Pedrito healed bodies stressed from hard labor, a poor diet, violence, aging, overexposure to the sun, contagious diseases, and the consequences—written on their bodies and spirits—of the new Anglo domination and capitalist order. Don Pedrito emerged as a source of spiritual healing and material support for a transnational community facing social change, illness, and an increasingly oppressive racial regime. He filled a role that state and professional institutions such as medicine and the Church would not or could not. His healings and the stories of his healings (like the story of Doña Tomasita Canales) circulated widely among Tejanos during his lifetime and after, and made the curandero "a symbolic figure of dissent from the new social order and its values" by reiterating and validating a Mexican cultural practice and the values embedded within it, much like the story of how he received his *don*, the supernatural gift of healing.[12]

The *Don*

The story of how Don Pedrito received his supernatural gift of healing laid the foundation for his curanderismo practice, which began after he crossed the US-Mexico border into Texas and settled on Rancho de Los Olmos in 1881.[13] Before Don Pedrito crossed the border, he was a poor laborer who worked as a shepherd in Jalisco, Mexico, where he was paid half a bushel of corn and the equivalent of five dollars a month.[14] According to one story, while he was working on the outskirts of Guadalajara, Don Pedrito crashed into a tree limb, fell off his horse, and broke his nose. A different story has it that his nose was broken after he tried to evade conscription into the Mexican Army and was beaten by "bandits."[15] After the injury (regardless of the way it happened), the story continues, relating how Don Pedrito buried his face in a muddy pond to relieve the pain and lay unconscious by the water for three days with his nose covered in mud. After the third day in this position, a voice told him that he was healed and that he had been given the *don*, but he must share his gift freely. The voice told him that his boss was sick, and that Don Pedrito could cure him. When he awoke, Don Pedrito quickly prescribed a cure for his sick boss: a cold bath daily for three consecutive days. This cure healed him. The fact that Don Pedrito received his *don* while laboring outside and that his cure required mud and water foreshadowed his curanderismo practice in South Texas, where most of his cures called for water to heal ranchers, agricultural laborers, and their families. Don Pedrito would always heal for free, prescribing cures featuring not only water, but also other simple, easy-to-find, and inexpensive ingredients such as tea, lemons, tomatoes, beer, coffee, and cheap whiskey.[16]

Figure 3.1. "Pedro Jaramillo." Notice Jaramillo's broken nose, which came to be associated with his healing power because it happened when he fell off his horse after receiving his supernatural gift of healing, the *don*. Photo by S. Sandoval, San Antonio, Texas, 1894. Image courtesy of the University of Texas at San Antonio Libraries, Special Collections, #087-0239.

When Don Pedrito received his gift of healing, the voice he heard in his dream also demanded of him total faith. Don Pedrito asked for the same faith from his patients. Similar to those in Mexico and US cities who believed in the special healing gifts that Teresa Urrea received through her *don*, the Tejano community's belief in Don Pedrito's gift gave him legitimacy. Curanderos often receive the *don* through an illness or accident, and while unconscious, they are visited by a spirit or simply hear a voice telling them they have been specially chosen to cure in the name of God. This supernatural gift and the reciprocity it required was the foundation upon which Don Pedrito built his curanderismo practice. Whenever a sick person came to him for a cure, he would quickly assess him or her and then write a prescription, a *receta*, on a scrap of paper with the instruction to do the prescribed treatment "en el nombre de Dios" (in the name of God).[17] Even though he never charged for his cures, people often offered donations of money, food, and even land, and if Don Pedrito sometimes accepted these, he was known to redistribute the gifts back into the community. One person who knew him said that "lo que este hombre recibía con una mano, la daba con la otra" (what this man received with one hand, he gave away with the other).[18] His generosity earned him the appellation "Benefactor of Humanity," engraved on his tombstone.

It is not known for certain why Don Pedrito decided to leave Jalisco, cross the border into the United States, and settle at Rancho de Los Olmos in the heart of what was known as the Nueces Strip.[19] Perhaps South Texas offered opportunities for a curandero because there were very few doctors. The offerings people gave to Don Pedrito in gratitude for his gift of free spiritual healing greatly surpassed the wages he made in Mexico. Even though he poured most of those donations back into the community, he did amass enough money to purchase a small piece of land on which he grew crops that fed those who came to him for healing.[20]

When Don Pedrito crossed the border, he was traveling with a group of men smuggling liquor to sell to South Texas ranchers—probably mezcal, which is derived from the maguey plant, indigenous to his home state of Jalisco.[21] In fact, one of the deliveries that Don Pedrito and his friends made was to Rancho de Las Cabras, owned by the families of Doña Tomasita and Don Andrés Canales, who were hosting a celebration for St. John's Day, June 24, a holiday widely celebrated on Mexican ranches. Rituals included bathing in the nearest pond, river, or lake—or a tub or *acequia* (drainage ditch) if no body of water was near—to commemorate John the Baptist's baptism of Christ in the River Jordan.[22] Like many fiestas honoring saints' days in nineteenth-century Tejano communities, St. John's Day involved a religious celebration followed by a large party replete with feasting, dancing, gambling, cockfighting, and the drinking of spirits such as mezcal.[23]

Popular lore has it that when Don Pedrito arrived in South Texas, he was so taken with its particular beauty—sparsely populated ranchland covered with faded grasses and thorny prickly pear, maguey, and mesquite shrubs—that he decided to stay.[24] Before he could stake his place on the landscape,

Jaramillo first went back to Mexico to care for his sick mother, and there he made a *promesa*—a sacred vow—that if she died, he would leave Mexico and never return. After her death, he fulfilled his *promesa* and left Jalisco to begin his life on *el otro lado* as a curandero. He settled on Rancho de Los Olmos, in what is now Brooks County, near the Canales family's Rancho de Las Cabras. Over the years he healed many of the workers from Las Cabras as well as others from Los Olmos and the many other ranches scattered across South Texas and the Río Grande Valley.[25]

As Don Pedrito's fame grew, he maintained the humility dictated by his *don*. He insisted that he was one of the people—nothing special—and if his cure worked, he claimed it was the work of God. One resident of the Río Grande Valley recalled that Don Pedrito used to say, "I'm just anybody."[26] This same informant described how he would admonish those who attempted to worship him, revealing one of the tenets of curanderismo: that the healer who is bestowed with a *don* is merely a conduit for the power of God.

> Every now and then a person would come along, kneel before him, and try to kiss his hand. That much they thought of him. But he would not let them do this. "Get up" he would say seriously, "Get up. What are you doing? If the cures are effective (si las curas sirven), it is Providence. I am not the one who cures."[27]

If his cure was not successful, this reasoning worked equally as well. One gentleman recalled that Don Pedrito once told a woman whom he could not heal, "Well . . . mamacita, what can I do? I am not God."[28]

Pathways to Don Pedrito

The lines leading to Los Olmos on the "Map of the Río Grande Frontier Texas" (map 3.1) provide visual evidence of the significance of this curandero and his curanderismo practice to this community. It shows that (at least in 1892) there were more roads to Los Olmos than to some of the bigger towns and cities of this region. These roads were created by the people, by their many journeys to and from Don Pedrito's healing practice situated there. One resident of South Texas struggled to put into words how much Don Pedrito meant to this community, offering an analogy that, like the map, reveals how deeply connected Don Pedrito was to his South Texas community.

> It's hard to say. I don't know how to say it. (long pause) I would say that Don Pedrito was like a nerve, a part of me and of everybody. Even rich people

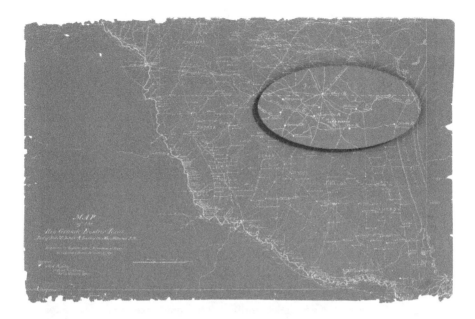

Map 3.1. "Map of the Rio Grande Frontier Texas, 1892." Notice all the roads leading to Los Olmos Ranch, the site of Don Pedrito's healing, revealing the significance of this curandero to this South Texas community. Thanks to Homero Vera for bringing this map to my attention. Map #4660, Archives and Records Program, Texas General Land Office, Austin.

thought of him in this way, like that family in (names nearby town). Don Pedrito was their God.[29]

Don Pedrito's curanderismo as a kind of central nervous system for this community suggests the many kinds of roads and pathways to and from Don Pedrito: some, like the lines on the map, were actual roads created by wagon wheels, horses' hooves, and the feet of those who made journeys to and from Los Olmos for healing; some pathways to Don Pedrito came from within individual bodies, unseen illnesses traveling through blood and synapses; some were spiritual pathways of prayer and faith through which health seekers made sense of illness and healing. There were also communal pathways to the curandero, shared by members of the social body who experienced collective trauma based on their gender, race, and the exploitative capitalist system making inroads into South Texas. An examination of Don Pedrito's curanderismo practice reveals the many roads and pathways people traveled for healing at Los Olmos. Those pathways reveal much about both the individual bodies and the broader social body that received healing at the hands of this curandero.

Don Pedrito's Curanderismo Practice at Los Olmos

Don Pedrito's healing drew many people from the South Texas Río Grande Valley region, as well as Mexico, to Rancho de Los Olmos, approximately seventy-five miles from the border. Don Pedrito treated these people—some who had crossed the border from Mexico, some who had made journeys from surrounding ranches and towns—for a wide variety of symptoms and illnesses that any healer of this period would have been confronted with: wounds, blindness, stomach ailments, fever, headaches, colds (called "catarrh" in turn-of-the-century parlance), toothaches, nosebleeds, and diseases such as tuberculosis. He also attended to people with diseases specific to that time period, such as dropsy (swelling); psychological afflictions, such as nervousness, anxiety, insanity, and addiction problems; and culturally specific ailments, such as *susto*, literally "fright," but suggesting a deeper loss due to trauma—a loss of the soul, which must be called back to the body.[30] Don Pedrito understood culturally specific illnesses, and he served his community with curanderismo—a system of healing that drew upon folk Catholicism, materials, rituals, and symbols that were culturally familiar to his adherents in South Texas, as well as gendered ideas about the body.[31]

At Los Olmos Don Pedrito not only healed sick bodies, but also offered his patients food, rest, and mental restoration, after which they returned to their communities to resume their labor on ranches and in fields, to tend households, and to raise families. As the numbers of people that came to Los Olmos for healing increased over the years, Don Pedrito continued to extend hospitality that made them feel welcome and cared for, like a good physician. One man remembered that when people arrived at Los Olmos, often after long and arduous journeys, the first thing Don Pedrito would say to them was "Go over there and have some coffee, rest awhile, then come over."[32] To the side of his *jacal* were *cocinas* (kitchens) where he worked side by side with women volunteers to provide people with coffee, water, and something to eat.[33] After the patient had rested and was ready to see Don Pedrito, he or she would enter his *jacal*, which one person described as simple, adorned with Virgin Mary statues and filled with letters requesting *recetas*.[34] Don Pedrito would sit at a table, and a male assistant would lead the supplicant to him. He would listen to their request, quickly make a diagnosis, and then give the person a *receta*. People might leave a dona-

Figure 3.2. "Don Pedrito, Far Right With White Shawl Around Shoulders, Feeds Followers," ca. 1900. This photograph, made by a traveling photographer at Los Olmos, belongs to Lino Treviño's heirs. Image courtesy of the Falfurrias Heritage Museum and Lourdes Treviño-Cantu.

tion on the table if they wished, but it was not required. Sometimes Don Pedrito would not take a donation if he felt the person could not afford it or needed it for other purposes. He might say, "No, take your money. You need it for your trip." Or, "No, return it to the one who loaned it to you."[35] Some remember that Don Pedrito would prescribe very quickly, "rápido, rápido," and in this way he would efficiently diagnose and offer cures to supplicants in most need of relief. This fast, efficient, yet hospitable style of healing accommodated the growing numbers of health seekers who came to Rancho de Los Olmos between 1881 and Don Pedrito's death in 1907.

Don Pedrito also came to possess an intimate knowledge of his community and an engagement with the natural world in order to heal effectively. For example, José Lozano, who in the early twentieth century was postmaster at Concepción, a small ranching community in Duval County, recalled one cure that Don Pedrito made for his uncle, who had been a mail carrier "right in the heart of South Texas brush country" and had delivered mail to Don Pedrito at Los Olmos.[36] He also had a drinking problem. One day, after he was so "borracho" (drunk) with mezcal and tequila that he fell off his horse and left the mail in the middle of the road, he realized he needed to see Don Pedrito for a cure for his drinking or he would lose his job.[37] To the postman's amazement, Don Pedrito seemed to know what the problem was before he said anything. Don Pedrito told him, "*Hijo*, you are the *borracho* that carries the mail from Los Olmos to Concepcion and you want a *remedio* to cure this problem."[38] He then told him that he should bathe in a lake near his house three times, once every three days, and he would be cured only if he did it *con fe* (with faith). Don Pedrito's cures often contained an instruction that specified the number of times an act was to take place—usually three, a number his patients likely would have recognized for its significance in Judeo-Christian symbolism.[39] When Don Pedrito instructed Doña Tomasita Canales to take three baths, a Tejano suffering from migraine headaches to take three pills, and a Tejana suffering with extreme abdominal pain to drink a cup of tequila for three mornings, he was using a familiar Catholic symbol that held meaning for them.[40] José Lozano followed Don Pedrito's instructions, taking one bath a day for three days, with faith, and was cured of his drunkenness.[41]

Gendered Pathways to Los Olmos

At the turn of the nineteenth century, prevailing gender ideals in the United States dictated that women and men should operate in separate spheres: women in the warmth and safety of the household, men in the cold, competitive, capitalistic world. Women, it was believed, were naturally moral, spiritual, and emotional—qualities that served the home and hearth—whereas men were considered rational and emotionally detached, having the qualities needed to navigate and succeed in the capitalistic world. When J. T. Canales recounted how Don Pedrito healed his mother, Doña Tomasita, he was invoking this turn-of-the-century gender convention that asserted women were essentially spiritual and emotional, whereas men were rational and thus could perhaps be better trusted: ". . . I was not present when my mother was sick, yet I have heard the account of her sickness and cure both from her own lips *and from my father's, especially from my father, who was very accurate in his statements* and who was not a believer in Don Pedro as a faith healer until this incident took place" (emphasis added).[42] Yet when it came to healing and religious faith in ethnic Mexican households, women—in particular, the grandmother, the matriarch (such as Doña Tomasita's mother, Eulalia Tijerina, who told Don Andrés to send for Don Pedrito)—held the power to make the most important decisions.[43]

Separate spheres ideology did not apply equally to all women. In the United States, women of all races and classes faced a variety of challenges and opportunities in the post–Civil War era. In the defeated South, for example, African American women freed from slavery took advantage of new opportunities in which they could marry, move about freely, and choose to whom to sell their labor. Yet they also faced dangers from Anglos insistent upon keeping them in a subordinate position through Jim Crow laws that segregated them from Anglos and restricted their movements, while their former white mistresses claimed the privileges of white supremacy. In South Texas, Tejanas worked just as hard as their men, in and outside of the home, in a variety of jobs: as household servants, agricultural laborers, mothers and housekeepers, and producers and sellers of goods such as tortillas. While the capitalist system provided more leisure and wealth for middle- and upper-class white women, working women from Native American, Mexican American, Asian American, and African American communities all had to fight to hold on to their unique cultural traditions as they faced exclusionary laws and the challenges imposed by second-class citizenship (or, in the case of Native Americans, non-citizenship).

While Don Pedrito's cures revealed the separate spheres ideology, his healing reflected gender norms and ideologies in other ways as well. For example, his curanderismo was similar in many ways to the social medicine practiced by women in the eighteenth-century United States, where "social" healers, especially midwives, practiced healing by building personal relationships and developing local reputations as gifted healers.[44] Another way his curanderismo incorporated gender ideologies was his application of humoral therapy, which reflected ideas about hot and cold and the theory of the opposites. An analysis of his cures reveals the popular notion that women were too passionate, thus hot and in need of cooling down, while men were losing their manhood, becoming too cold and rational, and thus needed heating up. This simplified version of humoral therapy—which stressed hot and cold, and the theory of opposites—had become very popular throughout Latin America, including Mexico and, by extension, South Texas.[45]

When Don Pedrito prescribed for women—who made up an estimated 39.2 percent of his recorded cures—he disproportionately prescribed water cures, especially cold or unheated water, as he did for Doña Tomasita Canales.[46] He not only prescribed unheated baths to women for general illnesses like fever, but also to treat "female problems" such as infertility and stomach pain. "Stomach pain" was a diagnosis that likely included pain and illness connected with childbirth, menstruation, and miscarriage, but prevailing ideas of modesty and decorum would likely have prohibited a nineteenth-century woman from describing in detail such a private illness to a male healer.[47]

Doña Petra Rocha de Hernández came to Don Pedrito because she had been married for seven years and had not yet conceived. He prescribed a bath in cool water at sunset for three days, instructing her to throw out the water after each bath. Doña Petra reported that one year after she performed Don Pedrito's cure, she conceived and bore a son.[48] Mrs. Minnie Alexander, "an American lady who lived in San Antonio," sought a cure for fatigue. Don Pedrito gave her a *receta* that instructed her to eat one onion without salt or water for three mornings, then for the next three mornings take a bath in cold water that had been left out in the night air, and then repeat this whole process once more. Mrs. Alexander told her interviewer that this cure, though hard to do, healed her lethargy.[49] Both conditions, the inability to conceive and fatigue, could have been attributed to "female hysteria," a popular nineteenth-century diagnosis that connected women's health to their reproductive organs and was associated with a wide variety of symptoms, including sexual and reproductive issues as well as mood swings and lethargy. One popular nineteenth-century treatment for hysteria was hydrotherapy—more specifically, the application of water in the area of the reproductive organs, not unlike the immersive water therapy Don Pedrito prescribed for women.[50]

Turn-of-the-century gender ideology included men as well as women. Don Pedrito prescribed hot or heated cures at a much higher rate for men than women. Even the cold water cures that he prescribed for men were consistent with this gendered ideology. A writer for the *Dallas Morning News* reported one cold water cure that Don Pedrito prescribed for a man who was "a consumptive in the last stages." He wrote that although the man had bathed nude in cold water and lay on the ground outside all night, he did not chill but "steamed with heat."[51]

Historians have examined the ideology that described how many Anglo men in urban areas of the United States in the late nineteenth century experienced a threat to their manhood because they had become "overcivilized" in desk jobs and had lost their "primitive" connection to land, nature, and the untamed and competitive nature that pioneering, farming, and fighting "Indians" had kept alive in them. Thus, these men needed to increase their vitality, heat up their blood, and revive a diminishing manhood by getting back to nature, going to war, or perhaps using a new device such as an electric belt or some other popular treatment to stimulate their masculine nature.[52] In South Texas, some men experienced a challenge to their sense of manhood in a different way than their urban counterparts. Because Anglos were buying up ranching land, many Tejanos were forced off their land and into jobs working for Anglos as ranch hands and agricultural laborers. One historian of South Texas describes this challenge while defending the manhood of Mexican laborers: "If *vaqueros* knew that other men profited from their talents and that the ranches of southern and western Texas prospered because of them, they also knew that such an arrangement did not make them any less manly."[53]

Don Pedrito treated some of these Tejanos to revive their sense of manhood and dignity. Priscilliano Martínez came to Don Pedrito because he had taken a serious "blow to the head" while working as overseer for a large ranch where he was in charge of a group of men carrying posts to make fences.[54] Martínez explained that his men were resentful of him because of his position (he was employed as a middleman between the Anglo ranch owner and the Mexican laborers) and they beat him very badly, especially with punches to his head. He felt depression as well as fright and anger—all symptoms of *susto*, or soul loss—not only because of the physical harm, but also because of the emotional wound and feelings of shame at being abused by other men who were taking out their frustrations on him. Don Pedrito looked at Martínez and told him nothing was wrong, and he should simply take a bath in lukewarm water when he got home. According to the prevailing gender ideology, this simple cure would have revived the heat in his body as well as his sense of manhood. Don Pedrito also provided what a therapist or a priest would: a familiar, comforting, and authoritative presence that eased his anxiety and affirmed that everything would be fine. Martínez remembered that he began to feel better on his way to Don Pedrito—perhaps anticipating the healing to come—and claimed that he "became completely well" after he saw him and performed the cure.[55]

The Journey Is Part of the Cure

An important feature of Don Pedrito Jaramillo's curanderismo revealed in the analysis of his cures is that the actual journey to see him—including the decision to make the journey—was an integral part of the cure. Of the recorded and published cures, most involved a journey: some by foot, others by horseback, wagon, or, after 1903, train.[56] While most of the recorded cure stories indicate travel within South Texas, some people traveled from towns and ranches on both sides of the border to be seen and healed by Don Pedrito.[57] Around this same time, in various parts of the world, many people were making journeys or pilgrimages for miraculous healing. Catholic pilgrims made their way to Lourdes, France, to be healed in the miraculous water from the grotto where it is believed the Virgin Mary appeared to a young peasant girl in 1858.[58] In Mexico, thousands have made the pilgrimage, by walking or crawling on their knees, to the Basilica of the Virgin of Guadalupe in Mexico City on her feast day, December 12, in order to hear a mass, venerate her image, and offer a sacrifice in order to request a miracle or ask for their sins to be pardoned.[59] In the American Southwest, every year hundreds make a pilgrimage to El Santuario de Chimayó in northern New Mexico (a place some call "the American Lourdes") to repent of their sins and receive healing from the sacred dirt there, where a cross is said to have miraculously appeared in the early 1800s.[60] The similarities between journeys to Don Pedrito and other pilgrimages are worth noting. These pilgrimages involved many of the things Don Pedrito (and other curanderos) used to heal, blending the material and the spiritual: water (Lourdes), dirt (El Santuario de Chimayó), and faith (all). Another important similarity between these more famous healing pilgrimages and the journeys to Don Pedrito is the understanding that healing power is activated during the journey; power is unleashed because of the supplicant's expectation of healing and in the actions taken to obtain healing.[61] Many who seek supernatural healing, either through pilgrimage to a sacred place like Lourdes or a faith healer like Don Pedrito, do so only after doctors have failed, and the supplicant is willing to seek out other healing possibilities as a "last resort." Thus, expectation is heightened, as well as the willingness to take more extreme action, such as a long journey or pilgrimage.

Often this is a choice the patient has made at the persuasion of friends and family who shared stories of the successful healings that happened at a pilgrimage site or at the hands of a faith healer. The story at the beginning of this chapter, the healing of Doña Tomasita Canales, is an example of this.[62] Don Pedrito was summoned only after two physicians had failed to cure her. (Not everyone agreed, as the Canales story also shows that it was Doña Tomasita's mother, Eulalia, who was more willing to send for Don Pedrito than Tomasita's husband, Don Andrés.) The important point here is that the destination of a healing pilgrimage often represents a last hope and, as such, increases the supplicant's belief and faith in the object of the pilgrimage/journey.

In addition to the *decision* to seek healing from this alternative source, behavioral and medical research demonstrates that the *belief* someone has in the power of a saint to heal them (or the medical treatment they are about to receive) can produce real physiological changes in the body: the supplicant can actually begin to feel better simply having made the decision to seek healing.[63] In this way, the decision to seek a cure works as a placebo: it triggers the release of endorphins in the brain in response to the expectation of relief from pain, thus causing the supplicant to feel better. According to this theory, the placebo only works in proportion to the belief a supplicant has in it. The more powerful and deep the belief in the object of devotion, the more relief from pain and feelings of well-being can be expected. Accordingly, the prestige of the object of devotion, in large part based on the many stories told about it, will increase the belief of the adherent.[64] One of the physiological responses the body produces at the expectation of healing, according to scholar Robert A. Scott, is the positive response of the immune system to "self-efficacy," defined as taking action to effect changes.[65] In other words, the moment one decides to make the journey to seek healing and begins to take action in that direction, the ability of his or her immune system to ward off illness increases, and the process of recovery begins.

The decision to seek healing is powerfully influenced by immediate context, culture, and the stories one has heard about a particular saint, shrine, doctor, treatment, or curandero. The stories of Don Pedrito's healing as well as shared cultural knowledge act as scripts that frame the experience: they lay out a map that tells the sick person how it should go and affirm their cultural and spiritual beliefs.[66] Anne Harrington, a historian of medicine, explains that stories of healing "are not just talk . . . the best ones are also scripts, or guides to action."[67] The stories of how Don Pedrito received his *don*, the cures he prescribed, and how he helped the community in other ways all function as scripts about how healing—both in the individual body and the social body—could happen in this South Texas community. How people experience healing and social change depends in part on such scripts; they can work as framing devices for experiences that provide a model of how to understand, process, and contextualize experiences of pain, loss, or joy, and even how to be sick and how to heal. Then, as believers repeatedly share their healing stories or scripts, the stories gain authority and authenticity for the whole community.[68] Take, for example, the oft-repeated story of the healing of Dionisio Rodríguez.

The Healing Journey of Dionisio Rodríguez

In 1884, Don Pedrito cured Dionisio Rodríguez—a sheepherder working on a ranch in South Texas—of chronic migraine headaches.[69] Before seeking healing from Don Pedrito, Rodríguez had consulted a doctor several times, but the physician had not been able to provide Dionisio any relief. Finally, during one migraine attack, a friend told Rodríguez he should see the curandero Don Pedrito Jaramillo and get a *receta* from him. Together, Rodríguez and his friend traveled by *calash* (a four-wheeled carriage on springs) sixty miles from Rancho Las Parrillas, where Rodríguez worked, to Rancho de Los Olmos. When the men arrived at Los Olmos late in the afternoon, Rodríguez greeted Don Pedrito and told him about his headaches. The first thing Don Pedrito did was to hand Rodríguez a glass of water. When he reached for the water with his right hand, Don Pedrito told him to take it with his left. Rodríguez remembered that he "immediately felt well-being" throughout his body when he drank the water.[70]

Don Pedrito invited the two men to stay at his *jacal* for dinner and spend the night. The next morning he gave Rodríguez three pills and the following instructions: on his journey back to Las Parillas he was to stop and gather the *cenizo* (purple sage) covering a particular hill he would pass. He told him that when he arrived at his home, he should boil the *cenizo* leaves in water, let the water cool and then strain it, bathe in that water, and then wrap himself up warmly to sweat. Don Pedrito's cure for Rodríguez incorporated natural materials from South Texas: water (the material Don Pedrito used most often) and *cenizo*, the type of sage indigenous to the area.[71] Don Pedrito instructed Rodríguez that after the sweat, he was to take one pill, an hour later the second, and an hour after that the third. Rodríguez completed his *receta* and claimed that he was healed.[72]

Like many who traveled to Los Olmos to seek healing from Don Pedrito, Rodríguez embarked on a journey to and from Los Olmos, and that journey was part of the healing process. Yet it was only after Rodríguez made at least two failed trips to a physician that his friend was able to persuade him to go to Don Pedrito for a cure for his migraine headaches. Thus, the prestige of the doctors who had no cure for him declined, while the prestige of Don Pedrito was enhanced for Rodríguez. His faith likely increased on the journey to Los Olmos as his friend continued to encourage him, telling him more stories about how Don Pedrito cured, and as Rodríguez anticipated the relief Don Pedrito would soon provide, perhaps his brain began releasing endorphins while his immune system began to work harder because of the action he took. This could explain why, upon arriving at Los Olmos after the journey, Rodríguez "immediately felt well-being throughout his body" after drinking the glass of water offered to him by Don Pedrito. The familiar and comforting cultural context, and Rodríguez's willingness to believe combined with his desire to heal and the action he took—based on his faith in Don Pedrito—grew on the journey and surely influenced his body and feelings.

Américo Paredes has shared several stories told about curanderismo in South Texas. He calls them *casos*, or "belief tales"—very short stories of extraordinary events, such as miracle cures, that happened to someone the teller knows.[73] Paredes explains that even though *casos* sometimes poke fun at what some acculturated middle- and upper-class Mexican Americans think of as the slow acculturation and poverty of many Mexicanos, he argues that their more important function is to foster belief in Mexican folk medicine, especially as it was being threatened by modern science and technologies that tended to dismiss it as "backward" and "superstitious" in the late nineteenth and early twentieth centuries.[74] Paredes describes a series of *casos* about Don Pedrito foiling doctors, dubbing them "intercultural jests," and argues that they demonstrate the validity not only of his curanderismo, but also Mexican American culture.[75] Call them *casos*, jests, scripts, stories, folklore, or mythology; in the end, these stories, like the story of how Don Pedrito acquired the *don*, function as guides to frame and make sense of a sometimes painful and sometimes joyful existence while leaving a record for following generations to do the same while valuing their culture.

Seven-year-old Manuel Hernández had an experience similar to Rodríguez's in his journey to Don Pedrito.[76] Manuel and his parents lived on a ranch on the Nueces River, seventy miles north of Los Olmos. The only son of Feliciano Hernández and his wife, Manuel was sick with an unidentified illness and was described as "weak, pale, and without appetite."[77] His parents had taken him to doctors, tried various home remedies, and even took the medical advice of the "American owner of the ranch" where they lived, but the boy remained very sick.[78] It was at this point, when "they saw they could do nothing to help him," that they decided to make the journey to Don Pedrito. Feliciano and his wife put Manuel's bed on a cart, and as they traveled to Los Olmos, they told their boy about Don Pedrito and "helped him believe he would be healed."[79] The story relates that as the journey progressed, Manuel began to feel better, and his appetite even returned. When they stopped to spend the night at Alice, he asked for food. When the family arrived at Los Olmos the following evening, many people were crowded into Don Pedrito's *jacal*, and they had to wait a long time to enter, but they explained that Manuel was already feeling much better. When it was finally their turn, Don Pedrito took hold of the boy's right hand, pulled his fingers, and said, "In the Name of God." He did the same to his father and mother. This was the only remedy Don Pedrito administered. By his parents' account, Manuel was healed.[80]

Don Pedrito, the "destination" of the pilgrimages described here, was a man—not a statue, relic, or shrine (although a shrine was built in his honor years after his death). He was a curandero (and, some believed, a living saint), and when supplicants and pilgrims came to him—bringing their pain, faith, and hope for healing—he ministered to them from a skill set that contained a variety of tools that were familiar to them. As one historian said, "It is not enough to cure the sick; you have to cure them with methods accepted by their community."[81] Don Pedrito's first and most important tool was the faith of his patients. He practiced a materialistic and experiential medicine that called for the immersion of bodies in hot or cold water (as in the case of Tomasita Canales), wrapping an herb-soaked body in blankets so that illness might sweat out through the pores of the skin (as in the case of Dionisio Rodríguez), as well as simple faith cures involving prayer (as in the case of Manuel Hernández). Yet, even in the case of Manuel, it was recounted that Don Pedrito grasped the boy's hand (even pulling his fingers) when he said "In the Name of God," and he also did the same to his parents, healing the whole family through touch and faith.[82]

Don Pedrito also gave Dionisio Rodríguez three pills—a form of modern allopathic medicine—which defies the stereotype of curanderos utilizing only herbs, touch, ritual, and prayer.[83] Yet, rather than making Rodríguez's case an anomaly, these apparent inconsistencies demonstrate that Don Pedrito's curanderismo was a creative, fluid, and sophisticated healing system. In the words of Robert Trotter, who has studied curanderismo in the Río Grande Valley, ". . . curanderos understand complexity and chaos," and so their system of healing includes what may seem like contradictory methods, such as healing with herbs and pills as well as utilizing science and faith. Yet they know that while these categories seem oppositional, they are not mutually exclusive, but blend together.[84] Don Pedrito blended techniques and methods in order to come up with the best cure for each individual. Trotter says that one trait all successful curanderos must have is "cultural competency."[85] That is, they must understand the culture of the people they are healing and walking among. Don Pedrito's cures demonstrate that he not only understood the Mexicano culture of South Texas, but also that he himself was a part of that culture.

Don Pedrito did not heal only individual bodies; he also healed the social body as he helped to sustain a community on the margins of state and institutional power.

Internal Colonialism in the South Texas Río Grande Valley

In 1881, when Don Pedrito arrived in South Texas, the Río Grande Valley was a place where Mexicans were the majority of the population, Spanish was the predominant language (both spoken and written), Mexican money circulated alongside US currencies, and Mexican cultural practices prevailed.[86] However, since 1848 and the signing of the Treaty of Guadalupe Hidalgo, which ended the Mexican-American War (1846–1848), the situation of Mexicans in Texas—now known as Tejanos—began to deteriorate as many lost their land to Anglo newcomers who used the US political and legal systems to take control of the land, politics, and social life of South Texas.

The discriminatory treatment of Mexicans living in Texas had actually begun even earlier, after Texas won independence from Mexico in 1836. Mexicans living in Texas, regardless of whether they fought for or against the Mexican Republic, faced a virulent reaction from Anglo Texans. Many even left the region they helped to build, fearing for their lives and property. The Texas Republic (which Mexico never recognized) existed from 1836 until 1845, when the United States admitted Texas as a state. However, disputes between Mexico and the United States over the international border between Texas and Mexico sparked the Mexican-American War, which ended with the defeat of Mexico, the signing of the Treaty of Guadalupe Hidalgo, the loss of half of Mexico's territory to the United States, and the establishment of the (eastern) border on the Río Grande, making Mexicans north of it American citizens.[87]

During these political transformations, Texas—and especially the South Texas Río Grande Valley—continued to be predominantly Mexicano and Tejano demographically and culturally as people crossed easily back and forth across the border.[88] Despite this, Anglo incursions into the area—usually motivated by business interests—began to erode the power of Mexicanos and Tejanos, particularly their access to and ownership of land.[89] Some scholars have described this Anglo invasion as "internal colonialism."[90] Like other forms of colonialism, internal colonialism involved not only the taking of land and resources of the colonized, but inscribing a racial system that defined the colonizers as the legitimate inhabitants and the colonized as the "other," the invader, the lesser, the dangerous.

Although the Treaty of Guadalupe Hidalgo provided stipulations to protect the land grants of ethnic Mexicans in ceded territories, many Tejano landowners ended up selling to Anglos at very low prices. This can partly be explained by the radically different views of land ownership possessed by Mexicans and Anglos. Mexican elites did not view land simply as a commodity to be bought and sold as the market dictated (as the newcomer Anglo ranchers did). For them, families and lineages owned land, and this formed the basis of a deeply valued traditional lifestyle. The Anglo commercial ranchers and land developers took advantage of these values and purchased land at very low prices because Tejanos would sell only when desperate for money—for example, during a drought or when they could not afford the cost of surveying or sinking wells on their land. Sometimes Anglo entrepreneurs took what they wanted through the imposition of expensive land surveys and legal proceedings required to defend Spanish and Mexican land grant titles, or through intimidation, violence, and illegal fencing.[91]

For example, Mifflin Kenedy, owner of the sprawling Kenedy Ranch, fenced in the lake of his neighbor, Doña Eulalia Tijerina (Doña Tomasita Canales's mother), owner of the La Atravesada land grant, without her permission and without paying her, simply because he needed water and she had it on her land.[92] Another Anglo rancher in the Río Grande Valley, Richard King, would simply take the land of his neighbors by illegal fencing or intimidation with the help of the Texas Rangers, who became known as "los rinches de la Kiñena" (the King Ranch Rangers).[93]

In some cases, the violence and intimidation by Anglo ranchers and the Texas Rangers sparked border wars, such as the Cortina Wars of 1859–1860 and the Caterino Garza Rebellion of 1890–1891. In the years following the Mexican–American War (1846–1848), Juan Nepomuceno Cortina, a wealthy Tejano rancher from the lower Río Grande Valley, spoke out against the Anglo judges and officials who he felt were exploiting Tejanos: "Many of you have been robbed of your property, incarcerated, chased, murdered, and hunted down like wild beasts, because your labor was fruitful, and because your industry excited the vile avarice which led them."[94] When Cortina shot a Brownsville marshal who was beating one of his *rancheros*, he sparked a yearlong war between ethnic Mexicans and the Texas Rangers. He eventually rallied approximately six hundred men to his cause. They raided Brownsville, proclaiming "Death to the Americans!" and "¡Viva México!," and seized control of the city until the US Army sent troops in.[95]

Decades later, Mexicanos and Tejanos were still fighting the oppressive actions of Anglo ranchers and Texas Rangers. In 1891, Caterino Erasmo Garza (1859–1895), a radical Mexican journalist, launched a transnational, cross-border rebellion against both Mexico and the United States.[96] Garza and the Garzistas wanted to overthrow the government of Mexican president Porfirio Díaz and defend ethnic Mexicans in South Texas against the Texas Rangers and the Anglo ranchers whose interests they protected.[97] Caterino Garza's Tejana wife, Concepción González Garza, came from a wealthy family that had two ranches near Don Pedrito's at Los Olmos. One, Palito Blanco, was about twenty miles from Los Olmos; the other, Rancho El Canelo, about ten miles away. Concepción's father, Alejandro, supported the Garzistas with guns, money, and horses. While clear documentation of a connection between Don Pedrito and the Garzistas has not been uncovered, some people from this region today assert that Don Pedrito must have known this family well and likely assisted the Garzistas, perhaps providing cover for them or hiding guns.[98]

What the cases of Garza, Cortina, and Doña Eulalia reveal is that in the period of Don Pedrito, a system of internal colonialism was imposed by Anglo newcomers in the Río Grande Valley, a racial system that positioned Anglos above Mexicans and hardened the social border between them. While it may be impossible to find out if Don Pedrito supported the Garzistas' armed rebellion, he would have been as aware of them as any other inhabitant of South Texas at this time—and why they were mobilizing against the forces of internal colonialism. He supported the health and well-being of those surrounding him in other ways.

An Informal Welfare System in the Río Grande Frontier

Returning to the "Map of the Río Grande Frontier Texas" (map 3.1): the year this map was produced, 1892, is significant. It was the year this region saw a time of hardship due to a depression, drought, and a surge of Anglo incursions. Despite their cultural and numerical dominance, many Tejanos suffered under the new Anglo order in the valley—not only poor *rancheros*, but elite Tejanos as well. Doña Tomasita Canales's son, José Tomás Canales, remembered this time as a painful one during which Protestant Anglos became a forceful presence in the mostly Mexican Catholic Río Grande Valley. In his memoir he wrote:

> most of the Anglo-Americans, who lived around us in Nueces County,
> Texas, were of the Protestant faith . . . they were not only very prosper-
> ous but some were officers in the County. I recollect how, in my childhood
> prayers to God, I used to complain to Him because He would permit such a
> heretic people to *govern over us*" (emphasis added).[99]

During this time, Don Pedrito Jaramillo helped elite Tejanos such as the Canales family as well as less fortunate ones with his cures. He assisted the state by providing food for starving Tejanos. He also helped Tejano ranchers and cowboys find water for their cattle, especially during the drought of 1893 and the Great Die-Up of 1892–1896.

Ruth Dodson, the author of *Don Pedrito Jaramillo, Curandero*, remembered that the first time she heard of him was during the "terrible drought year of 1893."[100] Her father and brother were searching for pasturage for their starving cattle when they passed Rancho de Los Olmos and came upon a naked Mexican man lying in the middle of an almost-dry lake "wallowing around in the muddy water."[101] When they asked him what he was doing, he told them he was simply following a prescription, or *receta*, given to him by Don Pedrito, the curandero at Los Olmos.[102] In South Texas, water held a particular, practical significance to the people who lived there: water (or the lack of it) was a matter of life and death. Even during the Great Die-Up, Don Pedrito continued to prescribe water cures for his clients—calling upon their faith in God to provide and restore not only their health, but also that of their land and cattle. Although residents of South Texas likely rationed water due to the drought (or fear of drought), Don Pedrito's water prescriptions gave them permission to indulge in several glasses of water or baths that they otherwise would not have permitted themselves. In any case, he prescribed water cures for a wide variety of ailments, including headaches, fever, alcoholism, and anxiety.[103]

At the same time that South Texas was suffering a severe drought, which devastated cattle ranchers, the national economy plunged into the worst depression the United States had yet seen.[104] In 1893, the European market for imported goods (including those made in the United States) contracted, and financial panic in England spread across the Atlantic to the United States, where several factors—including falling agricultural prices, federally funded over-expansion of railroads, tightening credit, and a weak banking system—fueled an economic collapse that has come to be known as the Panic of 1893. For the cattle market, the depression that started that year was the culmination of a longer trend in declining prices that began in the mid-1880s: cattle prices dropped from twenty-five dollars per head in 1884 to six dollars per head in 1893.[105] In South Texas, the years between 1892 and 1896 came to be known as the time of the Great Die-Up. A severe drought in 1893 produced a famine in South Texas that nearly destroyed the ranching business as massive numbers of cattle starved to death or were killed because they were no longer worth anything on the market.[106] One man from Falfurrias, Texas, Ramiro Rodríguez, remembered that his grandfather used to tell him stories about the "terrible drought years" when the only thing his grandfather could salvage from his cattle to sell was the tongue.[107]

Anglo ranchers with ample access to credit took advantage of struggling Tejano cattle ranchers and bought their land at give-away prices. Edward C. Lasater, for example, the founder of the town of Falfurrias and owner of the biggest Jersey dairy farm in the world, took advantage of the 1893 panic to invest in cattle: "That was the very year I had chosen to become ambitious. I was determined to make a fortune."[108] Lasater bought land from desperate land-rich but cash-poor Tejano ranchers who, without the same access to credit, could not afford to sink wells and keep their cattle alive.[109] Elite Tejanos who held large land grants, including Don Andrés Canales, sold off acreage to ranchers such as Richard and Henrietta King, who, like Lasater, took full advantage of the situation produced by the Great Die-Up.[110]

The 1893 drought was so devastating to the population of South Texas that a sense of hopelessness and desperation led some to anticipate the coming of the end of the world. Sixto García, a Tejano rancher who lived and worked on Rancho Agua Nuevo in Starr County, wrote a letter to the *San Antonio Express* in 1894 expressing this feeling, explaining that many in the Río Grande Valley had lost everything: their cattle, horses, and land.[111] The economic situation had worsened the already desperate state of affairs for those, like García, without access to capital or credit: "the refusal of credit by the merchants and the depreciation of the Mexican silver coin, make things harder still for the poor people."[112] García described how both cattle and humans were starving to death, and he pleaded with the governor of Texas to come see the situation for himself. He ended his letter by describing his daughter Pilar's vision.

> Sky very clear and blue and between the sky and the earth she saw on the east side, the moon very bright and clear and to the right of it were the bright colors of the rainbow, three times repeated. The first figure represented exactly an arch or the rainbow, the other went across it in the form of an arrow and the last in the form of a scroll, and next still to the right was an inscription in very black letters written in the Spanish language. . . . "En 1895 habra un día en que habra mucha mortandad de queate a causa de los rigors de hambre" [In 1895 there will come a day when many will die because of the rigors of hunger].[113]

Sixto García believed Pilar's vision was from God and prophesied the end of the world. The clearness of the sky, the vision in the east (the direction he believed the Lord would come from), the brightness of the moon, and the repetition of the colors of the rainbow all meant that God had suspended rainfall. The division of the sky between one-third of a rainbow and two-thirds outside the rainbow presaged the death of two-thirds of all living things, which (he believed) would occur before the end of the world. Garcia believed this prophesy would be fulfilled in South Texas, where even two more months without rain would drive people to unthinkable acts or death.[114] Comforting himself with faith in the face of this apocalyptic vision, García wrote, "I am not afraid myself to suffer with my family, as the Lord

Los Quintanillas Store 1896 — Don Pedro Jaramillo, famed curandero of Los Olmos, first man at left, standing Los Olmos (Paisano) once a community of 300 dates back to 1827 and the post office there came before Don Pedrito.

Figure 3.3. Don Pedrito and members of the Los Olmos community in front of Las Quintanillas dry goods store in 1896. Don Pedrito (far left, standing with horse) would buy large amounts of food to use in his cures as well as to feed those who came to him for a cure. "Dedication Ceremonies: Los Olmos Historical Marker," *Falfurrias Facts*, July 21, 1976. Courtesy of the Falfurrias Heritage Museum, Falfurrias, Texas.

is my trust, my help, and strength."[115] Like so many, García tried to make sense of a desperate situation through a combination of religious faith, interpretation of the scriptures, and his understandings of sickness and disease.

> the great and almost indescribable dying of the stock on account of the drought in this country . . . has absorbed all the fever and germs of all sorts of sickness on the bodies of the dying quadrupeds, and common sense teaches me that when the rain comes it will make sickly vapors that will develop a wholesale sickness through the country that will surely take many lives away.[116]

During the Great Die-Up, Don Pedrito helped the community of Tejanos by healing sick bodies, assisting struggling *rancheros* in finding water and digging wells, and providing food and sustenance in a kind of "informal welfare system" for the community.[117] At Los Olmos, he provided coffee, tortillas, and beans to those who came to him, or whatever he had cultivated on his small piece of land or purchased from the grocery store in the nearby town of Alice.[118] Doña Tomasita's son Albino Canales remembered that during this time of major food shortage and starvation, "Don Pedrito practically fed the northern part of Starr County."[119] In fact, during the

Great Die-Up the state of Texas took advantage of Don Pedrito's popularity as a healer and his informal welfare system and chose him to distribute rations of corn and beans to the famine-stricken population at Los Olmos— something he was already doing, but now with support and more provisions from the state.[120] Rather than taking advantage of the desperate situation of Tejanos in this period and enriching himself as the prominent Anglo ranchers Lasater, King, and Kenedy did, Don Pedrito provided a place of refuge, sustenance, and healing for those struggling to survive, fulfilling the obligation required by his *don*.[121]

Indigenous Roads to Don Pedrito

There are a few things that the "Map of the Río Grande Frontier Texas" (map 3.1) does not show: the Indigenous roads to Don Pedrito. He did not heal only Tejanos and Mexicanos. Like Teresa Urrea, Don Pedrito also healed Native people of this region, including the Lipan Apache, on whose sacred land Rancho de Los Olmos had been built. Don Pedrito was known to speak the Indigenous language of his home region in Mexico, Tarasco (Purepecha), as well as Lipan, Jicarilla, and Western Apache dialects. Jicarilla and Mescalero Apaches have traditions that tell of Don Pedrito, and later, Pimas and Navajos were known to visit Jaramillo's shrine. Among his Indigenous adherents, Don Pedrito was known for three special skills: true plant spirit medicine (peyote was a part of this, although not mentioned in any of his published cures likely due to its questionable legality), true hydrotherapy, and quickness—he could identify plants quickly and diagnose quickly. Although these Indigenous roads to Don Pedrito do not show up on maps produced by the state, according to oral histories and traditions, they are there. The name of Falfurrias, the closest town to Don Pedrito's healing practice, is a Lipan Apache word designating a type of flower that grows there, and the area was a historical Lipan Apache encampment, "from the Salt Flats on the south end of Falfurrias to past Olmos Creek," and also a trading area. In fact, the Spanish name for this region, La Apachería, reveals the historical and continuing significance of the Apache people to the region.[122]

The many roads—visible and invisible—to Don Pedrito Jaramillo reveal that curanderismo was central to this South Texas Río Grande Valley community. Those who lived in these borderlands navigated the dynamic and sometimes violent landscape as they worked, loved, worshipped, fought, got sick, and sought healing by negotiating among the competing authorities, ideas, and institutions available to them, often choosing the healing of Don

Pedrito. His successful cure of Doña Tomasita Canales in 1889 (the story that opened this chapter) is just one example of how Mexican and Indigenous cultural practices like Don Pedrito's curanderismo were equal to, if not superior to, professional medicine—an argument that J. T. Canales, Doña Tomasita's son, made in 1928, the subject of the next chapter.[123]

In the Clutches of Black Magic: Curanderismo and the Construction of a Mexican American Identity in the US-Mexico Borderlands

On February 8, 1928, Mexican president Plutarco Elías Calles left Mexico City, the center of federal power, and traveled to a small village on the northeast edge of the nation to be healed by a popular curandero, Niño Fidencio (1898–1938). Fidencio was known throughout Mexico and, especially, the South Texas–northeast Mexico borderlands for performing miraculous healings and surgeries with his hands, dirt, water, and broken glass at his makeshift hospital in Espinazo, Nuevo León. El Niño (as his adherents called him) treated Calles for a chronic skin disease by spreading honey all over his body and wrapping him in bandages.[1] After six hours with Fidencio on *Olivo*, the elegant presidential train that transported Calles to Espinazo, the president claimed he was healed.[2] Calles tried to keep it secret, but news of his consultation with a curandero traveled across the border, where it sparked a debate about curanderismo, Don Pedrito Jaramillo, and Mexican identity in South Texas.

Almost immediately after Calles visited Fidencio, *La Prensa*, a Spanish language newspaper in San Antonio, Texas, published a story that sharply criticized the president. "Mexico en las Garras de la Magia Negra" (Mexico in the Clutches of Black Magic) described curanderismo as *brujería*—black magic—and said the president's visit to Fidencio was an embarrassment to Mexicans on both sides of the border.[3] According to this article, Calles had misrepresented Mexico by seeking the healing of Fidencio because, in 1928, Mexicans no longer went to "superstitious" healers like curanderos. They were now modern and patronized professional doctors. This journalist contended that the practice of curanderismo should have expired in 1907 with the death of South Texas curandero Don Pedrito Jaramillo, described in this article not as a competent and respected curandero who healed and supported his community, but a *brujo* who "presided over this supernatural world in a rundown cabin adjacent to the Río Grande . . . unraveling secrets, hatching spells, perfecting the occult science."[4]

The article inspired a debate among readers of *La Prensa* about curanderismo, Don Pedrito, and Mexican identity, revealing that curanderismo was central to the modern Mexican identity on both sides of the border. An examination of this debate—including the voices, subjects, and ideologies imbricated in it—sheds light on how national identities are built, maintained, and contested not only by hegemonic institutions, such as the state and professional medicine, but also by cultural practices less obviously powerful yet no less important, such as Don Pedrito's curanderismo.

La Prensa founder Ignacio E. Lozano, along with the paper's journalists and many readers, thought of themselves as "méxicanos de afuera"—Mexicans abroad.[5] They identified as Mexican, not Mexican American or Tejano, and had no interest in becoming American citizens.[6] In the pages of *La Prensa*, they defended Mexican nationalism, the Mexican people, and a particular kind of national identity that was focused on Mexico City, the country's center of power, modernity, and scientific progress. Many were exiled Porfiristas and *científicos*, and their writings demonstrated continuity with the conservative, positivistic beliefs of the Porfirian age.[7] They believed that the current age was stuck in a phase of ignorance and fanaticism, represented by Calles leaving modern Mexico City to visit a curandero in a far northern outpost of the country.[8] In the imaginings of these elites, the Mexican north had long been associated with backwardness, barbarity, and superstition: it was the place of *indios bárbaros* as opposed to the exalted Aztecs of Mexico City.[9] Don Pedrito, described in *La Prensa* as a *brujo* "venerated in the frontier area," was yet another example of this.[10] Calles, "nothing less than the President of the Mexican Republic, fleeing from the authorities of the Aztec capital, some of whom are men of science," to secretly consult the curandero "el Niño Fidencio," "a type of *brujo* and curandero that science cannot take seriously," was an embarrassment.[11] Calles was the face of Mexico to the world, and by seeking out the healing of a curandero, he was showing the world their nation was not modern but "stuck in the clutches of black magic," like those who believed in Niño Fidencio, Don Pedrito Jaramillo, and curanderismo.

Not all Mexicans shared these feelings about curanderos, especially the Tejanos who had known Don Pedrito personally. In fact, this article inspired many impassioned letters to the editor of *La Prensa* defending his legacy, including one by prominent South Texas lawyer and legislator José Tomás (J. T.) Canales.[12] Don Pedrito had cured Canales's mother, Tomasita, in 1889 (as described in chapter 3) after professional physicians had given

Figure 4.1. "Mexico en las Garras de la Magia Negra," *La Prensa*, March 11, 1928.

up. In response to the outcry provoked by the article, *La Prensa* published a guest editorial by Canales. In it, he defended Don Pedrito and curanderismo. He also claimed an identity for Tejanos that did not designate curanderismo as "backward" or "ignorant." Instead, Canales argued that the scientifically superior curanderismo practiced by Niño Fidencio and Don Pedrito proved ethnic Mexicans, including Mexican American Tejanos like

Figure 4.2. "Pedro Jaramillo." Photo by S. Sandoval, San Antonio, Texas, 1894. Image courtesy of University of Texas at San Antonio Libraries, Special Collections, #098-1955.

himself, were modern, progressive, rational, and capable of being exemplary national citizens.[13]

In his editorial, titled "Don Pedrito Jaramillo curaba a los enfermos pobres, desahuciados" (Don Pedrito Jaramillo cured sick poor people, the terminally ill), Canales challenged the newspaper's critique of curanderismo as well as the characterization of Don Pedrito as a *brujo*. He explained that those who knew him revered his memory, and perhaps even still prayed to him, and they were deeply angered by the depiction of their beloved curandero as a sorcerer and *brujo*. Canales described Don Pedrito as a powerful healer, a humble laborer, and an honorable man who practiced the "Christian virtues" of caring for the poor.[14] In fact, he had done so much good for his community that he had come to be called the Benefactor of Humanity, the epitaph engraved on his tombstone.[15] The depiction of Don Pedrito as a *brujo* was especially upsetting to many Tejanos and Mexicans in the South Texas Río Grande Valley who understood *brujería* and curanderismo as oppositional practices with very different intentions: a *brujo* harms through the power of demons; a curandero heals through the power of God.[16] Don Pedrito was a curandero who healed, not a *brujo* who harmed. In his editorial, Canales explained why he was supremely qualified to defend the reputation of Don Pedrito. Not only was he a member of the Tejano community Don Pedrito healed, he also knew, firsthand, how effective his cures were because he had healed his own mother in 1889. Further, in his position as a lawyer, Canales had successfully defended the curandero before.[17]

Don Pedrito and *Médicos Científicos*

In 1901, Don Pedrito Jaramillo was accused of fraud by the US Post Office and the American Medical Association. His attorney and friend, J. T. Canales, defended him against these charges. Not only did Canales prove that Don Pedrito was not engaging in any fraudulent practices, he turned the tables on the "médicos científicos," as he called the physicians accusing Don Pedrito, by arguing that his curanderismo was superior to the scientific medicine because in 1899 Jaramillo healed his mother after two physicians had tried and failed. Ultimately, Canales succeeded in having the case dismissed for a clear reason: Don Pedrito "never charged a single cent for his cures. . . . All of this I proved with irrefutable information, at the General Office of the Mail, in Washington."[18] It was because of the considerable significance of Don Pedrito's curanderismo to his Tejano and Mexicano community, as Canales demonstrated in his 1928 editorial in *La Prensa*, that he came to the attention of the American Medical Association and the US Post Office.

Don Pedrito's successful curanderismo practice inspired both suspicion of fraud by the local postmaster and the resentment of professional physicians who sought to gain dominance and authority in the medical marketplace by exposing fraudulent practices of "quacks" and "charlatans." Although Don Pedrito's healing practice started small—at first he healed residents at Los Olmos and nearby ranches or traveled on horseback to make house calls and visit nearby ranches where he would diagnose and make cures, play some *malia* (a card game), and perhaps have a drink of mezcal from his *bota* (sheepskin sack) with the men—his popularity increased.[19] As his reputation grew, Don Pedrito began to receive letters asking for cures, or *recetas*. Some accounts suggest that by 1900 he was receiving up to two hundred such letters a week.[20] They usually contained stamps for Don Pedrito to send a *receta* in response, and often money or money orders as tokens of reciprocity. The local postmaster's suspicions were aroused when the number of letters mailed from the post office did not equal the number of stamps sold, suggesting something fraudulent might be going on. In addition, some doctors in the area tried to stop Don Pedrito's successful healing practice by alerting the AMA that he was receiving money orders for purportedly fraudulent cures. Consequently, in 1901 the federal post office ordered an investigation.[21]

The US Post Office—through which most mental healers, patent medicine salespeople, and companies peddled new and questionable inventions—was at the vanguard of an effort that began in the nineteenth century and continued into the twentieth to combat medical fraud and "quackery."[22] One example of a fraud case successfully prosecuted by the US Post Office and the AMA is that of Dr. Bye and his mail-order cancer cure business. Dr. Bye claimed to have a vegetable compound that would miraculously heal cancerous growths on the skin.[23] He solicited potential customers through the mail, asking twenty-five dollars for the compound. If the potential customer did not respond at first, he would reach out again, but the second time ask only twelve dollars, and with each subsequent request, he decreased the price. The Department of Agriculture analyzed Dr. Bye's compound and discovered that it was only a mix of cottonseed oil and ordinary tonics—not a cure for cancer. In this case, the AMA and the US Post Office successfully issued a fraud order in 1910 that denied Dr. Bye the use of the mail.[24] Don Pedrito was nothing like Dr. Bye. He did not advertise his cures, nor did he make the kinds of claims that Dr. Bye did. Don Pedrito also did not charge for his cures, all part of the dictates of his *don* that, according to the sources, he followed faithfully. However, Don Pedrito did pose a threat to the "médicos científicos" accusing him of fraudulent practices. He possessed something that professional Anglo physicians did not: cultural authority. In this predominantly Mexican region, cultural practices such as curanderismo prevailed. Don Pedrito was a popular healer not only because his cures were effective, but also because he shared the culture of the community he served. This posed a unique threat to the medical establishment in South Texas, which was predominantly Anglo. On top of that, at the beginning of the twentieth century in Texas and across the nation, the medical profession did not inspire the confidence that it would in the second half of the century. Don Pedrito, like any healer during this period, was judged more by the success of his cures (or the ability to alleviate symptoms) than by which particular school of medicine he was associated with, if any. As other rural physicians did, he treated a wide variety of illnesses and afflictions. In nineteenth-century rural South Texas there were few specialists; curanderos and rural doctors treated everything.

Dr. Strickland, a rural physician who covered much of the same territory as Don Pedrito—and may have been the only regular doctor serving people between Corpus Christi, Laredo, and San Diego at this time—hinted at the state of medical knowledge when, after being asked his opinion of the validity of Don Pedrito's medicine, he replied, "Now, how do I know that Don Pedrito's prayers don't do more good than my pills?"[25] As a rural doctor, Dr. Strickland had surely witnessed his share of the failures of nineteenth-century medicine, and he knew that sometimes the curandero succeeded and the physician failed, as in the case of Doña Tomasita Canales. Importantly, Dr. Strickland did not want to alienate the community that embraced Don Pedrito, nor ascribe to himself sole power to heal ailments.[26] However, unlike Dr. Strickland, many "regular" physicians, with the help of their professional organizations, sought to establish themselves as the sole professional healing authorities by denouncing alternative or "irregular" healers such as Don Pedrito.[27]

Another reason Don Pedrito presented a threat to professional medicine was because he did not ask for money for his cures. He survived on an economy of reciprocity. Some historians have argued that although the stated purpose of the AMA was to raise the standards of medicine and protect the public from the dangers of quackery, the real purpose was to defend the incomes of medical professionals against competition from other kinds of healers.[28]

Indeed, national and state medical journals such as the *Journal of the American Medical Association* (JAMA), *Daniel's Texas Medical Journal,* and the *Texas State Journal of Medicine* filled their pages with articles calling for the professionalization of medicine in order to increase physicians' incomes. JAMA, for example, published articles entitled "Why Is the Profession Poor in the Purse?" and "Does It Pay to Be a Doctor?," which compared the median income of a physician practicing at that time ($750 per year) to that of federal employees ($1,000) and ministers ($759), and lamented that physicians would never get rich at this rate.[29] *Medical News* featured an article explaining "Causes of the Decline of Physicians' Income" and calling for all physicians to professionalize in order to combat "irregular" healers and "quacks"—and increase incomes.[30] In 1905 the dean of the medical department at Tulane University wrote that alternative doctors and "quacks" were the "greatest foe to the medical profession," not because they could mistreat or hurt patients, but because they were "an obstacle to the financial success of the reputable medical practitioner."[31] Certainly not all physicians were concerned with becoming wealthy, but the lack of earning potential was a significant issue for them, and the threat of sectarian or "irregular" healers taking patients from them was real.

Curanderos such as Don Pedrito confounded institutions like the AMA and the US Post Office because they did not fit neatly into any of their categories, although their presence and popularity in the borderlands continued to pose a significant challenge to professional medicine. Starting in the 1890s, the AMA became more involved in local medical organizations, including the Texas Medical Association (TMA), encouraging them to attack the problem of competition posed by "irregular" healers by pursuing "fraudulent" healers in their region through the courts, and by creating laws and specialized licenses that would prohibit healers from infringing on their business.[32] At the TMA meeting in Austin in April 1894, physician members passed legislation that would require examinations by state boards for all "irregular" medical practitioners before they could officially practice and charge fees.[33] They wanted to make practicing any kind of medicine without having passed state examinations a criminal offense.[34]

The underlying assumption of strategies deployed by the AMA and local organizations such as the TMA echoes the argument made in the article "Mexico en las Garras de la Magia Negra": science (and modern civilization) belonged to professional medicine, not curanderos and faith healers. *Faith Cures and the Law*, a pamphlet written by a physician and published in 1901, the same year Don Pedrito was accused of fraud, reflects on the state of medicine and science at the turn of the century in light of what the author deemed fraudulent, superstitious healers.

> One would suppose now, at the beginning of the twentieth century, when men generally think sanely and reasonably, when we have come to substitute for superstition the habit of accounting for physical manifestations

DON PEDRITO.

Figure 4.3. This sketch of Don Pedrito accompanied an article about him published in the *San Antonio Daily Express* that attributed his healing power to his "Aztec blood" ("Flurry Over Don Pedrito," April 22, 1894).

upon scientific bases, when science has made evident the value of sanitation, hygiene, and clean living in inducing happiness and well-being and in dispelling disease, that these peculiar movements would be impossible.[35]

This physician argued that "superstitious" and "peculiar" healers—such as "Mind Curists," "Magnetic Healers," and "Psychic Scientists" who operated outside of the bounds of scientific medicine—threatened not only the medical profession, but also "the national life."[36] He did not mention Don Pedrito or the practice of curanderismo in his list of "pernicious movements," but he referred to Francis Schlatter, an itinerant faith healer popular in the Southwest who was very similar to (and often compared to) a curandero.[37] As in the 1928 *La Prensa* article, the sentiment in *Faith Cures and the Law* is that if modern civilization and nation-states are to progress, they must leave these kinds of healers in the past. And the past is where, some argued, Don Pedrito's healing power came from.

He Is an Aztec

Another factor contributed to Don Pedrito Jaramillo's threat to professional medicine as well as "the national life": his race. This became evident on one of his trips to San Antonio, when several journalists observed his healing and wrote about him in local newspapers.[38] A writer for the *San Antonio Express* asked, "Is it faith cure? This is the generally accepted theory, if there be any theory at all. The Mexicans do not try to advance any. The white people do, as they naturally wish to show some cause from indisputable effects."[39] Unable to find a scientific theory to explain Don Pedrito's healing power, the writer came to the conclusion that it must be his Aztec blood:

> He is an Aztec. The blood of seers of that practically extinct but wonderful race flows in his veins. He does not know why he is chosen, but impelled by something unaccountable, he is exercising a power that the Aztecs are said to have excelled in centuries ago. . . . The occult power of a prehistoric and advanced race has been transmitted to the present day through the humble body of an ignorant Mexican who barely looks at his patient while he tells him how to cure diseases that have baffled the skill of modern science.[40]

Don Pedrito may have been part Tarascan, an Indigenous group from his home state of Jalisco, Mexico, who were rivals of the Aztecs in the precolonial period, but there is no evidence he possessed Aztec heritage. How-

ever, the journalist did not need evidence of whether Don Pedrito had Aztec heritage. It simply was part of the broad racialization of Mexicans at
this time. In fact, one journalist justified Teresa Urrea's extraordinary healing power in a similar way, explaining that she was "a type of the Mexican
whose blood has come down through Aztec and Spanish ancestors."[41]

Journalists were not alone in their attempts to explain the healing power
of curanderos through something other than their skill. In 1894, US Army
captain John Gregory Bourke (1843–1894), while stationed in South Texas to
quell Caterino Garza's cross-border rebellion, studied the culture of border
Mexicans and published his observations in an article for *Scribner's Magazine* entitled "The American Congo."[42] Foreshadowing *The Heart of Darkness* (1899), Joseph Conrad's novel about Belgian colonialism in Africa,
Bourke compared the Río Grande to the Congo River in West Africa and
suggested that both river valleys were populated with people of a "degraded,
turbulent, ignorant, and superstitious character."[43] He juxtaposed the "civilizing" forces of Anglos against the "barbaric" and "savage" ways of the Tejanos and Mexicanos in order to justify economic exploitation and colonization of their lands.[44] Bourke describes being repulsed by the "penury,
filth, and ignorance" of nineteenth-century "Rio Grande Mexicans," but at
the same time he was fascinated with their traditional cultural practices, or
"survivals" as he called them, especially curanderismo.[45] As others did, he
explained that the power of curanderos came from the ancient Aztec past
rather than from their own medicinal knowledge and intelligence, and he
believed that South Texas and northern Mexico were ideal places to study
"cultural survivals" because "The Mexican . . . is the descendant of five different races, each in its way conservative of all that had been handed down
from its ancestors."[46] He described the five races as Roman, Teuton, Arab,
Celt, and Aztec, and stated that the lower Río Grande Valley was an ideal
place to study the "lore and custom of the folk" for clues to their "original
purpose and design."[47]

Captain Bourke, journalists, and professional doctors all touched upon
one of the anxieties at the center of the turn-of-the-century world: how to
resolve the problem of the achievements of contemporary Mexicans, Indigenous people, and other people of color in a racialized world in which non-
white people were considered incapable of understanding science, modernity, and progress, and even more ominously, they were dangerous to the
health of nations. Consequently, the strategy of invoking an ancient Indigenous past to explain the achievements of ethnic Mexicans such as Don Pedrito coincided with the rise of another racial ideology: tropical medicine.

Adherents of tropical medicine viewed the bodies of non-white peoples as potential reservoirs of diseases that could infect and weaken the nation. This type of medicine was a medico-racial view that emerged in the late nineteenth century in tandem with European colonialism in Asia and Africa, and US imperial efforts in Latin America. Tropical medicine viewed tropical diseases such as yellow fever as especially dangerous to white people not accustomed to tropical climates. These diseases needed to be eradicated, or at least contained, so that colonial and imperial projects—such as Belgian mining in the Congo, construction of the Panama Canal, US imperial wars in Cuba and the Philippines, and Anglo commercial interests in South Texas and Mexico—could succeed.[48] Tropical medicine provided a racial explanation of disease and hygiene that was well suited to colonial expansion and imperial domination. In the ideology of tropical medicine, the tropics—Africa, Asia, and Latin America—were seen as breeding grounds for diseases that threatened Europeans and Anglo Americans. A chilling racial corollary to this ideology was that the Indigenous bodies in these places were somehow different: they were viewed as dangerous, dark, dirty, and vectors of disease, and thus needed to be kept separate from European and Anglo bodies. This ideology extended to the South Texas Río Grande Valley—a place that many have argued was (and is still) an internal colony of the United States. In South Texas, concerns over yellow fever epidemics were combined with commercial interests. Mexicanos and Tejanos, whose labor was essential to the economic development of the valley, came to be seen as vectors of disease endangering the nation's health at the border.[49] Armed with this ideology, the physicians, scientists, and public health officials who worked in the field of tropical medicine assisted state institutions with imperial and colonial projects that promoted European expansion overseas and US hegemony in the Americas.

In the South Texas Río Grande Valley, a chorus of voices—including Anglo physicians, military men, lawyers, and scientists—clamored that ethnic Mexicans, "the laboring classes of the Río Grande," were causing similar disease outbreaks in places like Laredo and Corpus Christi. August Spohn, a Canadian-born physician who worked for the King Ranch, the Texas-Mexican railway, and the city of Corpus Christi, described ethnic Mexicans as "a filthy set" who "pay no attention to cleanliness or sanitary matters."[50] Spohn was laboring under the accepted (but mistaken) medical knowledge of the time that the cause of the spread of yellow fever was through germs or miasma, produced by filth, and thus must be fought with enforced sanitary measures.[51]

Federal, state, and local authorities shared Spohn's opinion of how the disease spread, as well as the view that ethnic Mexicans were a "filthy set," and so began working together to implement quarantines (enforced by mounted guards) throughout the Texas-Mexico borderlands.[52] In 1890, one Anglo American lawyer voiced his concern over the threat of yellow fever traveling from Mexico to the border city of Brownsville, harming "Americans" or "white men" living there: "I have been assured there are still cases of yellow fever in Matamoros. We should not raise the quarantine for any reason, even if it is starving or harming the working poor. We must stop the invasion of yellow fever to prevent any American deaths. . . . Since one white man is worth ten Mexicans."[53] As with yellow fever epidemics in other places throughout the colonized world, the colonizers—in the case of South Texas, Anglo newcomers, businessmen, and opportunists—strove to eradicate epidemic diseases. Yet they did so not out of concern for the health of the colonized—in the case of South Texas, the ethnic Mexican Tejanos—but to ensure the success of commerce and empire.[54]

In their desire to eradicate the diseases causing epidemics in South Texas in this period—and to protect the health of "white men"—federal, state, and local public health officials took controversial and coercive measures, including the deployment of armed guards to enforce quarantines.[55] For example, when a yellow fever epidemic broke out in Brownsville in 1882, the US Marine Hospital Service (USMHS) set up a 190-mile military-enforced quarantine along the Texas-Mexico railroad line that connected Laredo to Corpus Christi, medically isolating this region from the rest of Texas. They called it "Mexican Texas," a designation that consigned South Texas to Latin America, a place populated with what they considered strange and foreign people, and outside the medical boundaries of the United States.[56] As historian John Mckiernan-González explains, "the on-going presence of the armed USMHS quarantine guard provided visual evidence that—regardless of the causes of yellow fever—Mexicans were a dangerously diseased, potentially criminal, and transnationally connected population that required either expulsion or violent supervision."[57] The impact on the lives of Tejanos living under the 1882 Brownsville Quarantine was immense. Not only did they fear a painful death from yellow fever, but one nearly as horrible: death by starvation as unemployment skyrocketed and relief committees could not keep up with the demand.[58]

However, even in Mexico, curanderos such as Don Pedrito Jaramillo were seen as a threat to public health. Especially during the early years of the Porfiriato (1876–1910), officials explained that the high incidence of infectious diseases was caused by the lack of professional physicians and rural Mexicans' reliance on curanderos.[59] Some of the country's health officials believed that despite efforts of the state to eliminate yellow fever (endemic in some places in Mexico, including the port city of Veracruz, from 1890 to the early 1900s) through such invasive means as quarantines and forced disinfection and fumigation of homes, it persisted largely because folk healers convinced people that "they had been immunized by nature and that the illness was caused by supernatural spirits."[60] Yet, despite this discourse that painted traditional healers such as curanderos as backward, superstitious, and dangerous to the health of the nation, many people preferred their healing over a professional physician's. The reasons for this preference were varied. Sometimes the curandero was successful when the physician was not, as in the case of Doña Tomasita Canales; in many cases, people desired a healer who was embedded in the community and understood the culture, like Don Pedrito Jaramillo.

La Raza Cósmica in South Texas

J. T. Canales's defense of Don Pedrito in the pages of *La Prensa* against charges of fraud in 1901 and, in 1928, against characterizations of him as an outdated *brujo* was part of his larger mission to defend his "race," Mexican Americans, against the racist ideologies that informed the ways in which ethnic Mexicans were discriminated against and characterized as outside the bounds of US citizenship. Canales formulated a conception of Mexican American identity that drew from a constellation of ideas about identity and national belonging that claimed Mexican Americans were actually supremely qualified US citizens and so should have all the rights, protections, and opportunities of any American citizen. Canales's ideas about Mexican American national identity were important because during the first part of the twentieth century a racial regime had come to dominate people of Mexican descent living in the United States—whether legal US citizens or not—and reinscribed them as "illegal aliens."[61] In his position as a prominent Tejano politician and lawyer, Canales defended the rights of Mexican Americans and their culture in South Texas with his words and actions, just as he defended Don Pedrito in 1901 and 1928.

In his conception of Mexican American identity, Canales was inspired by ideas of *mestizaje* and indigeneity put forth by prominent Mexican intellectuals such as Justo Sierra, Manuel Gamio, and especially José Vasconcelos. In 1902, historian and journalist Justo Sierra (1848–1912) described Mexican national identity as a product of racial fusion: "We Mexicans are the sons of two countries and two races. We were born of the Conquest; our roots are in the land where the aborigines lived and in the soil of Spain. This fact rules our whole history; to it we owe our soul."[62] Sierra argued that the blending of Natives and Spaniards created the Mexican race and located the Mexican national identity in this mixture. However, reflecting the influence of Social Darwinism among Mexican intellectuals during this period, Sierra promoted European immigration to Mexico in order to "obtain a cross with the indigenous race, for only European blood can keep the level of civilization . . . from sinking, which would mean regression, not evolution."[63] A colleague of Sierra proclaimed, "Our national spirit is a consequence of the union of two races," but he emphasized that the Mestizos produced from such unions were "decidedly in favor of the Spanish type."[64]

During the period of the Mexican Revolution (1910–1920) and the postrevolutionary period, an articulation of national identity emerged that invoked the Aztec past while also addressing the contemporary Indigenous population. Revolutionary *indigenismo*, as it came to be called, advocated the progressive integration of Native people into mainstream Mexican society through education and celebration of their own culture.[65] Mexican anthropologist Manuel Gamio (1883–1960) argued that the postrevolutionary Mexican nation must build its unique identity upon pre-Hispanic Indigenous roots and combine the "many Mexicos"—the disparate Indigenous communities, each with its own distinctive language and cultural practices—into one unified Mexico.[66] Proponents of revolutionary *indigenismo* such as Gamio would help these varied indigenous peoples "forge . . . an Indian soul."[67] Echoing the positivistic evolutionary theory espoused by Sierra and other Porfirian thinkers (as did *La Prensa*'s "En las Garras de la Magia Negra"), Gamio explained the Native people's "lack of direction" and inability to achieve civilization not as a biologically determined inferiority, but rather the result of the "evolutionary state of our indigenous civilization," which, he believed, was stuck four hundred years in the past.[68] Gamio argued that most of the pre-Hispanic Indigenous practices, including religious beliefs and artistic tendencies, were "backward, anachronistic, impractical, inappropriate" in the present age, yet he made an exception for the "Indian sorcerer": this was the one pre-Columbian "survival" that surpassed contemporary knowledge. He compared the pre-Hispanic sorcerer to magnetizers, hypnotists, and mediums, explaining that these "contemporary sorcerers . . . approach the phenomena with the same vague knowledge" as a Native sorcerer.[69] Above all, Gamio articulated a nationalist cultural project in which the main goal was a unified Mestizo nation, and intellectual *indigenistas* such as Gamio would choose which pieces of Indigenous history and culture—like the "Indian sorcerer"—belonged in that nation.

Perhaps most significant to J. T. Canales's conception of Mexican American identity was José Vasconcelos and his 1925 book *La Raza Cósmica*. A lawyer, educator, and philosopher, Vasconcelos (1882–1959) challenged the idea of the superiority of one specific race and argued that in the "next great historical era" Mexico would lead the world because it embodied the "cosmic race," one constituted by *mestizaje*, the fusing of all races—Indigenous, African, and European.[70] Vasconcelos argued that this *mestizaje* was the nation's strength, not weakness, and it placed Mexico at the forefront of a new world epoch.[71] Vasconcelos's conception of *mestizaje* influenced ethnic Mexicans living across the border in Texas. In fact, in the 1920s, Vasconcelos published a weekly column in *La Prensa*, and the newspaper advertised his book, *La Raza Cósmica*, for decades.[72] Canales added a twist to Vasconcelos's ideas, claiming that the unique racial fusion of Latin Americans celebrated by Vasconcelos was exactly what would make Mexican Americans supremely qualified for US citizenship, and they should therefore embrace all the rights and privileges of US citizenship entitled to them as Mexican Americans.

In addition to creating and articulating an identity for Mexican Americans, Canales defended them against the depredations of Texas Rangers during the 1915 Plan de San Diego uprising. When ethnic Mexican revolutionaries, referred to as *sediciosos*, raided ranches and railroads in response to the exclusionary and racist treatment of ethnic Mexicans, Texas Rangers and Anglo vigilantes responded with extra-legal executions, deportations, and other bloody reprisals. At first Canales took the side of the US government and organized a company of Mexican American scouts to collect intelligence about the *sediciosos*. But his politics changed when he learned about the violence that *los rinches* (as some ethnic Mexicans called the Texas Rangers) were committing against Tejanos, including lynchings.[73] As state representative of the 95th District of Texas, he filed nineteen charges against the Rangers and called for a legislative investigation and reorganization of the force, proposing a bill that would drastically curtail their power and put them under stricter state authority and local control. Not only did the bill not pass, but Canales endangered his own life by prosecuting the Rangers, as his life was threatened by those who sought to defend the power of this institution.[74]

At this time, when Tejanos, Mexican immigrants, and Mexican Americans were experiencing racial discrimination in South Texas (and across the southwestern US), the United States entered the First World War. This global event had major effects on borderlands communities and the lives of Mexican Americans. Nativist and anti-immigrant sentiment rose, reflected in legislation passed in Congress, such as a 1917 Immigration Act, which, among other things, prohibited labor contractors from enlisting workers in Mexico, making the border states—Arizona, California, and Texas—desperate for farmworkers. Agribusiness leaders were able to persuade the secretary of labor to waive the provisions of the 1917 bill for Mexican migrants, yet even after 1921, when Congress restored the provisions of the 1917 act, hundreds of thousands of Mexicans entered the US, responding to the demand for agricultural laborers. Despite (or perhaps because of) the fluidity of Mexican workers moving back and forth across the border, the United States created the Border Patrol in 1924, a year that also saw Congress pass the Johnson-Reed National Origins Act, which restricted immigration from Europe by a system of quotas and ended immigration from Asia. However, no quotas were put on immigration from the Western Hemisphere (meaning Mexico) because agricultural, railroad, and mining industries needed "cheap labor" to build the economy of the US Southwest.[75]

Despite the importance of Mexican labor to the United States economy, many Anglo Americans during this period viewed Mexicans as a "health hazard," a threat to the "white race," and "illegal."[76] Lothrop Stoddard (1883–1950), a Harvard-trained historian and eugenicist, argued that Mexicans posed a threat to the nation because of the porous two-thousand-mile border, which allowed "the little brown peons" to "keep swarming in and spread far beyond our southern-border States--wherever, in fact there is a call for 'cheap labor' . . . the peon brings with him his ignorance, dirt, disease, and vice, which infect cities with slum plague-spots, depress wages, and lower the general tone of the community."[77] Stoddard wrote several influential books and articles on the threat of immigrants to white or "Nordic" civilization, including *The Rising Tide of Color Against White World-Supremacy* (1920) and *Re-forging America: The Story of Our Nationhood* (1927), which claimed racial mixing produced "mongrelized" Latin Americans and made their bodies "a battle ground of jarring heredities" that expressed itself in "hectic violence and aimless instability."[78] Such attacks were not limited to Mexicans, but included African Americans as well. Even as 1924 saw the creation of the Border Patrol to stem the flow of people across the border, the following year witnessed the height of Ku Klux Klan activity in the South and increased mob violence directed at Mexicans in the Southwest.[79]

In 1928, when J. T. Canales defended Don Pedrito's reputation in the pages of *La Prensa* against accusations of *brujería*, he and other Tejanos were in the early stages of developing the League of United Latin American Citizens (LULAC), a Mexican American civil rights organization dedicated to "combatting racism as an obstacle to community empowerment."[80] Founded on February 17, 1929, in Corpus Christi, Texas, LULAC claimed that the values of their Mexican ancestors and their loyalty to the United States made them worthy US citizens. A journalist described LULAC's goals in *La Prensa*: "Primero. To develop among the members of our race, the best, the most pure and perfect type of true and loyal citizen of the United States of America."[81] LULAC stressed the importance of speaking English, voting, and participating in the political system. One controversial requirement for LULAC membership was US citizenship, a provision sought by J. T. Canales. This may seem inconsistent with the ideology that Canales had crafted celebrating Mexican culture and racial fusion, ideas borrowed from Mexican thinkers. However, excluding Mexican citizens from membership had less to do with bias against them than with proving their loyalty as US-born Americans. Canales was justified in excluding noncitizens, according to historian Cynthia Orozco, because "In an era when cultural pluralism was nonexistent and English-only rules and assimilation were stated policy, national citizenship was a basis for racial justice."[82]

Throughout his life Canales continued to write to newspaper editors, politicians, clergy, and textbook authors to defend Mexican Americans, the Spanish language, and Tejano culture. He echoed the sentiments of Vasconcelos when, in an article for *Lulac News*, he attributed the success of the United States to the fact that "Americans" were not one singular Anglo-Saxon race, but a composite race, like Latin Americans. They were a mix of "Dutch, German French, Scandinavian, and other races."[83] Shortly after the creation of LULAC, Canales wrote to the author of a Texas history textbook, thanking her for writing a history that greatly improved upon the one Canales was taught as a boy. He wrote:

When I went to school in the [18]80's we had an abominable Texas History which I believe was Mrs. Pennybacker's that made us American citizens of Mexican and Latin extraction feel humiliated in the way she treated the war for Texas Independence. She never mentioned any single good quality on the Mexican character. All the glory went to the Anglo-Saxon and the Mexicans were painted as traitors, bandits and an altogether inferior race.[84]

Unlike Mrs. Pennybacker, when Canales defended Don Pedrito in *La Prensa* as an honorable representative of the "race" and a skilled healer superior to the *médicos científicos* who accused Don Pedrito of fraud, he reversed the prevailing assumption that Mexicans were inferior and Anglo Americans were the bearers of civilization, science, and progress.[85] Instead, he claimed that Mexican American and Mexican cultural practices such as curanderismo were just as good as, if not superior to, Anglo institutions and

Los Funerales de Don Pedrito

Figure 4.4. "Los Funerales de Don Pedrito." Charles I. Dryden Photographs, A1973-056.0005, South Texas Archives, James C. Jernigan Library, Texas A&M University–Kingsville.

identities. The *La Prensa* debate that Canales engaged in in 1928 shows how curanderismo was central to modern Mexican identity on both sides of the border, despite what elites and doctors said. Don Pedrito Jaramillo, Teresa Urrea, and Niño Fidencio's adherents—the sick, disenfranchised, and poor, as well as the political elite—constituted a dynamic source of power that flowed to the curanderos through their clients' belief and back to the people through their healing. It was precisely this fluid source of power encapsulated in the practice of curanderismo—with its unique mix of science, faith, and (what some believed) magic—that not only contributed to the vitality and health of borderlands communities, but also helped shape and maintain an ethnic Mexican transnational identity from the end of the nineteenth century into the twentieth.

"Ya murió Don Pedrito"

By defending Don Pedrito and curanderismo, J. T. Canales was also defending his community of Tejanos and Mexican Americans in South Texas, to whom Don Pedrito had been such a vital part, as the massive turnout at his funeral demonstrated. Ruth Dodson, an Anglo from the South Texas Río Grande Valley who collected the stories of Don Pedrito's cures, creating the largest archive of his healing, remembers when she learned Don Pedrito had died.

> Then one hot summer day, an old Mexican man I had known all my life came to my house to tell me that Don Pedrito had died. He told me the news in the manner of closing a story, which was the way I accepted it. "Ya murió Don Pedrito" Trinidad announced to me as I came in—"Now Don Pedrito has died." He seemed to imply that there was nothing more to be said of him, that his career has finished.[86]

When Don Pedrito passed away on July 3, 1907, his community mourned the loss and celebrated his life. Even though Dodson suggests there was nothing more to say at this point, there was more to say. One year after his death, a poem commemorating Don Pedrito, written by an eighty-five-year-old woman who lived near Los Olmos, was printed in a local newspaper. The very last stanza suggests his legacy to those in this community who believed in him:

> In order to depart this world
> And end his earthly stay
> To many many mothers
> He lavished consolation.
> Quickly, then, he went
> Up to the throne of God
> And with love he listens
> To all who petition contritely
> Because Pedrito is our mediator
> And Pedrito now belongs to all[87]

Conclusion

I'll tell you how I became a healer.
I was sick, my leg turned white.
Sobrino went to Juan Dávila
Asked if Juan Dávila knew
Anyone who could cure me.
Yes, Juan Dávila told him,
there is a healer in Mexico.

Juan Dávila crossed the border
To bring the healer.
GLORIA ANZALDÚA, "LA CURANDERA"

Gloria Anzaldúa described the US-Mexico borderlands as *una herida abierta*, an "open wound" created when two nations rub against each other and the less powerful one bleeds.[1] In her poem "La Curandera," the opening stanzas of which are quoted above, the healer's whitening leg suggests the sickness that manifests when the more powerful nation, the United States, exploits the less powerful, Mexico.[2] The US-Mexico borderlands are defined by the unequal power relationship that has existed between the two nations since the border was created in 1848. As "La Curandera" shows, however, there is more to this frictional dynamic. In this poem, a curandera crosses the border into the United States to cure the narrator, and by the end of the poem not only is the narrator healed of the sickness that caused her leg to whiten, but she becomes a curandera herself. She goes through death and rebirth while having visions of *la virgin santísima* (the blessed virgin) as she lay on her bed in a South Texas *jacal* surrounded by black snake spirit guides teaching her how to heal with the herbs that are always within arm's reach in the Río Grande Valley. A border-crossing curandera suggests that despite the violence that caused the white leg and the open wound, the borderlands are also a place of refuge and opportunity for subaltern peoples—a place filled with the possibility of personal and social transformation.[3]

Teresa Urrea and Pedro Jaramillo were transformed by their individual *don* experiences. As they practiced their curanderismo on both sides of the border, these border-crossing curanderos followed the mandate of their *don*. They healed communities of Indigenous peoples, ethnic Mexicans, Tejanos, and even some Anglos with the understanding that they were the conduits through which a larger spiritual force moved. Yet their own healing skills mattered too, as well as their knowledge of the struggles their communities faced. That is to say they healed individual sick bodies through the power of God as well as their own curative knowledge of medicinals and therapies; they also healed the social body in distress due to the failures of both nations to protect and respect communities of ethnic Mexicans and Indigenous peoples within their borders. This kind of healing contributed to their success and popularity, in a sense making Santa Teresa Urrea and Don Pedrito Jaramillo celebrity curanderos.

Borderlands Curanderos has also shown how the curanderismo of Santa Teresa and Don Pedrito was a nexus of interethnic interactions in a region of trans-regional/national mobility and intersecting global trajectories of medical/curative knowledge. The electric thrill coming from Santa Teresa's thumbs, like the electric belts and palpations from professional physicians, was part of the larger current of healing potentialities that crossed borders and oceans at the turn of the century, including the healing of espiritistas, Spiritualists, homeopaths, and curanderas. Don Pedrito's healing practice at Los Olmos served as a kind of central nervous system for the South Texas Río Grande Valley, his *recetas* providing healing for those living and working on the ranches and farms in this rural area. Yet his reputation spread even beyond this region, garnering him perhaps unwanted attention from the American Medical Association and US Post Office, yet demonstrating the reach and significance of this humble curandero.

To fully understand the power of the borderlands, it is important to remember that the transformations the region fosters come in waves embedded in communities that repeatedly seek out and embrace the borderlands as a blank slate. This space continually dissolves into a collection of places imbued with the evolving meanings, aesthetics, and values of these communities—places where the past and future stretch equally far in opposing directions, while the present is defined by both.

My time spent at the Don Pedrito Jaramillo Shrine in Falfurrias, Texas, and El Museo Urbano in El Paso, as discussed in the introduction, moved and inspired me. Seeing these two healers being celebrated proved what I wanted to argue: that they were significant historical actors, more than just cultural footnotes to borderlands history. However, there were some things that I did not see during my research trips.

What I did not see during my visits to Falfurrias were the mass graves of recent undocumented migrants from Central America and Mexico buried in Falfurrias's Sacred Heart Cemetery. Unlike the day in 1881 when Don Pedrito crossed the border into Texas while smuggling mezcal and likely avoiding customs agents at the border, Mexicans who cross the border in the twenty-first century risk their lives to arrive in *el otro lado*, and many die doing so. Brooks County—home to the Don Pedrito Shrine—had the highest number of migrant deaths in Texas from 2012 to 2018.[4] As part of the Border Patrol's vast Río Grande Valley sector, more migrant deaths happen in Brooks County than any other place in the borderlands. Hundreds of migrants die there every year of dehydration because they take a more dangerous route in order to avoid the interior border checkpoint in Falfurrias.[5] Some ranchers leave water out for migrants passing through their land, even though they might disapprove of their illegal crossing; others have no sympathy for "illegals" and would prefer to hunt them like animals.[6]

What I did not see while in El Museo Urbano, in Segundo Barrio, were the "revitalization" plans drafted by a development company and the city of El Paso that will substantially destabilize the historic neighborhood that edges up against the Juárez bridge, which has for years been home to many immigrant communities and those who cross the border daily for work.[7] The urban renewal project would raze much of the neighborhood, displace long-time inhabitants, and replace the thriving border culture with parking garages, lofts, condos, urban retailers, and a baseball stadium.[8] Residents of Segundo Barrio, historians, and even the Catholic Church have spoken in defense of keeping the neighborhood and its residents intact, trying to stop the coalition of developers, politicians, and planners from both sides of the border who see economic potential in gentrifying Segundo Barrio.[9] One opponent of the development plan, El Paso state senator José Rodriguez, argues that instead of gentrifying and homogenizing this historic neighborhood, "To capture what El Paso really is, you need to accept the Mexicanness, the Mexican America, and indigenous roots of El Paso."[10] Although El Museo Urbano is no longer situated in the former residence of Teresa Urrea at 500 South Oregon Street in Segundo Barrio, the organization, formed and led by Dr. Yolanda Leyva and Dr. David Dorado Romo, continues the work started in 2011 by accepting, embracing, and drawing attention to this deeper history of El Paso through community education and art exhibits that highlight the Mexican-ness and Indigenous history of El Paso.[11]

What I did not see during my visits was significant, because in the twenty-first century, debates about national identity, who gets to enjoy the opportunities and protections of American citizenship, and what cultural projects we celebrate and support in our communities continue to play out in the same borderlands that Santa Teresa Urrea and Don Pedrito Jaramillo inhabited at the turn of the twentieth century. As nativist Americans insist upon more firmly demarcating the edges of the nation and policing who belongs and who does not, ethnic Mexican cultural practices remain vibrant and important to transnational borderlands communities. The same holds true for the larger nation, particularly as the Hispanic population continues to outpace the national population growth rate.[12] As evidenced by the Don Pedrito Shrine in Falfurrias and El Museo Urbano in El Paso, Don Pedrito Jaramillo and Santa Teresa Urrea still provide refuge and inspiration to those of Mexican origin living in the United States and striving to keep alive their cultural practices while embracing a transnational ethnic Mexican identity—and perhaps also to those crossing the border seeking opportunity in the United States. The practice of curanderismo thus continues to have a vital, visible presence in the US-Mexico borderlands, both as a form of healing and cultural survival for ethnic Mexicans, and as a cure for the historical blindness of Anglo Americans.

In *Borderlands Curanderos* I have argued that in the US-Mexico borderlands, over the turn of the twentieth century, Santa Teresa Urrea and Don Pedrito Jaramillo participated in the creation and maintenance of transnational ethnic Mexican communities and identities in the US-Mexico borderlands. They helped shape national ideologies and identities, as well as spiritual and medical practices. Santa Teresa and Don Pedrito should be seen as more than mere cultural footnotes to history. These curanderos made history—and history looks different when seen through the lives of two borderlands curanderos.

Don Pedrito Jaramillo Cure Sample

This sample of Don Pedrito Jaramillo's cures performed from 1881 to 1907 represents every recorded and published cure I have discovered in my research. Although these 135 cures come from several sources, the majority come from Texas folklorist Ruth Dodson's *Don Pedrito Jaramillo, "Curandero"* (originally published in 1934), which is based on ethnographic research she did, recording stories of Don Pedrito's healing from residents of the South Texas Valley.[1] Some accounts say Don Pedrito saw hundreds of clients in one day, and on his bigger trips, like the one he made to San Antonio in 1894, newspaper accounts reported that he saw upwards of a thousand people a day. Even if these figures were exaggerated, it must be noted that this sample is still significantly small compared to the actual number of cures Don Pedrito performed in his twenty-six years of healing in South Texas.[2] It also must be noted that no Indigenous people, especially Lipan Apache, are represented in this sample. This likely has to do with the fact that many Lipan Apaches have Spanish names and so would not be visibly Indigenous in the sources I have used. It also most assuredly has to do with the bias of the sources, sources that focus on Anglos, Tejanos, and Mexicanos exclusively. There is still much work to be done on the Indigenous pathways to Don Pedrito Jaramillo.

Ruth Dodson

Texas folklorist J. Frank Dobie praised Ruth Dodson as a woman who "knows the Mexicans of that part of Texas better than they know themselves," yet she took a much more humble view of herself.[3] In the introduction to the original *Don Pedrito Jaramillo* (1934), Dodson wrote: "When I tell the Mexicans something about the occupation and work of this curandero it is not to tell them something that they do not know."[4]

Viola Ruth Dodson (1876–1963) was born and raised near Los Olmos, on Rancho Perdido in Nueces County. She came from one of the oldest Anglo ranching families in South Texas, descended from the "First Three Hundred" Anglos who came to Texas to join Stephen F. Austin's colony in 1821.[5] In the introduction to *Don Pedrito Jaramillo*, Dodson explains how she had always been interested in the Mexican culture that surrounded her on the ranch, and that she was fluent in both Spanish and English. She became friends with J. Frank Dobie later in life, and he was instrumental to the publication of *Don Pedrito Jaramillo*.[6] Dodson's stated purpose in recording stories about Jaramillo was to "have something written down for the Mexicans about him who from the beginning, is now and ever will be of interest to them." She humbly concludes, "I hope that my work will not be so badly written that interest will be lost."[7]

Table 1. Race and ethnicity breakdown of the Don Pedrito cure sample

Race/Ethnicity	Number of Cures	Percentage of Total
Mexican	90	66.6
Anglo	18	13.3
Other*	2	1.4
Unspecified	32	23.7

*One "mixed race" person of Mexican and Anglo parents; one Austrian.
Note: Ninety percent of the residents of the South Texas Valley were Mexican during the time Don Pedrito practiced medicine there. Arnoldo De León compares the Mexican American and Anglo American population statistics of the residents of Webb, Cameron, and Starr Counties in 1850 and 1900. By his estimations, taken from census data, in 1900, 92.4 percent of the residents of these counties were Mexican American, whereas only 6.1 percent were Anglo.
Source: De León, *The Tejano Community*, 36.

Table 2. Illnesses treated by Don Pedrito Jaramillo

Illness/Ailment	Appearances	Percentage of Total
Unspecified*	25	18.5
Wound	11	8.1
Stomach Ailments	10	7.4
Fever	9	6.6
Rheumatism/Arthritis	6	4.4
Toothache/Mouth Pain	6	4.4
Headaches/Migraines	4	2.9
Epilepsy	4	2.9
Anxiety/Nervousness	4	2.9
Insanity	4	2.9
Reproductive Issues (Infertility, Pregnancy)	4	2.9

Table 2. (*continued*)

Illness/Ailment	Appearances	Percentage of Total
Skin Problems	4	2.9
"Crippled"	4	2.9
Cold/Cough/Catarrh	4	2.9
Deafness/Muteness	4	2.9
Tumors/Growths	3	2.2
Vices (Alcohol, Tobacco, Food)	3	2.2
Tuberculosis	3	2.2
Dropsy	2	1.4
Nosebleeds	2	1.4
Asthma	2	1.4
Sunstroke	2	1.4
Eye Problems	2	1.4
Susto (Fright)	2	1.4

*The ailment that occurred most frequently in the sample is "unspecified," at 18.5 percent. This is likely because most of the stories of Don Pedrito's healing are focused on his cures rather than the clients and their maladies.
Note: Illnesses that occurred only once in the sample are not included in this table, but they are: fatigue, neuralgia, hemorrhage, bowlegs, clubfeet, curse, poverty, congestion of brain, and hair loss.

Table 3. Materials and instructions specified in Don Pedrito's cures

Material/Instruction	Times Used	Percentage of Total
Numeric Specifications	72	53.0
Water	57	42.4
Food*	28	20.7
"In the name of God"/Prayer	14**	10.3
Herbs and Medicinal Plants***	9	6.6
Alcohol	8	5.9
Coffee	7	5.1

*Includes tomatoes (7), cooking oil (4), onion (3), bread (2), eggs (2), and oranges (2). The following foods each appear once in the sample: lemons, canned fruit, fish (cooked without salt), pecans, potatoes, garlic, and chocolate.
**This number is very likely not representative. A significant part of Don Pedrito's legacy was that he prescribed "in the name of God." This was such a common part of his cures that Dodson and others who recorded these cure stories likely did not feel the need to include that aspect.
***Includes cenizo, soldier's herb (plantain), cumin seed tea, flor de agosto, mint tea, tobacco leaf, herbal ointment, prickly pear cactus, and nopal cactus.

Table 4. Gender constitution of the cure sample

Gender	Frequency	Percentage of Total
Male	80	59.2
Female	53	39.2
Unspecified	2	1.4

Table 5. Top four specified illnesses treated by Don Pedrito Jaramillo according to gender

Top Four Illnesses in Sample	Top Four Illnesses Attributed to Women	Top Four Illnesses Attributed to Men
Wounds (11)	Stomach Ailments (7)	Wounds (10)
Stomach Ailments (10)	Reproductive Issues (4) (Infertility and Pregnancy Complications)	Fever (7)
Fever (9)	Skin Irritations (3) Teeth/Mouth Pain (3)	Rheumatism /Arthritis (6)
Rheumatism/Arthritis (6)	Epilepsy (2)	Migraine Headaches (3)
Teeth/Mouth Pain (6)	Fever (2)	Cold/Catarrh/Cough (3)
	Insanity (2)	Stomach Ailment (3)
	Lump/Tumor (2)	

Note: The top illness for each category, "unspecified," is omitted from this table. See table 2.

Table 6. Top six cures prescribed by Don Pedrito Jaramillo according to gender

Top Six Cures in Sample	Top Six Cures for Women	Top Six Cures for Men
Bathe in Water (34)	Bathe in Water (14) Food Cure (14)	Bathe in Water (20)
Food Cure (29)	Drink Water (7)	Food Cure (15)
Drink Water (17)	Complex Cure (5) (a cure involving two or more prescriptives)	Drink Water (10)
Do Nothing (8)	Drink Coffee (4) Do Nothing (4)	Apply Plasters (5) Herbal Concoction (5)
Drink Liquor (7)	Drink Liquor (3)	Drink Liquor (4) Do Nothing (4)
Drink Coffee (6)	Unspecified (2)	Drink Coffee (2)

Acknowledgments

The path from dissertation to book manuscript is a long one. I could not have completed this journey without the assistance of generous colleagues, professors, advisors, archivists, librarians, curanderos, students, friends, and family who have guided and supported me along the way.

This journey started in graduate school at the William P. Clements Department of History at Southern Methodist University when David Weber suggested that the topic of curanderismo might be a good one for a dissertation. Over my years in graduate school I developed this project into my dissertation under the tutelage of an amazing group of scholars and advisors, including Crista DeLuzio, Alexis McCrossen, Sherry Smith, Ben Johnson, John Chavez, James Hopkins, and my dissertation advisor, Neil Foley. I am also indebted to Luis Urrea for agreeing to serve on my dissertation committee and providing invaluable feedback that would find its way into *Borderlands Curanderos*. I am also thankful for the support and inspiration from my wonderful cohorts in graduate school who continue to inspire me with their work, including Luis Garcia (who helped me navigate the archives in Mexico City), Ruben Arellano, John Gram, George Diaz, Aaron Sanchez, Joel Zapata, Carla Mendiola, Tim Bowman, Ryan Booth, and Margaret Neubauer.

In addition to the intellectual support and guidance I received from my professors and cohort, I received generous institutional support from the history department and the William P. Clements Center for Southwest Studies at Southern Methodist University. I am thankful for the Summerfield G. Roberts Dissertation Writing Fellowship, the Jim Watson Research Grant, the Advisory Panel Grant for research travel, the Graduate Dean Award for research travel, and the Levine/Advisory Panel Fellowship that provided funding that allowed me to travel to archives in Mexico and the southwestern United States to conduct research, as well as time to write. I realize now, as I am teaching history courses full-time, how crucial a gift the time to write is. I am especially grateful for this support.

Borderlands Curanderos would not have been possible without the help of archivists and librarians from the many institutions I visited to conduct research, including Rebekah Tabah at the Arizona Historical Society, Rob King and Randy Vance at Southwest Collections/Special Collections Library at Texas Tech University, and Lourdes Treviño-Cantu and Ramiro Rodríguez at the Falfurrias Heritage Museum. I am also thankful for the help of historians David Romo and Dr. Yolanda Chávez Leyva at Museo Urbano in El Paso, the staff at Archivo Histórico de Secretaría del Estado y Despacho de Relaciones Exteriores in Mexico City, and all the archivists and librarians who helped me at South Texas Archives at Texas A&M University–Kingsville; the university library at the University of Texas at El Paso; the El Paso Border Heritage Center; the National Archives in Forth Worth, Texas; the Special Collections Library at the University of Texas at San Antonio; the Historical Health Fraud and Alternative Medicine Collection at the American Medical Association; and the Special Collections at the DeGolyer Library at Southern Methodist University.

I must also thank those scholars and friends who provided important feedback during conferences, research presentations, and research trips. Lourdes Treviño-Cantu, from Falfurrias, Texas, has been a constant source of information about the history of Don Pedrito Jaramillo and his significance to the South Texas community he was such an important part of. Not only did Lourdes provide me with historical information about Don Pedrito, she introduced me to her beautiful mother, Maria Lemus Treviño, and allowed me to interview her. Born in 1910, Mrs. Treviño crossed the border from Mexico to the United States when she was thirteen years old and lived the rest of her life in South Texas. She shared tremendous insight into Don Pedrito's legacy in this region, as well as her deep faith. It is truly an honor to have met her. Like Lourdes and Maria, another knowledgeable resident of the valley, Homero Vera, provided vital information about this region, directing me to sources that I otherwise would have missed, especially the map of the Río Grande frontier that provides visual evidence of the significance of Don Pedrito Jaramillo to this region.

Like Lourdes Treviño-Cantu, Maria Lemus Treviño, and Homero Vera, the following scholars have also influenced the course of this manuscript through their support and feedback: Natalie Avalos and Brett Hendrickson, whom I met at the University of New Mexico's "Curanderismo: Traditional Medicine Without Borders Conference"; Mary Mendoza, whom I met at the

Newberry Seminar in Borderlands and Latino/a Studies; and Lisa Barnett, who encouraged me from very early on when I first formally presented my research at the Clements Center for Southwest Studies Brown Bag Lecture Series.

My colleagues in the Metropolitan State University of Denver History Department—especially Meg Frisbee, Monica Black, and Brian Weiser—have given me invaluable support and guidance as I revised the manuscript for publication. I am also thankful to James Drake and Chrystyna Banks for authorizing and organizing department funding to travel to conferences where I presented my research. I must also thank my amazing students at MSU who allowed me to share my research with them and, in turn, taught me the ongoing significance of curanderismo as a cultural practice affirming the values of those of Mexican descent living in the United States today.

In addition to researching the history of two famous curanderos, working on this book has put me in touch with curanderos who are active today and shared their thoughts about healing and history with me and my students. I want to thank Toñita Gonzales, a curandera from Albuquerque, New Mexico; Gonzo Flores, a curandero and present owner of the Don Pedrito Jaramillo Shrine, who shed light on aspects of Don Pedrito's healing that I did not find in the archives; and Danielle López. I am especially grateful to Danielle, a curandera and PhD student from the Río Grande Valley who continues to heal her community while pursuing her academic goals. She has shared stories about her healing practice and philosophy with me, and supported my scholarship. I am honored to have met and learned so much from these healers.

Finally, there are two people who deserve my deepest gratitude. My husband, Michael Seman, read countless chapter drafts, indulged me in endless conversations about this book, and often took care of any number of details in our lives while I wrote and revised. Without his kindness, humor, and support, I am not sure I could have completed this journey. My editor, Robert Devens, whom I met through Alexis McCrossen in graduate school many years ago, has given me unflagging support since then. It is because of Robert's guidance, patience, and literary insight that this project is now complete.

Notes

Introduction. Borderlands Curanderos

1. "Museo Urbano Opens," *El Paso Times*, May 8, 2011, 1B; Dr. Yolanda Leyva, interview by author, El Paso, TX, May 7, 2011; and David Dorado Romo, interview by author, El Paso, TX, May 7, 2011. Leyva and Romo are from the University of Texas at El Paso and are the main organizers of the El Museo. They are collecting oral histories of Segundo Barrio.

2. El Paso native David Dorado Romo has written extensively on the history of El Paso and the Segundo Barrio and their importance during the revolution. See his *Ringside Seat to a Revolution: An Underground Cultural History of El Paso and Juárez: 1893–1923* (El Paso: Cinco Puntos, 2005).

3. Frank Graziano, *Cultures of Devotion* (Oxford: Oxford UP, 2007), ix. One scholar describes folk saints as created by the people who venerated them, "unofficially beatified by the masses" who are inspired by a "desire to materialize the sacred in everyday life." Gastón Espinosa, "Mexican Madonna: Selena and the Politics of Cultural Redemption," in *Mexican American Religions: Spirituality, Activism, and Culture*, ed. Espinosa and Mario T. García (Durham: Duke UP, 2008), 367. Not every folk saint was a real person, as demonstrated by the latest scholarship focusing on Santa Muerte, among others. See Andrew Chestnut, *Devoted to Death: Santa Muerte, the Skeleton Saint* (Oxford: Oxford UP, 2012); and Desirée A. Martín, *Borderlands Saints: Secular Sanctity in Chicano/a Culture* (New Brunswick, NJ: Rutgers UP, 2014).

4. The most recent work on curanderismo is Brett Hendrickson's *Border Medicine: A Transcultural History of Mexican American Curanderismo* (New York: New York UP, 2014); Patrisia Gonzales, *Red Medicine: Traditional Indigenous Rites of Birthing and Healing* (Tucson: University of Arizona Press, 2012); and Elizabeth de la Portilla, *They All Want Magic: Curanderas and Folk Healing* (College Station: Texas A&M UP, 2009). Two foundational texts on curanderismo are Ari Kiev, *Curanderismo: Mexican-American Folk Psychiatry* (New York: Free Press, 1968); and Robert T. Trotter II and Juan Antonio Chavira, *Curanderismo: Mexican American Folk Healing* (Athens: University of Georgia Press, 1981). Two influential works that describe curanderismo as a female-empowering and fluid spiritual practice are

Elena Avila, *Woman Who Glows in the Dark: A Curandera Reveals Traditional Aztec Secrets of Physical and Spiritual Health* (New York: Tarcher/Putnam, 1999); and Bobette H. Perrone, Henrietta Stockel, and Victoria Krueger, *Medicine Women, Curanderas, and Women Doctors* (Norman: University of Oklahoma Press, 1989). Two books written for a popular audience by a practicing curandero are Eliseo "Cheo" Torres, with Timothy L. Sawyer, Jr., *Curandero: A Life in Mexican Folk Healing* (Albuquerque: University of New Mexico Press, 2005); and Torres, with Timothy L. Sawyer, Jr., *Healing with Herbs and Rituals: A Mexican Tradition* (Albuquerque: University of New Mexico Press, 2006). Ricardo A. Carrillo et al., in *Cultura y Bienestar: MesoAmerican Based Healing and Mental Health Practice Based Evidence* (CreateSpace Independent Publishing Platform, 2017), look at the efficacy of traditional healing practices such as curanderismo from the perspectives of several different scholars and healers, including clinical psychologist and curandero Dr. Ricardo Castillo.

5. For example, Teresa Urrea and Don Pedrito Jaramillo gained recognition as curanderos during their lifetimes, but even though they both practiced in the US-Mexico borderlands at the same time, from the 1880s to 1907, they did not heal in the same way. Some curanderos are primarily *yerberas* (herbalists), *parteras* (midwives), *sobardoras* (massage specialists, or "softeners"), *consejeras* (counselors), *espiritualistas* (mediums), *hueseros* (bone-setters; spinal and joint adjusters), and *señoras* (psychics, card readers)—but most incorporate all types of methods into their practice. Torres, *Healing with Herbs and Rituals*, 8-10; Perrone, Stockel, and Krueger, *Medicine Women, Curanderas, and Women Doctors*, 85.

6. Just as the "conquering" of one culture by another is never as complete or final as it might appear in the written word, the conquest of the Indigenous people of the Americas by Europeans did not happen in one fell swoop with the fall of Tenochtitlán in 1521. Although significant, disease only partially explains the Spaniards' swift success over the numerically superior Aztecs. The cultural transformations and exchanges, beginning in 1521, continued throughout the Spanish colonization of Mexico. David Weber, *The Spanish Frontier in North America* (New Haven: Yale UP, 1992), 29.

7. The primary source for the story of his captivity is Alvar Núñez Cabeza de Vaca, *The Narrative of Cabeza de Vaca* (Lincoln: University of Nebraska Press, 1999). The best secondary source that contextualizes his experience is Andrés Reséndez, *A Land So Strange: The Epic Journey of Cabeza de Vaca* (New York: Basic Books, 2007).

8. Cabeza de Vaca, *Narrative*, 93.

9. Cabeza de Vaca, 93.

10. Cabeza de Vaca, 93-94.

11. Rolena Adorno, "The Negotiation of Fear in Cabeza de Vaca's *Naufragios*," *Representations*, no. 33, special issue: *The New World* (Winter 1991): 166. In this article, Adorno describes this "complex web of negotiations between the shipwrecked survivors and the native peoples they encountered" and how the castaways were forced to adapt to the patterns of ritualized exchange and warfare.

12. Virgil Vogel, *American Indian Medicine* (Norman: University of Oklahoma Press, 1970), 6-10.

13. Cabeza de Vaca, *Narrative*, 93.

14. The Natives encountered by Cabeza de Vaca and the castaways lived in close

relationship to the land and, because of this, understood nature as sacred. Natalie Avalos, "Latinx Indigeneities and Christianity," in *The Oxford Handbook of Latino/a Christianities in the United States* (Oxford UP, forthcoming), 3–4.

15. Cabeza de Vaca, *Narrative*, 93–94.

16. Cabeza de Vaca, 125. María Luz López Terrada, "Medical Pluralism in the Iberian Kingdoms: The Control of Extra-academic Practitioners in Valencia," *Medical History* 29 (2009): 15–16. López Terrada is quoting a 1538 document describing *saludadores* entitled *Reprovación de las Supersticiones y Hechicerías* by Pedro Ciruelo.

17. Fabián Alejandro Campagne, "Charismatic Healers on Iberian Soil: An Autopsy of a Mythical Complex of Early Modern Spain," *Folklore* 118, no. 1 (2007): 47.

18. Cabeza de Vaca, *Narrative*, 93–94. However, even as his *relación* reveals similarities in the healing styles of Iberian and Indigenous healers, there was one distinct difference he noted that troubled him. Cabeza de Vaca describes his astonishment when their Indigenous captors first insisted that the Spaniards become healers. He called this a "mockery" because the castaways had not been trained in the university, nor had they been examined by the Protomedicato, the official medical licensing board in Spain. See Cabeza de Vaca, *Narrative*. The functions of the Protomedicato were twofold: they examined and granted licenses to physicians, surgeons, and apothecaries; and they controlled the exercise of the various medical professions, prosecuting and punishing unauthorized medical practice. Thus, in sixteenth-century Spain, a physician not only had to attend university and obtain a doctorate, but he also had to prove himself to the Protomedicato, and if accused of unethical or unauthorized practice of medicine, he might have had to come before the board again. Robin Price, "Spanish Medicine in the Golden Age," *Journal of the Royal Society of Medicine* 72 (November 1979), 864–865; López Terrada, "Medical Pluralism in the Iberian Kingdoms," 9–10; the classic study on the Protomedicato is John T. Lanning, *The Royal Protomedicato: The Regulation of the Medical Professions in the Spanish Empire* (Durham, NC: Duke UP, 1985).

19. Angelica Morales Sarabia, "The Culture of Peyote: Between Divination and Disease in Early Modern New Spain," in *Medical Cultures of the Early Modern Spanish Empire*, ed. John Slater, MariaLuz Lopez-Terrada, and Jose Pardo-Tomas (Burlington, VT: Ashgate, 2014), 23.

20. Noemí Quezada, "The Inquisition's Repression of Curanderos," in *Cultural Encounters: The Impact of the Inquisition in Spain and the New World*, ed. Mary Elizabeth Perry and Anne J. Cruz (Berkeley: University of California Press, 1991), 38.

21. Mark Goldberg, *Conquering Sickness: Race, Health, and Colonization in the Texas Borderlands* (Lincoln: University of Nebraska Press, 2016), 28–32.

22. For more on *susto*, see Avila, *Woman Who Glows in the Dark*, 63–69; and Trotter and Chavira, *Curanderismo*, 90–91. In addition to *susto*, other illnesses treated by curanderos are *mal de ojo* (sickness from being stared at by someone with an "evil eye"), *mal aire* ("bad air," a cold), *envídio* (sickness when someone envies you), *bilis* (sickness from rage), and *empacho* (stomach blockage). Avila, *Woman Who Glows in the Dark*, 23.

23. Danielle López, correspondence with the author, May 26, 2019. For more on her healing practice, see https://utrgvpulse.com/2018/09/19/danielle-lopez-grvs -millennial-curandera/.

24. Gonzo Flores, interview with the author in Denver, June 1, 2019. Flores lives in Portland, OR, but grew up in George West, a small town in South Texas. Flores comes from a long lineage of healers from this region, some who knew Don Pedrito Jaramillo.

25. Avila, *Woman Who Glows in the Dark*, 28. Others who share this point of view are Portilla (*They All Want Magic*, 5) and Gonzales (*Red Medicine*). The idea of sickness connected to the loss of the soul is not exclusive to Mexican culture, just as depression and PTSD are not illnesses only people in the West suffer from. For example, the Hmong, an ethnic group from Southeast Asia, also believe that the soul can be lost and cause illness. One Hmong woman explained it this way: "Your soul is like your shadow. . . . Sometimes it just wanders off like a butterfly and that is when you are sad and that's when you get sick. . . . Sometimes the soul goes away but the doctors don't believe." Foua Lee, quoted in Anne Fadiman, *The Spirit Catches You and You Fall Down: A Hmong Child, Her American Doctors, and the Collision of Two Cultures* (New York: Farrar, Straus, and Giroux, 1997), 100.

26. For the cross-cultural appeal of curanderismo, see Hendrickson, *Border Medicine*.

27. For the anthropological approach, see Portilla, *They All Want Magic*; and Gonzales, *Red Medicine*.

28. Avila, *Woman Who Glows in the Dark*; Carrillo et al., *Cultura y Bienestar*; Torres, *Curandero* and *Healing with Herbs and Rituals*.

29. Luis Alberto Urrea, *The Hummingbird's Daughter* (New York and Boston: Back Bay Books, 2005) and *Queen of America* (New York, Boston, and London: Little Brown and Company, 2011). Both of Urrea's novels are based on extensive research into Teresa Urrea's life. Urrea generously shared his research with the author. A different novelization of Teresa Urrea's life is Brianda Domecq, *La Insólita Historia de la Santa de Cabora* (Mexico City: Plantea, 1990). Domecq's novel employs a feminist, postmodern take on Teresa Urrea's life, questioning why she has not been integrated into the nationalist narrative of Mexico.

30. Recent examples of scholarship on the Tomóchic Rebellion include Rubén Osorio, *Tomóchic en Llamas* (Mexico City: Consejo Nacional para la Cultura y las Artes, 1995); Paul Vanderwood, *The Power of God Against the Guns of Government: Religious Upheaval in Mexico at the Turn of the Nineteenth Century* (Stanford: Stanford UP, 1998); and Jesús Vargas Valdez, *Tomóchic: La Revolución Adelantada: Resistencia y Lucha de un Pueblo de Chihuahua contra el Sistema Porfirista* (Juarez: Universidad Autónoma de Ciudad Juárez, 1994).

31. The most recent scholarship on Teresa Urrea examines the way novelists, performance artists, and historians have become "possessed" by her and interpreted her to suit their own purposes, in the process revealing perhaps more about the writer than Urrea. See Martín, *Borderlands Saints*, 32–65. Another scholar examines the ways in which she has been appropriated as a symbol for Chicanas; see Gillian E. Newell, "Teresa Urrea, Santa de Cabora and Early Chicana? The Politics of Representation, Identity, and Social Memory," in *The Making of Saints: Contesting Sacred Ground*, ed. James Hopgood (Tuscaloosa: University of Alabama Press, 2005), 90–106. The exception to this style of scholarship is Brandon Bayne, "From Saint to Seeker: Teresa Urrea's Search for a Place of Her Own," *Church History* 75, no. 3 (September 2006): 594–597.

32. Octavio Romano, "Don Pedrito Jaramillo: The Emergence of a Mexican-American Folk Saint," PhD diss., University of California at Berkeley, 1964. The latest work on Jaramillo consists of a few pages in a book chapter analyzing the cures he made for Anglos in Texas. See Hendrickson, *Border Medicine*, 61–69.

33. Particularly, book chapters by Desirée A. Martín, Yolanda Chávez Leyva, Gillian E. Newell, and Marian Perales examine Urrea and her legacy and cultural representations to demonstrate the ways in which she embodies Chicana feminist politics (in the case of Newell) and secular sanctity (Martín). Martín, *Borderlands Saints*; Leyva, "Healing the Borderlands"; Newell, "Teresa Urrea," 90–106; and Perales, "Teresa Urrea." See also Yolanda Broyles-Gonzáles, "Indianizing Catholicism: Chicana/India/Mexicana Indigenous Spiritual Practices in our Image," in *Chicana Traditions: Continuity and Change*, ed. Norma Cantú and Olga Nájera-Ramírez (Urbana: University of Illinois Press, 2002); Espinosa and García, *Mexican American Religions*; Graziano, *Cultures of Devotion*; Luis León, *La Llorona's Children: Religion, Life, and Death in the U.S.-Mexico Borderlands* (Berkeley: University of California Press, 2004); and Yolanda Chávez Leyva, "Healing the Borderlands Across the Centuries," in *Grace and Gumption: The Women of El Paso*, ed. Marcia Hatfield Daudistel (Fort Worth: Texas Christian University Press, 2011).

34. Nicole M. Guidotti-Hernández, *Unspeakable Violence: Remapping U.S. and Mexican National Imaginaries* (Durham, NC: Duke UP, 2011); Mark Goldberg, *Conquering Sickness: Race, Health, and Colonization in the Texas Borderlands*; John Mckiernan-González, *Fevered Measures: Public Health and Race at the Texas-Mexico Border, 1848–1942* (Durham: Duke UP, 2012); and Natalia Molina, *Fit to be Citizens? Public Health and Race in Los Angeles, 1879–1939* (Berkeley: University of California Press, 2006).

35. The idea to focus on "small worlds" and micro-histories in order to find new perspectives on larger historical transformations was, in part, inspired by James F. Brooks, Christopher R. N. DeCorse, and John Walton, eds., *Small Worlds: Method, Meaning, and Narrative in Microhistory* (Santa Fe: School for Advanced Research Press, 2008); and Carlo Ginzburg, *The Cheese and the Worms: The Cosmos of a Sixteenth-Century Miller* (Baltimore: Johns Hopkins UP, 1992).

Chapter 1. The Mexican Joan of Arc

1. The depositions taken by the Mexican government reveal that many of the witnesses to the Nogales customs house attack recalled the Teresistas proclaiming "¡Viva la Santa de Cabora!" Teresa Urrea Extradition File, 9–15–15, "Tomás and Teresa Urrea," 5–10, Archivo Histórico de la Secretaría de Relaciones Exteriores, Mexico City (hereafter referred to as SRE).

2. The detail about the mosquito netting and pink ribbon comes from A. M. Peck, "In the Memory of a Man," 374, Arthur Leslie Peck Manuscripts, MS 652, Arizona Historical Society. Peck was a rancher who lived in the border region and married a Mexican woman, and his papers provide his own recollections of events in this region, such as the Nogales raid of 1896, and include local newspaper clippings describing events.

3. "Asalto a Nogales, Sonora por indios yaquis adictos a la Santa de Cabora,"

1–3–670 (I), SRE. Included in the file are the following articles about the Nogales raid: "Modern Witch Is Their Saint," *San Francisco Examiner*, August 14, 1896; "El Asalto de Nogales," *El Fronterizo* (Tucson, Arizona Territory), August 15, 1896; "Nipped in the Bud," *The Oasis* (Nogales, AT), August 15, 1896; "El Asalto a La Aduana," *El Estado de Sonora* (Nogales, Sonora, Mexico), August 16, 1896.

4. "Modern Witch Is Their Saint," *San Francisco Examiner*, in "Asalto a Nogales, Sonora por indios yaquis," 1–3–670 (I), SRE.

5. Alice Kehoe, *The Ghost Dance: Ethnohistory and Revitalization* (Long Grove: Waveland, 2006), 7. See also David W. Grua, "In Memory of the Chief Bigfoot Massacre: The Wounded Knee Survivors and the Politics of Memory," *Western Historical Quarterly* 46 (Spring 2015): 31–51; Rani-Herik Andersson, *The Lakota Ghost Dance of 1890* (Lincoln: University of Nebraska Press, 2008); Heather Cox Richardson, *Wounded Knee: Party Politics and the Road to an American Massacre* (New York: Basic Books, 2011); and Jerome A. Greene, *American Carnage: Wounded Knee* (Norman: University of Oklahoma Press, 2014).

6. One historian who has examined photographs of lynched Yaquis published in newspapers and magazines, as well as the correspondence between Mexican and US officials concerning Yaqui movements across the border, finds that "The paper trail, or literal body of evidence, shows a wavering of consciousness and severe anxiety on the part of Americans, Sonoran Mexicans, and the central Mexican government about efforts to contain and exterminate the Yaqui because they posed a threat to a modern vision . . . of Mexico." Nicole M. Guidotti-Hernández, *Unspeakable Violence*, 175, 204.

7. Quoted in Kehoe, *Ghost Dance*, 14.

8. Quoted in Guidotti-Hernández, *Unspeakable Violence*, 173.

9. This quote comes from an interview recorded in New York City, where she was part of a traveling medicine show, years after the 1896 Teresista Rebellion. *New York Journal*, March 3, 1901, 1. This is just one of many comments by Urrea on the situation of the Yaqui. In a different interview she is quoted as saying: "I pity the Indians of Sonora. I wish they were cared for and protected as this country protects its Indians. But they have no rights and I fear they will be exterminated. I would do anything for them, but I do not pretend to have any power to lead them to better conditions. I can only heal their sick and that I am not allowed to do." "Santa Teresa Comes in Cause of Mercy, Mexican Girl Famed as the Joan of Arc of Yaqui Indians of Sonora is in San Francisco," *San Francisco Call*, September 9, 1900, 40. In yet another interview she says, "I had nothing to do with the Yaqui revolution. They were fighting always to keep their land." Helen Dare, "Santa Teresa, Celebrated Mexican Healer, Whose Powers Awe Warlike Yaquis in Sonora, Comes to Restore San Jose Boy to Health," *San Francisco Examiner*, July 27, 1900, 7. Teresa Urrea's own words prefigured muckraking socialist journalist John Kenneth Turner's 1910 expose of the Mexican government's genocidal policy towards the Yaqui. John Kenneth Turner, *Barbarous Mexico* (1910; reprint, Austin: University of Texas Press, 1969).

10. On the deportation of Yaquis, see Ignacio Almada Bay, *Sonora: Historia Breve* (Mexico City: El Colegio de México, Fondo de Cultura Económico, 2010), 152–154; Hu-DeHart, *Yaqui Resistance and Survival*, chap. 6: "The Final Solution," 155–200; Guidotti-Hernández, *Unspeakable Violence*, 174–327; and John Kenneth Turner, *Barbarous Mexico* (1910; reprint, Austin: University of Texas Press, 1969).

11. Historian Nicole Guidotti-Hernández argues that the Yaqui's struggles and the state violence used against them are ignored in histories of the Mexican North, even as the state and corporations use sacred Yaqui symbols to promote Mexican nationalism. Guidotti-Hernández, "National Appropriations: Yaqui Autonomy, the Centennial of the Mexican Revolution and the Bicentennial of the Mexican Nation," *Latin Americanist* (March 2011): 69–92. Guidotti-Hernández elaborates on this argument by examining instances of state violence against Indigenous peoples in *Unspeakable Violence*, where she describes how, in 1908, *Harper's Weekly* published images of Yaquis hanging from trees with the title "The Scourge of the Yaquis." *Harper's* wanted this image to demonstrate the "barbarity" of Mexico and to show that the Mexican state would resort to violence and outright murder in order to "keep the Yaquis down." These images reinforced a popular idea in the United States: that Anglo-Saxon "civilization" stood in opposition to Mexican "barbarity," ignoring the US government's treatment of its own Indigenous populations as well as its acquiescence to hundreds of lynchings of black Americans from the Civil War well into the twentieth century. Guidotti-Hernández, *Unspeakable Violence*, 201–203.

12. *New York Journal*, March 3, 1901, 1.

13. The information on Teresa Urrea's birth comes from William Curry Holden, *Teresita*, 10; and Vanderwood, *Power of God*, 164. One source says that Cayetana Chávez worked for Miguel Urrea, an uncle of Don Tomás. For this version, see Perales, "Teresa Urrea," 98. Perales also provides a thoughtful discussion on the patriarchal relations between female workers and male bosses in this period and others (98–99).

14. This background is covered in many secondary sources, including Holden, *Teresita*; Vanderwood, *Power of God*; and Perales, "Teresa Urrea." Holden's interviews with Urrea's living relatives, which inform his hagiography, *Teresita*, and newspaper stories published during Urrea's life are the primary sources that provide this information.

15. Dare, "Santa Teresa," 7.

16. Perales, "Teresa Urrea," 98–99; Martín, *Borderlands Saints*, 40.

17. Perales, "Teresa Urrea," 98–99.

18. Background information on Teresa Urrea's parents comes from Vanderwood, *Power of God*, 162–164; and Perales, "Teresa Urrea," 98–100.

19. In an interview for the *San Francisco Examiner* in 1900, Teresa told the journalist Helen Dare, "When I was sixteen my father sent for me to come to his home. I went to his hacienda in Cabora." See Dare, "Santa Teresa." Don Tomás Urrea moved from Sinaloa to Sonora for political reasons. He had supported the anti-Díaz candidate in Sinaloa, and when the candidate lost, he no longer had protection and so moved his operations north to Sonora. For more on this, see Vanderwood, *Power of God*, 164–166; and Holden, *Teresita*, 13–28. For the teasing of Urrea by her family, see Holden, *Teresita*, 11–12.

20. Perales, "Teresa Urrea," 99.

21. María Sonora, or Huila, is discussed in many secondary sources, including Perales, 100.

22. The first mention of Teresa Urrea receiving the gift of healing at age sixteen is in *La Voz de Mexico*, December 21, 1889, 3, under the heading "Servicio Interior

De La República, Via los Telégrafos Federales." For more about the *don* (or gift), see Luis D. León, "Borderlands Bodies and Souls: Mexican Religious Healing Practices in East Los Angeles," in *Mexican American Religions: Spirituality, Activism, and Culture*, ed. Gastón Espinosa and Mario T. García (Durham, NC: Duke University Press, 2008), 301.

23. A detailed account of Teresa Urrea's *don* experience is in the Mexican Spiritist periodical *La Ilustración Espirita* (January 1, 1892): 256–257. The author of this story claims that Teresa's father, Don Tomás Urrea, provided this firsthand account.

24. Painter, *With Good Heart: Yaqui Beliefs and Ceremonies in a Pasqua Village* (Tucson: University of Arizona Press, 1986), 106–107.

25. N. Ross Crumrine, *The Mayo Indians of Sonora* (Tucson: University of Arizona Press, 1977), 124, 133.

26. For Urrea's insistence upon eating only dirt during the thirteen days of her attacks, see *La Ilustración Espirita* (January 1, 1892): 257.

27. *La Ilustración Espirita*, 257.

28. Urrea's *don* experience is described in many places, including Vanderwood, *Power of God*, and Holden, *Teresita*, but the original source is *La Ilustración Espirita* (January 1, 1892).

29. Dare, "Santa Teresa." Parts of this are quoted in León, *La Llorona's Children*, 144.

30. For Tenskwatawa, the Shawnee prophet, see Sami Lakomäki, *Gathering Together: The Shawnee People Through Diaspora and Nationhood, 1600–1870* (New Haven: Yale UP, 2014).

31. Vanderwood, *Power of God*, 161–163; Crumrine, *Mayo Indians*, 17; Painter, *With Good Heart*, 53–59.

32. A. M. Peck, "In the Memory of a Man," Arthur Leslie Peck Manuscripts, MS 652, Arizona Historical Society, 373–375; Dare, "Santa Teresa."

33. For one example of the use of "fanatic savages" to describe the Yaqui Teresistas, see *El Estado de Sonora*, August 16, 1896 (copied in Maria Teresa Urrea File, 11-19-11, SRE); for "crazed on account of fanatical worship," see "Insurrection at Nogales," *Arizona Daily Star* (Tucson), August 13, 1896.

34. Dare, "Santa Teresa."

35. Brianda Domecq de Rodriguez, "Teresa Urrea: La Santa de Cabora," in *Memoria del VII Simposio de Historia y Antropología* (Universidad de Sonora, Departamento de Historia y Antropología: Hermosillo, Sonora, Mexico, 1982), 214–251.

36. One historian claims that the Yaquis were likely not involved in the 1896 Nogales *aduana* attack, that it was only sensationalist journalists on both sides of the border linking the rebellious Yaquis to other antigovernment political movements. However, I found the opposite to be true. Not only does the caption on the photograph taken of the dead Teresistas (contained in Mexican government files) describe them as Yaqui, but also in depositions many of the Teresistas are referred to as Yaqui. That the Teresistas were a mix of Mexicans and Yaquis, and perhaps other Indigenous groups such as the Pima, makes it even more compelling that the dead Teresistas in the photo are said to be Yaquis or, even if they are not, referred to as Yaquis. Evelyn Hu-Dehart, *Yaqui Resistance and Survival: The Struggle for Land and Autonomy 1821–1910* (Madison: University of Wisconsin Press, 1984), 148. Teresa Urrea Extradition File, 9-15-15, "Tomás and Teresa Urrea," 6–8, SRE.

37. The Yaqui refer to themselves as Yoeme, meaning "people." Outsiders and official nationalist discourse refer to them as "Yaqui." I use *Yaqui* for clarity and because all of the primary sources I have consulted use that designation. For the importance of understanding Yaqui/Yoeme history and culture on their terms, see David Delgado Shorter, *We Will Dance Our Truth: Yaqui History in Yoeme Performance* (Lincoln: University of Nebraska Press, 2009).

38. Hu-Dehart, *Yaqui Resistance and Survival*, 5.

39. Crumrine, *Mayo Indians*, 18; Hu-DeHart, *Yaqui Resistance and Survival*, 227.

40. Mary I. O'Connor, *Descendants of Totoliqouqui: Ethnicity and Economics in the Mayo Valley* (Berkeley: University of California Press, 1989), 11.

41. For the history of the Mayo, see Crumrine, *Mayo Indians*; O'Connor, *Descendants of Totoliqouqui*; and Barbara June Macklin and N. Ross Crumrine, "Three North Mexican Folk Saint Movements," *Comparative Studies in Society and History* 15, no. 1 (January 1973): 89–105. There is less written about the Tehueco, but they are mentioned in conjunction with the Yaqui, Mayo, and other Indigenous groups whose homelands are along the Fuerte River in Sinaloa, just south of the Yaqui and Mayo Rivers. See Edward H. Spicer, *The Yaquis: A Cultural History* (Tucson: University of Arizona Press, 1980), 15–16, 22, 26, 288.

42. Spicer, *The Yaquis*, 23–48, 59–65.

43. Spicer, 63–64.

44. O'Connor, *Descendants of Totoliguoqui*, 12.

45. The main history of Yaqui resistance is Hu-Dehart, *Yaqui Resistance and Survival*. Two books in Spanish on the deportation of Yaquis to southern Mexico and repatriation to their homelands are Raquel Padilla Ramos, *Yucatán, Fin del Sueño Yaqui: El Tráfico de los Yaquis y el Otro Triunvirato* (Hermosillo: Gobierno del Estado de Sonora, 1995), and *Progresso y Libertad: Los Yaquis en la Víspera de la Repatriación* (Hermosillo: Programa Editorial de Sonora/Instituto Sonorense de Cultura, 2006). Other works that touch upon the history of Yaqui resistance are Guidotti-Hernández, *Unspeakable Violence*, 173–235; and Shorter, *We Will Dance Our Truth*. For a look at the ways in which the Yaqui fit into the broader revolutionary history of Sonora, see Héctor Aguilar Camín, *La Frontera Nómada: Sonora y la Revolución Mexicana* (Mexico City: Ediciones Cal y Arena, 1971).

46. Painter, *With Good Heart*, 197–198.

47. Spicer, *The Yaquis*, 171, 327.

48. Painter, *With Good Heart*, 80; Shorter, *We Will Dance Our Truth*, 100–110.

49. Spicer, *The Yaquis*, 54, 66.

50. Painter, *With Good Heart*, 53–57.

51. Painter, 53–57; Shorter, *We Will Dance Our Truth*, 107.

52. Shorter, 219.

53. Shorter, 239.

54. Hu-DeHart, *Yaqui Resistance and Survival*, 17.

55. Friedrich Katz, "Mexico: Restored Republic and Porfiriato, 1867–1910," in *Cambridge History of Latin America*, vol. 5, ed. Leslie Bethell (Cambridge: Cambridge UP, 1986), 45–46. For more on the economic development of Sonora during the Porfiriato, see Miguel Tinker Salas, *In the Shadow of the Eagles: Sonora and the Transformation of the Border during the Porfiriato* (Berkeley: University of California Press, 1997).

56. For general histories of the Yaqui, see Hu-Dehart's *Yaqui Resistance and Survival* and *Missionaries, Miners, and Indians: History of Spanish Contact with the Yaqui Indians of Northwestern New Spain, 1533–1830* (Tucson: University of Arizona Press, 1981). Two of the foundational works on the Yaqui are Spicer's *The Yaquis*; and *People of Pascua* (Tucson: University of Arizona Press, 1988).

57. Quoted in Hale, *The Transformation of Liberalism*, 236.

58. Hale, 234.

59. Hale, 128.

60. Guidotti-Hernández, *Unspeakable Violence*, 196.

61. Peck, "In the Memory of a Man," 373.

62. Peck, 373.

63. "Modern Witch Is Their Saint," *San Francisco Examiner*, August 14, 1896, copied in Maria Teresa Urrea File, 11–19–11, SRE.

64. *La Ilustración Espirita*, January 1, 1892, 257.

65. The first mention of Teresa Urrea receiving the gift of healing at age sixteen is in *La Voz de Mexico*, December 21, 1889, 3, under the heading "Servicio Interior De La República, Via los Telégrafos Federales."

66. *La Ilustración Espirita* (September 1890): 159.

67. Ibid.

68. This story is recounted in *La Ilustración Espirita* (September 1892): 138–139; and Vanderwood, *Power of God*, 171.

69. E. J. Schellhous, MD, "Teresa Urrea, the Healing Medium of Cabora," in *Carrier Dove* (San Francisco) 7, no. 16 (August 1890).

70. Schellhous, "Teresa Urrea." The scene at Cabora is described in detail in Vanderwood, *Power of God*, 159–170.

71. Schellhous, "Teresa Urrea."

72. Schellhous, "Teresa Urrea."

73. For the history of Spiritism in Mexico, see Lia Theresa Schraeder, "The Spirits of the Times: The Mexican Spiritist Movement from Reform to Revolution" (PhD diss., University of California, Davis, 2009). For Spiritism in France, see John Warner Monroe, *Laboratories of Faith* (Ithaca, NY: Cornell UP, 2008); and Lynn L. Sharp, *Secular Spirituality: Reincarnation and Spiritism in Nineteenth-Century France* (Lanham, MD: Lexington Books, 2006).

74. Keith Brewster and Claire Brewster, "Ethereal Allies: Spiritism and the Revolutionary Struggle in Hidalgo," in *Faith and Impiety in Revolutionary Mexico*, ed. Matthew Butler (New York: Palgrave Macmillan, 2007), 95.

75. Macklin and Crumrine, "Folk Saint Movements," 97.

76. "De Ultra-Tumba," *El Independiente* (El Paso), August 7, 1896. Kardec's emphasis on charity did not challenge social inequality in the ways that Urrea and her Spiritist cohort would. Rather, he accepted it as a necessary condition of life on Earth. Even though *spiritisme* posited that all souls were equal, the doctrine of reincarnation justified inequality by suggesting that some souls had more sins to atone for, and in a subsequent life these unfortunate earthly souls would reach a higher social status.

77. Monroe, *Laboratories of Faith*, 107.

78. But they need not overthrow the system or challenge existing gender, class, and racial hierarchies to create a better and more equal world for everyone, as the

1848 radicals in France and the suffragists and abolitionists in the United States sought to do. Monroe, 106–107.

79. Although the Catholic Church in France condemned it as a heretical practice. Monroe, 120–121.

80. Porterfield, *Healing in the History of Christianity* (Oxford: Oxford UP, 2005), 182.

81. For the influence of France on Mexican Spiritists, see Schraeder, "Spirits of the Times," 5. For the influence of France on Mexican elites and culture generally, see Hale, *Transformation of Liberalism*; and Mauricio Tenorio-Trillo, *Mexico at the World's Fairs: Crafting a Modern Nation* (Berkeley: University of California Press, 1996).

82. Brewster and Brewster, "Ethereal Allies." *Espiritismo* was distinct from another form of Spiritualism practiced in Mexico at the time, the Iglesia Mexicana Patriarchal Elías, a religion founded by Roque Rojas Esperza, whom his adherents knew as Padre Elías. Followers of Padre Elías viewed themselves as the ten lost tribes of Israel and believed Mexico was the new Jerusalem. Iglesia Mexicana Patriarchal Elías, which in Mexico came to be known as Spiritualism or *espiritualismo*, appealed more broadly to the lower classes and the rural population, as it incorporated popular Indigenous healing practices into its belief system. Social position often determined whether one was an espiritista or an espiritualista, revealing the influence of European culture on the Mexican elite in the nineteenth century. Mexican elites and intellectuals were typically followers of Kardec's *espiritismo*, while the middle and lower classes chose Padre Elías's *espiritualismo*. For a brief overview of the history of spiritualism and Padre Elías in Mexico and an in-depth analysis of spiritualist healing practices, see Kaja Kinkler, *Spiritualist Healers in Mexico* (South Hadley, MA: Bergin and Garvey, 1985). See also Brewster and Brewster, "Ethereal Allies," 95. Interestingly, Spiritualists in the South Texas–northeast Mexico borderlands have been channeling Don Pedrito Jaramillo since his death in 1907. See, for example, Ruth Dodson, "Don Pedrito Jaramillo," 65–66. Folklorist Américo Paredes discovered members of a Texas-Mexican Spiritualist society who channeled and prayed to Don Pedrito while he was doing research in the 1950s on border folksongs of the Río Grande Valley. In fact, through these Spiritualists, Paredes learned of "Don Pedrito Jaramillo," a song that was sung in farewell to his spirit when a Spiritualist séance ended. Paredes, *A Texas-Mexican Cancionero: Folksongs of the Lower Border* (Austin: University of Texas Press, 1995), 114; for the song "Don Pedrito Jaramillo," 120–121.

83. Kardec had organized, systematized, and popularized Spiritism so that it could be practiced anywhere in the world, adhering to the guidelines he set out in his books and in the Spiritist magazine he founded, *Revue Spirite*. Kardec wanted Spiritism to be a worldwide movement, and he worked to coordinate one through his publications. Monroe, *Laboratories of Faith*, 112.

84. Schraeder, "Spirits of the Times," 21. For the period of liberal reforms in Mexico, see Jan Bazant, *Alienation of Church Wealth in Mexico*; and Luis González, "El Liberalism Triunfante," in *Historia General de México*.

85. Schraeder, "Spirits of the Times," 21.

86. Schraeder, 26; Brewster and Brewster, "Ethereal Allies," 95.

87. Schraeder, "Spirits of the Times," 27.

88. Schraeder, 48. See also *La Ilustración Espirita*, March 1, 1892, 327–328.

89. Schraeder, "Spirits of the Times," 47.

90. "Acerca de La Medium Teresa Urrea," *La Ilustración Espirita*, March 1, 1892, 315.

91. Schraeder, "Spirits of the Times," 86. Schraeder explains that Spiritists vehemently denied the role of the supernatural in healing: there were no miracles, only science.

92. Schellhous, "Un Problema Para La Medicina," 50.

93. Schellhous, 50.

94. Schellhous, 50.

95. Schellhous, 51.

96. Schellhous, 50.

97. Crumrine, *Mayo Indians*, 132–133.

98. Robert S. Fogarty, *All Things New: American Communes and Utopian Movements, 1860-1914* (Lanham, MD: Lexington Books, 2013), 120–128; and Ray Reynolds, *Catspaw Utopia: Alfred K. Owen, the Adventurer of Topolobampo Bay, and the Last Great Utopian Scheme* (San Bernardino, CA: Borgo, 1996). For an explanation of the colony from the perspective of the Mayo, see David Yetman and Thomas Van Devender, *Mayo Ethnobotany: Land, History, and Traditional Knowledge in Northwest Mexico* (Berkeley: University of California Press, 2002), 56–57.

99. Schellhous, "Un Problema Para La Medicina," 50.

100. Schellhous, 50; and "Important Letter," *Carrier Dove* (San Francisco) (July 1892): 223.

101. "'Saint' Teresa Shot," *Carrier Dove* (July 1892): 218.

102. Schellhous, "Important Letter," *Carrier Dove* (July 1892): 223.

103. Schraeder, "Spirits of the Times," 48.

104. *La Ilustración Espirita*, September 1, 1892, 138.

105. For a discussion of the paradoxical role of women in Modern American Spiritualism as passive mediums finding a voice in the public sphere, at once challenging gender norms and confirming them, see Molly McGarry, *Ghosts of Futures Past: Spiritualism and the Cultural Politics of Nineteenth-Century America* (Berkeley: University of California Press, 2008), 28–48; for the Mexican Spiritist context, see Schraeder, "Spirits of the Times," 118–120.

106. For two examples of this kind of critical evaluation of Teresa Urrea, see *La Voz de Mexico*, December 21, 1889, 3; "Una Santa en Pleno Siglo XIX," *El Monitor Republicano*, January 3, 1890, 3.

107. "La Medium de Cabora," *La Ilustración Espirita*, May 1, 1890, 28.

108. "La Medium."

109. Schraeder, "Spirits of the Times," 133–144; and Vanderwood, *Power of God*, 178–184, 299–302.

110. "La Medium de Cabora," *La Ilustración Espirita*, May 1, 1890, 29.

111. "La Srta. Urrea Y Un Observador," *El Independiente*, August 7, 1896. Original in Spanish, translation is by the author.

112. Teresa Urrea is connected to another rebellion that took place in Chihuahua, Mexico: the 1892 Tomóchic Rebellion. Although she did not live in Mexico at the time the rebellion took place, her name was connected to it, especially through the leader Cruz Chávez. There is a significant amount of scholarship addressing the

Tomóchic Rebellion, which was fought in the name of God and La Santa de Cabora; see, for example, Francisco R. Almada, *La Rebelión de Tomóchic* (Chihuahua: Talleres Linotipográficos del Gobierno del Estado, 1938); Jose Carlos Chavez, *Peleando en Tomóchic* (Ciudad Juárez: Imprenta Moderna, 1957); Rubén Osorio, *Tomóchic en Llamas* (Mexico City: Consejo Nacional para la Cultura y las Artes, 1995); and Vanderwood, *Power of God.*

113. Macklin and Crumrine, "Folk Saint Movements," 102.

114. O'Connor, *Descendants of Totoliquoqui,* 23.

115. O'Connor, 24–25.

116. Crumrine, *Mayo Indians,* x; and O'Connor, 23.

117. This story is related in Crumrine, ix–x; Macklin and Crumrine, "Folk Saint Movements," 102; Domecq de Rodriguez, "Teresa Urrea," 219–220; O'Connor, *Descendants of Totliguoqui,* 23; Spicer, *Cycles of Conquest,* 75–76; and Vanderwood, *Power of God,* 195–198.

118. John Milton Hawkins, "She Is Not a Saint: Neither a Joan of Arc, An Indian Queen nor a Nun," *Los Angeles Times,* September 20, 1896.

119. Domecq de Rodriguez, "Teresa Urrea," 220–221.

120. The story of the Urreas' deportation from Mexico and relocation to Arizona is covered in several issues of *La Ilustración Espirita* from July to December 1892, and Vanderwood, *Power of God,* 226–229.

121. "La Mexicana Teresa Urrea," 9–17, report from Felipe A. Zabadie, Mexican consul in Nogales, AT, to Señor Secretario de Estado y del Despacho de Relaciones Exteriores, Mexico, July 5, 1892, II-19-11, SRE.

122. Hawkins, "She Is Not a Saint," *Los Angeles Times,* September 20, 1896. Hawkins's article provides the most detailed description of her healing practice, but by all accounts Urrea was healing hundreds of people in Nogales as well.

123. Hawkins, "She Is Not a Saint."

124. In a letter, Mallén, the Mexican consul in El Paso, reported that Teresa Urrea arrived in El Paso "último sábado" (last Saturday) and went on to describe her whereabouts and activities in El Paso, showing particular concern over the favorable impression Teresa received in the US press, causing the Mexican government to look bad for expelling a humanitarian healer who "only wanted to do good." Letter from Francisco Mallén, Mexican Consul in El Paso, to the Secretario de Relaciones Exteriores in Mexico City, June 18, 1896, 20–21, Maria Teresa Urrea File, 11-19-11, SRE.

125. Letter from Charles A. Rose to Francisco Mallén, September 7, 1896, 25–26, Maria Teresa Urrea File, 11-19-11, SRE.

126. Letter from Rose to Mallén.

127. One historian of Mexico describes *revoltosos* as a word used by both the Mexican and US governments to describe Mexican insurgents living in the United States and using it as a base for insurrections into Mexico. He includes Lauro Aguirre and Teresa Urrea in his group of *revoltosos.* Ratt, *Revoltosos,* 33.

128. Letter from Rose to Mallén, September 7, 1896, Maria Teresa Urrea File, 11-19-11, SRE.

129. Lauro Aguirre, "Señorita Teresa Urrea, Juana De Arco Mexicana" (Miss Teresa Urrea, The Mexican Jeanne d' Arc), copied in the letter from Rose to Mallén, September 7, 1896, María Teresa Urrea File, 11-19-11, SRE.

130. Letter from Rose to Mallén, September 7, 1896.

131. Letter from Francisco Mallén, Mexican consul in El Paso, to Sr. Juez de Distrito an el Estado, October 19, 1896, II-19-II, SRE; and "Santa Teresa Blamed, Old Texas Ranger Charges the Uprising to the Saint," *Los Angeles Times*, August 7, 1899.

132. Letter from Louis M. Buford to William W. Rockwell, Assistant Secretary of State, Paso del Norte, September 9, 1896, Despatches From United States Consuls in Ciudad Juarez (Paso Del Norte), 1850–1906, RG 59, microfilm reel #5, General Records of the US Department of State, National Archives of the United States (hereafter referred to as RG 59).

133. For the economic impacts of *orden y progresso*, see John Coatsworth, "Obstacles to Economic Growth in Nineteenth-Century Mexico," *American Historical Review* 83, no. 1 (February 1978): 80–100; Stephen Haber, *Industry and Underdevelopment: The Industrialization of Mexico, 1890–1940* (Stanford, CA: Stanford UP, 1995); and John Tutino, *From Insurrection to Revolution in Mexico: Social Bases of Agrarian Violence, 1750–1940* (Princeton, NJ: Princeton UP, 1986).

134. In an interview in 1901, Urrea described seeing Yaqui children "hanged from trees" near her father's hacienda in Cabora. *New York Journal*, March 3, 1901, 1.

135. For gender ideology in Mexico during the Porfiriato, see Nichole Sanders, "Gender and Consumption in Porfirian Mexico: Images of Women in Advertising, *El Imparcial*, 1897–1910," *Frontiers: A Journal of Women Studies* 38, no. 1 (2017): 1–30; and Carmen Ramos Escandón, "Señoritas Porfirianas: Mujer e Ideología en el México Progresista, 1880–1910," in Ramos et al., *Presencia y Transparencia: La Mujer en la Historia de México* (Mexico City: El Colegio de México, 1987).

136. For *la reforma* in Mexico, see Bazant, *Alienation of Church Wealth*.

137. Hale, *Transformation of Liberalism*, 12.

138. The "Plan Restaurador de la Constitución Reformista" is reprinted in Rubén Osorio, *Tomóchic en Llamas* (Mexico City: Consejo Nacional Para La Cultura Y Las Artes, 1995), 379–389.

139. Perales, "Teresa Urrea," 106–107.

140. Lauro Aguirre published *¡Tomochic!* serially in *El Independiente* (El Paso) in 1896 and also in *El Progresista* (El Paso) in 1901 under the title *Tomochic and the Role of the Saint of Cabora (The Mexican Joan of Arc)*. Lauro Aguirre and Teresa Urrea, *¡Tomochic!, El Independiente*, an imprint of *The Evening Tribune*, El Paso, TX, 1896. Amador Collection, University of Texas at El Paso Library, Special Collections.

141. Aguirre and Urrea, *¡Tomochic!*, 3. Quoted in Romo, *Ringside Seat*, 31.

142. Quoted in Hale, *Transformation of Liberalism*, 49. Hale finds that both groups thought of themselves as heirs to the liberal tradition, and that *científicos* were Constitutionalists and not merely apologists for the authoritarian regime of Porfirio Díaz.

143. Quoted in Hale, 34–35.

144. Quoted in Hale, 35.

145. Sierra's influential history of Mexico, *The Political Evolution of the Mexican People* (1902), explained that Mexico's history was not determined by outside forces—God, Spain, the United States—but by unchanging scientific laws that must pass through stages: the Indigenous, or pre-Hispanic; the colonial; and finally the period of the Mestizo in which the Indigenous and Hispanic became one unique people. It was first published as a two-part essay, *México: Su Evolución Social* (Mexico City: J. Bellescá y Cía., 1900–1902). The complete essay was published as *Evolución Política del Pueblo Mexicano* by Casa de España (Mexico City) in 1940. Justo

Sierra, *The Political Evolution of the Mexican People*, trans. Charles Ramsdell (Austin: University of Texas Press, 1969), 3.

146. Letter from Mexican consul in El Paso to Roberto U. Culberson, Auxiliary Promoter of the West, October 10, 1896, 72, Maria Teresa Urrea File, 11–19–11, SRE. "La llamada Santa Teresa, es una joven Mexicana sin educación é ignorante, que tiene algun poder magnético curativo semejante al de los dotoras llamados de la Fe. La clase baja de los Mexicanos consideran á esta mujer una santa."

147. The original Spanish: "Esto es lo positivo; no hay tal santa, no tal inspirada, sino sencillamento uno de aquellos hechos en la ignorancia aparece en todos su apogeo. . . . Los santos no pertenecen á esto tiempo; pasó su época, que afortunadamente para honra de la civilización y del progreso, no volverá jamás." "La Santa de Cabora," *El Monitor Republicano*, January 10, 1890, 3.

148. "De Ultra-Tumba," *El Independiente*, El Paso, TX, August 7, 1896.

149. Cynthia Monter Recoder, "'Vieja a los Trienta Años': El Proceso de Enjeicimiento Segun Algunas Revistas Mexicanas de Fines del Siglo XIX," in *Enjaular los Cuerpos*, ed. Julia Turñon (Mexico City: El Colegio de México, 2008), 281–232.

150. Urrea spoke about her failed marriage in many interviews, including one in the *San Francisco Examiner*: "I was married . . . on the 22nd of June—last month—to Guadalupe N. Rodriguez. He is Mexican. I had known him eight months. The next day after we were married he acted strangely: he tore up some things of mine, packed some of my clothes in a bundle, put it over his shoulder, and said to me, 'Come with me!' The people who saw him said for me not to go, but I followed him. He walked on the railroad track. I did not know where he wanted to go, but I would follow. Then he began to run. I ran, too. He had his gun and started to shoot. The people ran out and made me come back. Then they caught him. He was insane and they put him in jail. There is where he is now." Dare, "Santa Teresa," *San Francisco Examiner*, July 27, 1900.

151. Journalists from the *Los Angeles Times* not only referred to her as the Mexican Joan of Arc, but also the Modern Joan of Arc, the Joan of Arc of the Yaquis, and various iterations of this identity that linked Teresa with the Yaqui revolt. "Santa Terese, Story of the Famous Mexican Joan of Arc," *Los Angeles Times*, August 16, 1896; "Santa Teresa, The Modern Joan of Arc," *Morning Times* (DC), September 6, 1896; "A Mexican Joan D' Arc, Teresa Urrea, the Warrior Saint of the Yaquis," *Washington Post*, September 6, 1896; "Old Mexico's Joan of Arc," *Kansas City (MO) Journal*, September 18, 1896. In an obituary published in the *Tucson Citizen* in 1906 (the year Teresa Urrea died), she was remembered as "Joan d'Arc with the Yaquis." The usage of "Juana de Arco Mexicana" was not as common in newspapers published in Mexico. An article from *El Popular*, a newspaper published in Mexico City, stated that Teresa Urrea used the title of "Juana de Arc" to exploit the "yanquis" who were devoted to her, and to raise an army for her own purposes. "Las Mentiras Yanquis," *El Popular*, February 9, 1900.

Chapter 2. Laying on of Hands

1. Helen Dare, "Santa Teresa," *San Francisco Examiner*, July 27, 1900, 7.

2. K. David Patterson, "Meningitis," in *Cambridge World History of Human Disease*, ed. Kenneth F. Kiple (Cambridge: Cambridge UP, 1993), 876.

3. Patterson, 877–878.

4. Dare, "Santa Teresa," *San Francisco Examiner*, July 27, 1900, 7.

5. For cerebrospinal meningitis, see Patterson, "Meningitis." For tuberculosis, it was not until 1944, with the discovery of streptomycin, that there was a specific, effective drug therapy for sufferers. William D. Johnston, "Tuberculosis," in *Cambridge World History of Human Diseases*, ed. Kenneth F. Kiple, 1059. There still is no cure for yellow fever, only supportive care. https://www.mayoclinic.org/diseases -conditions/yellow-fever/diagnosis-treatment/drc-20353051.

6. Dare, "Santa Teresa," *San Francisco Examiner*, July 27, 1900.

7. "Santa Teresa, the Yaqui Idol, A Cause of Fierce Indian Uprisings, Has Come to Heal Diseases," *San Francisco Examiner*, September 9, 1900.

8. A fascinating exploration of this theme that focuses on film is Kristin Whissel, *Picturing American Modernity: Traffic, Technology, and the Silent Cinema* (Durham, NC: Duke UP, 2008).

9. All advertisements can be found in *San Francisco Call*, Friday, September 21, 1900, 4.

10. The Electric Coronet was advertised in many newspapers, including the *Progressive Thinker* 4 (August 29, 1891), 4.

11. All of the advertisements in this sample come from issues of the *San Francisco Call* in 1900 that also featured stories on Teresa Urrea.

12. Peruna Tonic was advertised in many newspapers, including the *San Francisco Call* (July 1, 1900, 14).

13. The Foo and Wing advertisement comes from Patricia Palma, "Unexpected Healers: Chinese Medicine in the Age of Global Migration (Lima and California, 1850–1930)," *Hist. cienc. saude-Manguinhos* (online) 25, no. 1 (2018): 13–31. The Dr. Chas Clayton advertisement was found in the American Medical Association Historic Health Fraud Collection, Box 106, Folder 6.

14. "Santa Teresa, the Yaqui Idol," *San Francisco Examiner*, September 9, 1900.

15. William Bynum, *The History of Medicine: A Very Short Introduction* (Oxford: Oxford UP, 2008), 10–14.

16. For an examination of the complexities of heroic medicine and what it meant to the medical professional in the nineteenth century, see John Harely Warner, *The Therapeutic Perspective: Medical Practice, Knowledge, and Identity in America, 1820–1885* (Cambridge, MA: Harvard UP, 1986).

17. Warner explains how, in this period, traditional medical practices were "founded on assumptions about disease shared by doctor and patient and oriented toward visibly altering symptoms of sick individuals." Warner, *Therapeutic Perspective*, 1. For these reasons, from the late eighteenth century until after the Civil War (1861–1865), bloodletting was the standard treatment of heroic medicine, and physicians used it to treat almost every ailment: fever, hernia, even amenorrhea (failure to menstruate), a condition the physician might treat by inserting leeches into the vagina and placing them on the cervix to promote blood flow. Stage, *Female Complaints: Lydia Pinkham and the Business of Women's Medicine* (New York: W. W. Norton, 1979), 48–49.

18. Warner, *Therapeutic Perspective*, 13.

19. One Ohio settler had this to say about the aggressive therapies of heroic doctors: "He purged, he bled, he blistered, he puked, he salivated his patient. He never cured him." Quoted in Stage, *Female Complaints*, 50.

20. For the history of Indigenous medicine on the American continents, see Virgil J. Vogel, *American Indian Medicine* (Norman: University of Oklahoma Press, 1970).

21. Botanical medicine inspired significant formalized movements that offered a different kind of therapeutics than heroic medicine. For example, in 1805, Samuel Thomson (1769–1843) founded a system of botanical therapeutics that spread with an almost evangelical passion throughout the northeastern, southern, and midwestern United States in the early nineteenth century. See John S. Haller, Jr., *Kindly Medicine: Physio-Medicalism In America, 1836–1911* (Kent, OH: Kent State UP, 1997).

22. For vitalism as it relates to homeopathy, see Jethro Hernández-Berrones, "Revolutionary Medicine: Homeopathy and the Regulation of the Medical Profession in Mexico, 1853–1942" (PhD diss., University of California, San Francisco, 2014), 30–32; for vitalism as it relates more broadly to other alternative botanical healing practices, see Haller, *Kindly Medicine*, 89–110.

23. Haller, 9.

24. John S. Haller, *The History of American Homeopathy: The Academic Years, 1820–1935* (New York: Pharmaceutical Products Press, 2005).

25. Hernández-Berrones, "Revolutionary Medicine," 1–2.

26. Hernández-Berrones, 1–2.

27. The Medical Code of Ethics, established at the 1846 and 1847 American Medical Association national conventions, stated that it was the responsibility of the physician to "enlighten the public on these subjects, to expose the injuries sustained by the unwary from the devices and pretensions of artful empirics and imposters." Quoted in Arthur W. Hafner, *Guide to the American Medical Association Historical Health Fraud and Alternative Medicine Collection* (Chicago: American Medical Association, 1992), vii.

28. Jethro Hernández-Berrones argues that homeopathy functioned as a subaltern medical movement during the Porfiriato and postrevolutionary period in Mexico ("Revolutionary Medicine," 19–20); Ana María Carrillo, "Profesiones Sanitarias y Lucha de Poderes en el México del Siglo XIX," *Asclepio* 50, no. 2 (1998); Ana María Carrillo, "¿Indivisibilidad o Bifuración de la Ciencia?: La Institucionalización de la Homeopatía en México," in *Continuidades y Rupturas: Una Historia Tensa de la Ciencia en México*, ed. Francisco Javier Dosil Mancilla and Gerardo Sánchez Díaz (Morelia, Michoacán: Instituto de Investigaciones Históricas, Universidad Michoacana de San Nicolás de Hidalgo, Facultad de Ciencias, Universidad Nacional Autónoma de México, 2010); and Yolia T. Cervantes, "Madero, Francisco I.," in *Encyclopedia of Mexico: History, Society and Culture*, ed. Michael S. Werner (London: Routledge, 1998), http://literati.credoreference.com/content/entry/routmex/madero_francisco_i/0, accessed May 2, 2015.

29. For Madero's involvement with Spiritism, see Schraeder, "Spirits of the Times," 148–161.

30. "Federación Universal De La Prensa Espiritista y Espiritualista," *La Ilustración Espirita*, May 1, 1890, 2–6.

31. *San Francisco Call*, October 5, 1900, 10. Urrea's brief advertisement—"Santa Teresa, the Mexican healer, removed to 1610 California St."—is listed under the heading "Spiritualism" with other mediums who advertised healings, readings, advice, and Spiritualist circles.

32. James Wyckoff, *Franz Anton Mesmer: Between God and the Devil* (Englewood Cliffs, NJ: Prentice Hall, 1975), 10–12. For a general history of mesmerism, see Robert Darnton, *Mesmerism and the End of the Enlightenment in France* (Cambridge, MA: Harvard UP, 1968); Monroe, *Laboratories of Faith*; and Anne Taves, *Fits, Trances, and Visions: Experiencing Religion from Wesley to James* (Princeton, NJ: Princeton UP, 1999).

33. Despite his emphasis on the scientific, rational nature of magnetism, Mesmer was considered a charlatan by many in the medical profession and was eventually expelled from the medical faculty at the University of Vienna for conducting a "fraudulent practice." Wycoff, *Franz Anton Mesmer*, 63.

34. This description of mesmeric healing comes from Darnton, *Mesmerism*, 3–7; and Monroe, *Laboratories of Faith*, 67–68.

35. Monroe, 67.

36. Intrinsic to the power of mesmerism was the relationship between the "magnetizer and the magnetized." This relationship would prove to be very influential to physicians such as Jean-Martin Charcot (1825–1893) and Sigmund Freud (1856–1939), who laid the foundation for theories about hypnosis as a treatment for hysteria and other emotional illnesses. Porterfield, *Healing in the History of Christianity*, 174–177.

37. Catherine L. Albanese, *A Republic of Mind and Spirit: A Cultural History of American Metaphysical Religion* (New Haven, CT: Yale UP, 2007), 194.

38. Albanese, 195.

39. Quoted in Albanese, 195.

40. Porterfield, *Healing in the History of Christianity*, 164.

41. Anne Braude, *Radical Spirits: Spiritualism and Women's Rights in Nineteenth Century America* (Bloomington: Indiana UP, 1989), 11. Sojourner Truth first attended a séance in Rochester with the Posts in 1851. Nell Irvin Painter, *Sojourner Truth: A Life, A Symbol* (New York: W. W. Norton, 1996), 146. Several scholars of religion have argued that the significance of Modern American Spiritualism has been undervalued in the religious and political history of the United States. Molly McGarry claims, "That Spiritualism did not become the religion of America says less about the power and appeal of the movement at the time than about what counts as 'religion' and where historians tend to look for and find its traces in the past." McGarry, *Ghosts of Futures Past*, 3. For ways in which Spiritualism informed the politics of the era, particularly the women's rights movement, see Braude, *Radical Spirits*; and Barbara Goldsmith, *Other Powers: The Age of Suffrage, Spiritualism, and the Scandalous Victoria Woodhull* (New York: Alfred A. Knopf, 1998).

42. McGarry, *Ghosts of Futures Past*, 53–54, 118–119.

43. McGarry, 29.

44. Schraeder, "Spirits of the Times," 154.

45. Hernández-Berrones, "Revolutionary Medicine," 47.

46. Quoted in Krauze, *Mexico: Biography of Power*, 248. Madero applied the concept of purification to the nation and also to his own body and spirit. In a Spiritist transmission from Raúl to Madero dated January 9, 1901, the spirit of Raúl admonished Madero to "stop smoking, because such a foolish vice does not do any good to you [and] it profoundly harms your health." Quoted in Hernández-Berrones, "Revolutionary Medicine," 47.

47. Hernández-Berrones, 50–51.

48. Hernández-Berrones, 52–53.

49. For Madero's reluctant radicalism, see Gilbert Joseph and Jürgen Buchenau, *Mexico's Once and Future Revolution: Social Upheaval and the Challenge of Rule since the Late Nineteenth Century* (Durham, NC: Duke UP, 2013), 33–36.

50. Dare, "Santa Teresa," *San Francisco Examiner*, July 27, 1900, 7.

51. "Santa Teresa, the Yaqui Idol," *San Francisco Examiner*, September 9, 1900.

52. David E. Nye, *Electrifying America: Social Meanings of a New Technology, 1880–1940* (Cambridge: MIT Press, 1990), 153.

53. For the policy of assimilation, see David Wallace Adams, *Education for Extinction: American Indians and the Boarding School Experience, 1875–1928* (Lawrence: University of Kansas Press, 1995); and Katherine Ellinghaus, *Blood Will Tell: Native Americans and the Assimilation Policy* (Lincoln: University of Nebraska Press, 2017).

54. "Santa Teresa, The Yaqui Idol," *San Francisco Examiner*, September 9, 1900.

55. "Teresa Comes in Cause of Mercy, Mexican Girl Famed as the Joan of Arc of Yaqui Indians of Sonora Is in San Francisco," *San Francisco Call*, September 9, 1900.

56. There were, of course, women physicians in the United States. In fact, by 1900, women were approximately 5 percent of the male-dominated profession of medicine. Ellen Carol DuBois and Lynn Dumenil, *Through Women's Eyes: An American History with Documents*, vol. 1: *To 1900*, 3rd ed. (Boston and New York: Bedford/St. Martins, 2012), 458.

57. See, for example, Sherman J. Bonney, *Pulmonary Tuberculosis and Its Complications: With Special Reference to Diagnosis and Treatment For General Practitioners and Students* (Philadelphia: W. B. Saunders Company, 1908), 174.

58. "Exiled Patron Saint of Thousands Is in St. Louis on Tour of the World," *The Republic*, January 13, 1901.

59. One account that describes her healing with oils and herbs is Hawkins, "She Is Not A Saint," *Los Angeles Times*, September 20, 1896, 19.

60. Teresa Urrea spoke in Spanish, so her interviews in the United States were translated into English by interpreters.

61. "Exiled Patron Saint."

62. "Exiled Patron Saint."

63. "Exiled Patron Saint."

64. "Exiled Patron Saint."

65. "Exiled Patron Saint."

66. "Exiled Patron Saint."

67. "Santa Teresa Uses Her Healing Powers, Mexican Girl Benefits a Number of Sick People With Her Gentle Manipulations," *San Francisco Call*, September 13, 1900, 12. The estimated audience number is based on the description in the article of the "half-filled hall" and *Doxey's Guide to San Francisco and Vicinity* (San Francisco: Doxey and Co., 1881), 26, which describes the main hall as having a capacity of up to two thousand and a lecture hall with a capacity of up to eight hundred.

68. "Santa Teresa Uses Her Healing Powers."

69. "Santa Teresa Uses Her Healing Powers."

70. The Metropolitan Temple had been a Baptist church in 1877, but by 1900 it

featured a variety of secular, political, and other kinds of cultural entertainment like vaudeville shows, lectures, and even the California State Woman Suffrage Convention in 1896. Perales, "Teresa Urrea," 112; and Elizabeth Cady Stanton and Ida Husted Harper, eds., *The History of Woman Suffrage, 1883–1900* (Indianapolis: Hollenbeck, 1902), 482.

71. Brandon Bayne suggests that "her performances resembled the presentations of Mary Baker Eddy, Henry Steele Olcott, and Aimee Semple McPherson more than the theatrics of the Kickapoo Medicine Company." Bayne, "From Saint to Seeker," 622.

72. "Santa Teresa Uses Her Healing Powers," *San Francisco Call*, September 13, 1900, 12.

73. "Fight for Possession of Santa Teresa Begun, J. H. Suits, Her Manager, Arrested for Detaining Alleged Divine Healer as Prisoner," *San Francisco Call*, September 23, 1900, 21.

74. The judge dismissed the lawsuit, but did advise Suits that he could sue Urrea in civil court for damages, "provided she possessed any money." It was revealed that Urrea had only received fifty dollars of the $833.33 she was promised to receive every month. "Divine Healer Urrea Breaks Her Contract," *San Francisco Call*, September 25, 1900, 14.

75. "Divine Healer Urrea Breaks Her Contract."

76. For Madame Young and the Mediums Protective Association, see the advertisement for a meeting to be held at her "hall" in the *San Francisco Call*, July 5, 1899, 11.

77. For a discussion of the historical importance of women supporting one another, see Gerda Lerner, *The Creation of a Feminist Consciousness: From the Middle Ages to Eighteen-seventy*, vol. 2 of *Women in History* (Oxford: Oxford UP, 1993), 226–230.

78. A very insightful analysis of Teresa Urrea's tour is Bayne, "From Saint to Seeker."

79. "Exiled Patron Saint of Thousands Is in St. Louis on Tour of the World," *The Republic*, January 13, 1901. Several contemporary newspapers commented on Urrea's declaration to travel to Europe and Asia and discover the source of her powers, including: *San Francisco Call*, October 5, 1900, 10; "Santa Teresa Will Next Go To Europe," *San Francisco Call*, February 24, 1901; and "Santa Teresa in New York," *Brownsville Herald*, March 7, 1901.

80. "Exiled Patron Saint of Thousands Is in St. Louis," *The Republic*, January 13, 1901.

81. "Exiled Patron Saint."

82. Bayne, "From Saint to Seeker," 624.

83. Brandon Bayne points this out in "From Saint to Seeker," 625. For the links between Spiritualism and Theosophy, see Stephen Prothero, "From Spiritualism to Theosophy: 'Uplifting' a Democratic Tradition," *Religion and American Culture: A Journal of Interpretation* 3, no. 2 (Summer 1993): 197–216.

84. "Sociedad Teosófica en America: Su Segunda Convencion Annual," *El Independiente*, May 13, 1896, 2.

85. One example of her discussions of traveling the world is "Santa Teresa: Magnetic Healer," *Denison Review*, March 29, 1901.

86. Teresa's relationship with John Van Order is covered in many places, including Perales, "Teresa Urrea," 113–114.

87. Marian Perales discusses the possible reasons that Urrea left New York City and relocated to Los Angeles in Perales, "Teresa Urrea," 113.

88. The *Los Angeles Times* describes how García "was induced by neighbors to spend almost his last dollar to make the trip to Los Angeles, in the hope that Teresa could help him to get well, when recovery was impossible." "Dies Unattended. Tomas Garcia Comes to Take Treatment from 'Santa' Teresa and Refuses Medical Attention," *Los Angeles Times*, December 19, 1902, A7.

89. Sheila M. Rothman, *Living in the Shadow of Death: Tuberculosis and the Social Experience of Illness in American History* (New York: Basic Books, 1994), 2.

90. "Flocking to See Mystic Santa Teresa," *Los Angeles Times*, December 15, 1902; "Santa Teresa's Home Ruined By Fire," *Los Angeles Times*, August 27, 1903; "Santa Teresa a Loser," *Los Angeles Express*, August 27, 1903; and "A Saint's Divorce," *Minneapolis Journal*, August 28, 1903, 11.

91. "Dies Unattended," *Los Angeles Times*, December 19, 1902, A7.

92. "Dies Unattended."

93. William Curry Holden interviewed living family members of Teresa Urrea, as well as people that knew her, for his book *Teresita*, and in several interviews, people mentioned how she used her hands to heal. "Teresita V.II" and "Teresita: Interviews with the family, Jan. 1962," William Curry Holden Papers, Box 52, Folder 16, Southwest Collection/Special Collections Library, Texas Tech University. In Mexico, journalists and observers also commented on this. For one example from newspapers published in Mexico, see "Teresa Urrea, La 'Santa De Cabora,'" *El Mundo* (Mexico City), March 22, 1901. Just a few of the many examples of the numerous mentions of Teresa's magnetic and electric hands are: "Santa Teresa, The Yaqui Idol, A Cause of Fierce Indian Uprisings, Has Come To Heal Diseases," *San Francisco Examiner*, September 9, 1900; "Santa Teresa Uses Her Healing Powers," *San Francisco Call*, September 13, 1900; "Santa Teresa in New York," *Brownsville Herald*, March 7, 1901; "Flocking to See Mystic Santa Teresa," *Los Angeles Times*, December 15, 1902; and "Un Problema Para La Medicina," *La Ilustración Espirita*, June 1, 1891, 51.

94. "She Is Not a Saint," *Los Angeles Times*, September 20, 1896.

95. "Santa Teresa Uses Her Healing Powers," *San Francisco Call*, Thursday, September 13, 1900.

96. "Flocking to See Mystic Santa Teresa," *Los Angeles Times*, December 15, 1902.

97. "Flocking."

98. William D. Johnston, "Tuberculosis," in *Cambridge World History of Human Diseases*, ed. Kenneth F. Kiple (Cambridge: Cambridge UP, 1993), 1016.

99. Not until 1944, with the discovery of streptomycin, was there a specific, effective drug therapy for tuberculosis sufferers. Johnston, 1059.

100. At the turn of the twentieth century, tuberculosis was the leading cause of death in the United States. One physician estimated that tuberculosis accounted for approximately one-seventh of all deaths in the early twentieth century. Bonney, *Pulmonary Tuberculosis*, 57.

101. "Dies Unattended," *Los Angeles Times*, December 19, 1902, A7.

102. Important scholarship on the racialization of disease and the ramifications of that for public health is Natalia Molina, *Fit to Be Citizens?* See also Emily Abel,

Tuberculosis and the Politics of Exclusion: A History of Public Health and Migration to Los Angeles, 68–73; and Alan M. Kraut, *Silent Travelers: Germs, Genes, and the Immigrant Menace*.

103. For segregation of Mexicans in the US Southwest, see Cynthia Orozco, *No Mexicans, Women, or Dogs Allowed: The Rise of the Mexican American Civil Rights Movement* (Austin: University of Texas Press, 2009).

104. Rothman, *Living in the Shadow of Death*, 2-4.

105. Mexicans who had tuberculosis were viewed as an unfair economic burden on state resources. Abel, *Tuberculosis*, 70–73.

106. Abel, 1–4; Rothman, *In the Shadow of Death*, 4.

107. For the way these racial ideologies coincided with the broad eugenics movement (a movement that gained authority in the decades following 1900, as the field of professionalized scientific medicine gained authority), see Nancy Leys Stepan, *"The Hour of Eugenics": Race, Gender, and Nation in Latin America*. For the ways these racial ideas concerning disease and public health played out in Los Angeles in the progressive and post–Mexican Revolution era as well as the Great Depression, see Molina, *Fit to Be Citizens?* For a compelling examination of the ways tuberculosis was perceived and used metaphorically throughout history, see Susan Sontag, *Illness as Metaphor and AIDS and Its Metaphors* (New York: Doubleday, 1989), 31–36.

108. Bonney, *Pulmonary Tuberculosis*.

109. Bonney, 57.

110. Nancy Leys Stepan, *"The Hour of Eugenics,"* 21–34.

111. Abel, *Tuberculosis*, 29–38; Kraut, *Silent Travelers*, 50–77; Molina, *Fit to be Citizens?*

112. Bonney, *Pulmonary Tuberculosis*, 59.

113. Bonney's racial hierarchy of tuberculosis susceptibility shows slippage between race and nationality. From most resistant to least, Bonney lists Poles (most resistant), Jews, "Americans," English, Russians, Italians and Hungarians, Germans, French, Scotch and Canadians, Swedes, Irish, American Indians, and the most susceptible, African Americans. He makes no mention of Mexicans, Asians, or Spaniards. Bonney, 60–75.

114. Abel, *Tuberculosis*, 68–69.

115. Emily Abel, *Suffering in the Land of Sunshine* (New Brunswick, NJ: Rutgers UP, 2006), 83–84.

116. Abel, 83–84.

117. For more on the biography of Charles Dwight Willard, see Abel, *Suffering*.

118. Bonney, *Pulmonary Tuberculosis*, 153. Based on the description of Tomas García dying "suddenly in a fit of coughing," it sounds like he may have experienced a severe pulmonary hemorrhage as described here by Bonney.

119. John Hunt, "National Register of Historic Places Inventory/Nomination: Los Angeles Plaza Historic District/El Pueblo de Los Angeles," National Park Service, August 14, 1982. It was mostly Mexicans who worked laying track for railroads and electric city cars in the Southwest in the late nineteenth and early twentieth centuries, especially in Los Angeles. Charles Wollenberg, "Working on El Traque: The Pacific Electric Strike of 1903," *Pacific Historical Review* 42, no. 3 (August 1973): 358–369. The following articles published in the *Los Angeles Herald* all describe Mexican laborers at the lodging house at 418 North Main (usually said to be en-

gaged in criminal activity or heavy drinking, contributing to the demeaning cultural stereotypes of Mexicans prevalent at that time): "Acrobatic Mexican Thief," *Los Angeles Herald*, August 17, 1903; "Chain Gang for Theft," *Los Angeles Herald*, December 8, 1906; and "Mystery of a Black Eye Starts Vengeful Hunt," *Los Angeles Herald*, August 18, 1907. California bought the Pico House (as it is now known) in 1953, and now it belongs to the El Pueblo de Los Angeles State Historic Monument.

120. Pio Pico built the Pico Hotel in 1869 but lost it to the bank in 1876. Hunt, "National Register," 5. For Pio Pico, see Carlos Manuel Salomon, *Pio Pico: The Last Governor of Mexican California* (Norman: University of Oklahoma Press, 2010).

121. Jeffrey Marcos Garcilazo, *Traqueros: Mexican Railroad Workers in the United States, 1870–1930* (Denton: University of North Texas Press, 2012), 95.

122. Beginning in the 1900s, Mexicans became the major immigrant group in Los Angeles. One historian of Los Angeles quotes a tourist pamphlet that described Los Angeles in the 1880s as a "sleepy semi-Mexican *pueblo* of 11,000," and how the "contrast between Anglo-Saxon energy and Mexican lassitude demonstrated the fits between whites and the land." Abel, *Tuberculosis*, 3, 61.

123. Carey McWilliams, *North From Mexico: The Spanish-Speaking People of the United States* (New York: Praeger, 1948), 88–89.

124. Abel, *Tuberculosis*, 71–72. When the deputy coroner arrived, the men surrounded his body and refused to let it be moved, and the deputy responded by threatening to have the crowd arrested. "Dies Unattended," *Los Angeles Times*, December 19, 1902, A7.

125. I thank the reader who helped me clarify this.

126. Teresa Urrea's involvement in this strike is mentioned in the only in-depth look at the 1903 Pacific Electric Strike: Charles Wollenberg, "Working on El Traque: The Pacific Electric Strike of 1903." Jeffrey Marcos Garcilazo refers to Wollenberg's work in his book about Mexican track workers, and writes a bit more about Teresa Urrea's involvement, citing the same source as Wollenberg, an article in the *Los Angeles Record*, April 28, 1903. Garcilazo, *Traqueros*, 98–99. The following sources only briefly mention Urrea and the P.E. strike of 1903 but do not add anything new to Wollenberg and Garcilazo: Carlos Larralde, *Mexican-American Movements and Leaders*, 68; and Perales, "Teresa Urrea," 113–114.

127. *Los Angeles Record*, April 28, 1903, cited in Jeffrey Marcos Garcilazo, *Traqueros*, 95–102. For the Mexican flag at the UFM headquarters, see "This Smacks of Treason," *Los Angeles Times*, April 28, 1903.

128. "Santa Teresa Takes Hand in the Strike," *Los Angeles Record*, April 28, 1903.

129. "This Smacks of Treason," *Los Angeles Times*, April 28, 1903; "Public Down on Agitators: Citizens Favor Driving Them From Los Angeles," *Los Angeles Times*, May 1, 1903. For the background on the strike, see Garcilazo, *Traqueros*, 95–102.

130. "Only Women Interfered," *Los Angeles Times*, April 26, 1903, 8; Garcilazo, *Traqueros*, 98–100.

131. Wollenberg, "Working on El Traque," 358, 366–367.

132. "Santa Teresa Takes a Hand in the Strike," *Los Angeles Record*, April 28, 1903, 1.

133. Garcilazo, *Traqueros*, 97. One journalist for the *Los Angeles Times* described the heavy police presence at the site of the strike and explained that it was to protect the workers from the strikers and "prevent trouble that it would have been un-

healthy for any man or body of men to have attempted to interfere with the work." This same journalist quoted the police chief, who explained, "We are prepared for any emergency and while we are not looking for trouble, should trouble occur we will not take to the wood." "Only Women Interfered," *Los Angeles Times*, April 26, 1903.

134. It is not known why the home burned down. Some scholars speculate it could have been arson, but the reason remains unclear. "Santa Teresa a Loser, Flames Burn Cottage Occupied by Woman Supposed to Possess Miraculous Healing," *Los Angeles Express*, August 27, 1903. For speculation on causes, see Perales, "Teresa Urrea," 114–115. For her divorce, see "Santa Teresa Divorced," *Los Angeles Times*, January 4, 1904.

135. Deed for the sale of land from Henry and Rose Hill to Teresa Urrea for $300 in the "Henry Hill Addition to Clifton," copied in William Curry Holden Papers, Box 51, Folder 5, Southwest Collection/Special Collections Library, Texas Tech University.

136. In this period of her life, it seems that John Van Order was not around much. Perales, "Teresa Urrea," 115.

137. The information on this period of Urrea's life comes from William Curry Holden Papers, Southwest Collection/Special Collections Library, Texas Tech University. In December 1902, a little more than three years before her death, the tubercle bacillus was most likely in her lungs and probably had been for a while. Teresa had just given birth to her daughter, Laura, and pregnancy was known to greatly exacerbate the dangers of tuberculosis for women. As a pregnancy progressed, and the uterus pushed against the diaphragm and lungs, the disease was known to progress rapidly, and many tubercular women died within days of delivering. In the early twentieth century, physicians often performed abortions to save the lives of tubercular mothers. Bonney wrote that "Pregnancy as a complication of pulmonary tuberculosis is almost universally believed to be distinctly detrimental to the health of the consumptive, regardless of the extent or activity of the disease." Bonney, *Pulmonary Tuberculosis*, 310–311. Another physician estimated that by the beginning of the twentieth century almost 1.5 percent of all pregnant women suffered from tuberculosis. Judith Walzer Leavitt, *Brought to Bed: Childbearing in America 1750 to 1950* (New York and Oxford: Oxford UP, 1986), 68–69.

138. Brandon Bayne cataloged the scholars who have discussed this period of her life as a fall from grace, an abandonment of her true Mexican borderlands curandera nature. Bayne, "From Saint to Seeker," 613. See also Frank Putnam, "Teresa Urrea: The Saint of Cabora," *Southern California Quarterly*; William Curry Holden, *Teresita*; Carlos Larralde, *Mexican American Movements and Leaders* (Los Alamitos, CA; Hwong, 1976); Luis León, *La Llorona's Children*; and Vanderwood, *Power of God Against the Guns of Government*.

139. Luis Alberto Urrea, *The Queen of America* (New York: Little, Brown, 2011), 455.

140. My argument here builds on the work of scholars who have taken a more nuanced approach to interpreting her identity. See Bayne, "From Saint to Seeker"; Hendrickson, *Border Medicine*; Martín, *Borderlands Saints*; Newell, "Teresa Urrea"; and Perales, "Teresa Urrea." I borrow the phrase "enchanted modernity" from Lia Schrader, who uses it to explain how religion and spirituality did not necessarily de-

cline with the rise of scientific modernity in the nineteenth century, but rather modernity remained enchanted through the rationalization of spiritual experience as expressed in Mexican Spiritism. Schraeder, "Spirits of the Times," 11.

Chapter 3. All Roads Lead to Don Pedrito Jaramillo

1. The honorific terms of respect *don* and *doña* are used before the names of Andrés Canales, Pedro Jaramillo, and Tomasita Canales because that is how they are most often addressed in the literature. Elders and those with social distinction or high status in Mexican and Latin American cultures are respectfully addressed as *don* or *doña*.

2. The story of Don Pedrito Jaramillo healing Doña Tomasita Canales comes from J. T. Canales, "Don Pedrito Jaramillo curaba a los enfermos pobres, desahuchiados," *La Prensa*, March 21, 1928, 1; and Ruth Dodson, *Don Pedrito Jaramillo, "Curandero"* (San Antonio: Casa Editorial Lozano, 1934), 17–18. This was subsequently published in English with some revisions and expansion as "Don Pedrito Jaramillo: The Curandero of Los Olmos," in *The Healer of Los Olmos and Other Mexican Lore*, ed. William M. Hudson (Dallas: Texas Folklore Society and Southern Methodist UP, 1951). Unless otherwise stated, the original 1934 Spanish version, *Don Pedrito Jaramillo, "Curandero,"* is used. Doña Tomasita came from an elite Tejano family, heirs to the Spanish El Espiritu Santo land grant. For a history of Doña Tomasita and the Canales family, see Richard Henry Ribb, "José Tomás Canales and the Texas Rangers: Myth, Identity, and Power in South Texas, 1900–1920" (PhD diss., University of Texas at Austin, 2001). The term *Tejana* refers to a woman of Spanish/Mexican descent from Texas; *Tejano* is used for a male.

3. There were other people besides Don Andrés Canales who did not believe in Jaramillo's healing power, but respected him nonetheless. The curator of the Falfurrias Heritage Museum in Falfurrias, Texas, explained that her great-grandfather was a close friend of Jaramillo but did not believe in him as a curandero. Lourdes Treviño-Cantu, telephone interview by author, March 24, 2014; for Don Andrés Canales's feelings about Don Pedrito, see J. T. Canales, "Don Pedrito Jaramillo curaba a los enfermos pobres," 1.

4. Canales, 1.

5. For yellow fever outbreak in South Texas, see John Mckiernan-González, *Fevered Measures*.

6. The National Board of Health report explained that words such as "malignant" and "pernicious" were used in place of yellow fever to conceal the number of cases: "A critical examination of the monthly statistics for several years shows that the so-called 'pernicious' and 'malignant' fevers almost always prevailed most when yellow fever did, and that the maximum deaths by these diseases occurred when yellow fever was most fatal." *Annual Report on the National Board of Health* (Washington, DC: Government Printing Office, 1881), 281. Mariola Espinosa, *Epidemic Invasions: Yellow Fever and the Limits of Cuban Independence, 1878–1930* (Chicago: University of Chicago Press, 2009), 25–26.

7. This description of the symptoms of yellow fever comes from Espinosa, *Epidemic Invasions*, 1–2.

8. Dodson, *Don Pedrito Jaramillo, "Curandero,"* 17–18. For Tomasita's age, see J. T. Canales, "Personal Recollections of J. T. Canales," Río TS, Center for American History, University of Texas at Austin, April 28, 1945, Appendix A, 6.

9. For the practice of medicine in nineteenth- and twentieth-century Mexico, see Claudia Agostoni, *Curar, Sanar y Educar: Enfermedad y Sociedad en México, Siglos XIX y XX* (Mexico City: Universidad Nacional Autónoma de México, 2008); Ana Maria Carrillo, "Médicos del México Decimonónico: Entre el Control Estatal y la Autonomía Professional," *Dynamis* 22 (2000), 351–375; and George M. Foster, *Hippocrates' Latin American Legacy: Humoral Medicine in the New World* (Amsterdam: Gordon and Breach Science Publishers, 1994). For a social history of the relationship between nineteenth-century medical practice and knowledge in the United States, see John Harley Warner, *The Therapeutic Perspective: Medical Practice, Knowledge, and Identity in America, 1820–1895* (Cambridge: Harvard UP, 1986); for women in medicine during this period, see Regina Markell Morantz-Sanchez, *Sympathy and Science: Women Physicians in American Medicine* (New York and Oxford: Oxford UP, 1985); for medical practice in Texas and the US West during this period, see Watson C. Arnold, "Home Remedies, Folk Medicine, and Mad Stones," *Southwestern Historical Quarterly* 117, no. 2 (October 2013); Sylvia Van Voast Ferris and Eleanor Sellars Hoppe, *Scalpels and Sabers: Nineteenth Century Medicine in Texas* (Austin, TX: Eakin, 1985); and Volney Steele, *Bleed, Blister, and Purge: A History of Medicine on the American Frontier* (Missoula, MT: Mountain Press, 2005).

10. Michael Worboys, "Tropical Diseases," in *Companion Encyclopedia of the History of Medicine*, vol. 1, ed. W. F. Bynum and Roy Porter (New York: Routledge, 1993).

11. For the history of South Texas during the period that Don Pedrito Jaramillo conducted his medical practice, see Daniel D. Arreola, *A Mexican Cultural Province: Tejano South Texas* (Austin: University of Texas Press, 2002); Arnoldo De León, *The Tejano Community*; De León, *They Called Them Greasers: Anglo Attitudes Towards Mexicans in Texas, 1821–1900* (Austin: University of Texas Press, 1983); and David Montejano, *Anglos and Mexicans in the Making of Texas, 1836–1986* (Austin: University of Texas Press, 1987). Seminal studies of South Texas folklore during this period are Américo Paredes, *Folklore and Culture on the Texas-Mexican Border* (Austin: Center for Mexican American Studies, University of Texas at Austin, 1993); Paredes, *"With His Pistol in His Hand": A Border Ballad and Its Hero* (Austin: University of Texas Press, 1958); and Ramón Saldívar, *The Borderlands of Culture: Américo Paredes and the Transnational Imaginary* (Durham, NC: Duke UP, 2006). Important feminist- and women-centered scholarship of this region includes Gloria Anzaldúa, *Borderlands/La Frontera* (San Francisco: Aunt Lute Books, 1987); Jovita González, *Life Along the Border: A Landmark Tejana Thesis*; and Sonia Saldívar-Hull, *Feminism on the Border: Chicana Gender Politics and Literature* (Berkeley: University of California Press, 2000). Among the newest scholarship on South Texas are the following transnational studies of the region: George Díaz, *Border Contraband: A History of Smuggling across the Río Grande* (Austin: University of Texas Press, 2015); Omar S. Valerio-Jiménez, *River of Hope: Forging Identity and Nation in the Río Grande Borderlands* (Durham, NC: Duke UP, 2013); and Aaron E. Sánchez, "From Pocholandia to Aztlán: Belonging, Homeland, Politics, and Citizenship in US-Mexican Thought, Texas 1910–1979," PhD diss., Southern Methodist University, 2012.

12. Quote from José E. Limón, *Dancing with the Devil: Society and Cultural Poetics in Mexican-American South Texas* (Madison: University of Wisconsin Press, 1994), 192–193. The main source on Jaramillo is Dodson, *Don Pedrito Jaramillo, "Curandero."* There are a few theses and dissertations about Jaramillo, including Refugio S. Garza, "En el Nombre de Dios y Don Pedrito Jaramillo," MA thesis, Texas College of Arts and Industry–Kingsville (later Texas A&M–Kingsville), 1952; and Romano, "Don Pedrito Jaramillo." See also Octavio Romano, "Charismatic Medicine, Folk-Healing, and Folk-Sainthood," *American Anthropologist* 67, no. 5, pt. 1 (October 1965): 1151–1173; Amelia Malagamba, "Don Pedrito Jaramillo, una Leyenda Mexicana en el Sur de Texas," in *Entre la Magia y la Historia: Tradiciones, Mitos y Leyendas de La Frontera*, ed. José Manuel Valenzuela Arce (Tijuana: El Colegio de la Frontera Norte, 1992), 63–74; and Limón, *Dancing with the Devil*, 187–198.

13. For the *don*, see León, "Borderlands Bodies and Souls," 301; Trotter and Chavira, *Curanderismo*, 27: and Torres, *Healing with Herbs and Rituals*, 10–12.

14. Dodson, "Don Pedrito Jaramillo: The Curandero of Los Olmos," 12–13.

15. For this version, see Garza, "En el Nombre de Dios," 9–12.

16. Dodson, *Don Pedrito Jaramillo, "Curandero,"* 10.

17. Dodson, 7; Garza, "En el Nombre de Dios," 11; Ann Reed Washington, "South Texas' Greatest Folk Healer," in *Roots by the River: A Story of Texas Tropical Borderlands*, ed. Valley By-Liners (Mission, TX: Border Kingdom, 1978), 94–95.

18. Dodson, *Don Pedrito Jaramillo, "Curandero,"* 12. All translations are the author's.

19. Called Los Olmos or Paisano, after the El Paisano land grant given to Ramón de la Garza by the Mexican state of Tamaulipas in 1830. Alicia A. Garza, "LOS OLMOS, TX," Handbook of Texas Online, http://www.tshaonline.org/handbook/online/articles/hvlat, accessed November 16, 2014, published by the Texas State Historical Association.

20. Don Pedrito Jaramillo purchased 289.5 acres of land from Luciano and Antonia Flores for $289.50. This land was part of the original Mexican Loma Blanca land grant, "originally granted to Francisco Guerra Chapa by the State of Tamaulipas and patented to him and his heirs by the State of Texas. State of Texas, County of Duval, *Warranty/Deed from Luciano Flores and Antonia Vela de Flores to Pedro Jaramillo*, San Diego, TX, November 24, 1896; Transcribed from Starr County Real Estate Records Book 'Q' page 314 to 316," Regional Historical Resource Depository Collection at South Texas Archives, Texas A&M–Kingsville.

21. Dodson, "Don Pedrito Jaramillo: The Curandero of Los Olmos," 11. Américo Parades, in his study of folklore in the Lower Río Grande region of Texas, explains that there was little stigma attached to smuggling at this time because smugglers were not flouting customs agents as a form of social protest; rather, it was simply commonplace to try circumventing customs to get goods into the United States. Parades, *Folklore and Culture*, 24–28. For more on liquor smuggling and *tequileros* during the Prohibition era, see Díaz, *Border Contraband*, 96–106.

22. De León, *The Tejano Community*, 142.

23. Rosario Torres-Raines, "The Mexican Origin of Rituals, Ceremonies, and Celebrations in South Texas," *South Texas Studies* 7 (1996): 153.

24. Dodson, "Don Pedrito Jaramillo: The Curandero of Los Olmos," 11.

25. The Canales family's Rancho de Las Cabras was in what is now Wilson

County; Jaramillo lived approximately forty-five miles away on Rancho de Los Olmos, in nearby Starr County.

26. Quoted in Romano, "Don Pedrito Jaramillo," 97–98.

27. Romano, 97–98.

28. Romano, 97–98.

29. Quoted in Romano, 97.

30. For more on *susto* and other folk illnesses, see Avila, *Woman Who Glows in the Dark*, 43–69; and Trotter and Chavira, *Curanderismo*, 89–92.

31. Portilla, *They All Want Magic*, 60. One anthropologist who specializes in ritual theory explains that the effectiveness of ritual—such as Don Pedrito's cures involving meaningful numbers and materials—"lies in its ability to have people embody assumptions about their place in a larger order of things." Catherine Bell, *Ritual: Perspectives and Dimensions* (Oxford: Oxford UP, 1997), xi.

32. Romano, "Don Pedrito Jaramillo," 97.

33. Romano, 97.

34. Of the Virgin Mary statues, the informant stated, "I don't recall which ones." Romano, 97. Robert Trotter suggests that the altars of curanderos are communication systems, filled with symbols that provide comfort and cultural congruence to their patients. Interview by author, Dallas, TX, October 29, 2014.

35. Dodson, "Don Pedrito Jaramillo: The Curandero of Los Olmos," 12.

36. The informant, José C. Lozano, related this story and others he remembered about Don Pedrito to Texas folklorist H. C. Arbuckle. H. C. Arbuckle III, "Don José and Don Pedrito," in *The Folklore of Texan Cultures*, ed. Francis Edward Abernethy and Dan Beaty (Austin: Encino, 1974), 84–87.

37. Arbuckle, 84–87.

38. *Hijo* means "son"; *borracho*, "drunk"; and *remedio*, "remedy."

39. Most Tejanos practiced Catholicism, albeit a folk or "frontier" version since the institution of the Catholic Church was not as strong in northern Mexico and the borderlands as it was in other regions of Mexico, yet the tradition of Catholicism and its attendant teachings, rituals, and practices were still deeply held by most in the Tejano community. De León, *The Tejano Community*; and Trotter and Chavira, *Curanderismo*, 32.

40. For the cure for the woman suffering stomach pain, see Dodson, *Don Pedrito Jaramillo, "Curandero,"* 31–32; for the man suffering migraines, see Dodson, 21–22. Mckiernan-González suggests that part of the appeal of Jaramillo's water-based cures was the "healing power of the South Texas landscape" through the exposure of his clients to night air and natural water. Mckiernan-González, *Fevered Measures*, 163.

41. Arbuckle, "Don José and Don Pedrito," 86.

42. Quoted in Dodson, *Don Pedrito Jaramillo, "Curandero,"* 21–23. On how turn-of-the-century gender ideals coincided with the concept of civilization and reinforced gender hierarchies and separate spheres ideology, see Gail Bederman, *Manliness and Civilization*; Kristin L. Hoganson, *Fighting for American Manhood: How Gender Politics Provoked the Spanish-American and Philippine-American Wars* (New Haven: Yale UP, 1998); and Carroll Smith Rosenberg, "The Woman as Androgyne: Social Disorder and Gender Crisis, 1870–1936," in *Disorderly Conduct: Visions of Gender in Victorian America* (New York: Alfred A. Knopf, 1985).

43. Palomo Acosta and Ruth Winegarten, *Las Tejanas*, 95–103; Romano, "Don Pedrito Jaramillo," 63–64. For the role of Tejanas as bearers of spiritual education and morals in the family, see Acosta and Winegarten, *Las Tejanas*, 96, 200. For a different interpretation of the separate spheres ideology as it applies (or does not) to Mexican American working-class women, see Ruiz, *From Out of the Shadows*, 24–25.

44. Another similarity between nineteenth-century curanderos and eighteenth-century social healers from the eastern United States is the paucity of records, letters, and archival sources about them. A rich study of one such social healer and midwife from eighteenth-century Maine who did leave a journal for the historical record is Laurel Thatcher Ulrich, *A Midwife's Tale: The Life of Martha Ballard, Based on Her Diary, 1785–1812* (New York: Vintage Books, 1990).

45. Foster, *Hippocrates' Latin American Legacy.*

46. For one examination of the ways in which gendered ideas affected female medical issues, see Laura Briggs, "The Race of Hysteria: 'Overcivilization' and the 'Savage' Woman in Late Nineteenth-Century Obstetrics and Gynecology," *American Quarterly* 52, no. 2 (2000): 246–273.

47. In one of the cures Don Pedrito made for infertility, the husband was present, although the cure (to drink a glass of water before going to bed every night for nine months) applied only to the woman. Juan Sauvageau, *Stories That Must Not Die*, 14–15.

48. Doña Petra told Dodson she knew about Don Pedrito because he had visited Refugio, Texas, "walking everywhere performing healings." But in the years Doña Petra consulted Don Pedrito (1905 and 1906) she explained that he was too old to do much traveling, so she had no choice but to travel the one hundred miles to Los Olmos to see him. Dodson, *Don Pedrito Jaramillo, "Curandero,"* 119.

49. Dodson, 135.

50. Rachel P. Maines, *The Technology of Orgasm: Hysteria, the Vibrator, and Women's Sexual Satisfaction* (Baltimore: Johns Hopkins UP, 2001), 44, 73–75.

51. "Saint Don Pedrito," *Dallas Morning News*, April 21, 1894.

52. For detailed examinations of the "crisis of American manhood" at the turn of the century, see Bederman, *Manliness and Civilization*; and Hoganson, *Fighting for American Manhood.*

53. The focus on Mexican male resistance fighters in South Texas legends and folklore may be attributed to this impulse to defend a threatened masculinity in late-nineteenth and early-twentieth century South Texas. See especially Américo Paredes, *"With a Pistol in His Hand"* and *A Texas–Mexican Cancionero*; and De León, *The Tejano Community*, 57.

54. Dodson, *Don Pedrito Jaramillo, "Curandero,"* 55–56.

55. Dodson, 55–56. For the many ways healers cure *susto*, see Hendrickson, *Border Medicine*, 125–126; for the potential of pilgrimage to heal feelings of shame, see Scott, *Miracle Cures*, 124–125.

56. According to the sample of 135 cures this chapter takes as its subject, 35 percent of them were obtained at Los Olmos (of those that specified where the cure took place) and of that 35 percent, 48 percent specify that the supplicant traveled 50 miles or more to receive the cure from Don Pedrito, and 13 percent involved a friend or relative sent, usually on horseback, to procure a *receta* from Don Pedrito. It is im-

portant to note that 50 percent of the cures in the sample do not specify where the cure took place. Thus, the fact that 35 percent—by far the largest percentage of cures that specify a location—took place at Los Olmos indicates the likeliness that a significant number of cures took place at Los Olmos and thus involved a journey.

57. Of the 135 cures analyzed for this chapter, only ten cures were made for people outside of Texas, or .7 percent of the total sample. This is likely due to the fact that Ruth Dodson collected these stories in Texas and therefore her sample is primarily representative of Texas. Dodson, *Don Pedrito Jaramillo, "Curandero,"* 137–148; Romano, "Don Pedrito Jaramillo," 95.

58. For a social history of Lourdes that puts the miraculous event in the context of the debate between science and religion, see Ruth Harris, *Lourdes: Body and Spirit in the Secular Age* (New York: Penguin, 1999).

59. Victor Turner and Edith Turner, *Image and Pilgrimage in Christian Culture* (New York: Columbia UP, 1978).

60. Jeremy R. Ricketts, "Land of (Re) Enchantment: Tourism and Sacred Space at Roswell and Chimayó, New Mexico," *Journal of the Southwest* 53, no. 2 (Summer 2011): 239–261; and Jill Dubish and Michael Winkelman, eds., *Pilgrimage and Healing* (Tucson: University of Arizona Press, 2005). Catholicism is not the only religion that has a history of pilgrimage as part of its official and unofficial devotional practices. For a transnational and transcultural look at pilgrimage, see Simon Coleman and John Elsner, *Pilgrimage: Past and Present in the World Religions* (Cambridge, MA: Harvard UP, 1995).

61. Robert A. Scott, *Miracle Cures: Saints, Pilgrimage, and the Healing Powers of Belief* (Berkeley: University of California Press, 2010).

62. In one ethnographic study of the Río Grande Valley (the southernmost counties of South Texas), the author claims that "the conservative Mexican-American consults a physician only as a last resort when all other curing techniques have failed." William Madsen, *Society and Health in the Lower Río Grande Valley: Based Upon the Findings of the Hidalgo Project on Differential Culture Change and Mental Health* (Austin: University of Texas Press, 1961), 25–26. A more nuanced version of this stance is offered in Trotter and Chavira, *Curanderismo*, 1–24.

63. Scott, *Miracle Cures*, 128–129.

64. Scott, 143–147. For the placebo effect, see Anne Harrington, *The Placebo Effect: An Interdisciplinary Exploration* (Cambridge: Harvard UP, 1997). In an interdisciplinary study of healing and pilgrimages to shrines containing holy relics in seventeenth century Spain, one scholar suggests that pilgrimages increased the currency and prestige of the object of devotion, and that especially for "desperate pilgrims who had begun to come to the Shrine as a last resort," the likelihood of a successful cure was greater. Katrina Olds, "Visions of the Holy in Counter-Reformation Spain: The Discovery and Creation of Relics in Arjona, c. 1628," in *The "Vision Thing": Studying Divine Intervention*, ed. William A. Christman Jr. and Gábor Klaniczay (Budapest: Collegium Budapest, 2009), 148–149.

65. Scott, *Miracle Cures*, 149–150.

66. Scott, 151–155; Harrington, *The Cure Within*, 22.

67. Harrington, 22.

68. One sociologist who has studied metaphysical practitioners in Massachusetts demonstrates that the sharing of "experiential narratives" that recount per-

sonal mystical experiences not only builds the authority of that particular narrative, but "indicate[s] individuals' abilities to narrate their lives according to shared norms and expectations." Courtney Bender, *The New Metaphysicals: Spirituality and the American Religious Imagination* (Chicago: University of Chicago Press, 2010), 58.

69. Dionisio Rodríguez related this story to Texas folklorist Ruth Dodson in 1934, when he was eighty-five years old. Dodson, *Don Pedrito Jaramillo, "Curandero,"* 21–22. Before Rodríguez made a journey to be healed by Don Pedrito Jaramillo, he had made the journey across the border to start a new life in South Texas. In 1882, after serving five years in the army of Mexican president Porfirio Díaz, Rodríguez left his home in San Carlos, Tamaulipas, Mexico, and crossed the border into the United States, entering a region that had been part of a variety of national projects and sovereignties, including Native ones, and was 90 percent or more Mexicano or Tejano. Rodríguez did not say why he choose to enlist in the army, but he did explain later, in 1934, to folklorist Ruth Dodson that "in those days when someone had committed some offense, for instance having killed someone . . . he went and enlisted in the army for five years, that freed him of all guilt." Dodson, *Don Pedrito Jaramillo, "Curandero,"* 21–23; and Dodson, "Don Pedrito Jaramillo: The Curandero of Los Olmos," 18–20. Porfirio Díaz, the president of Mexico during the period that Don Pedrito practiced curanderismo in South Texas, had a distinctive presence in Tamaulipas. Díaz launched his reformed Plan of Tuxtepec from Palo Blanco, Tamaulipas, in 1876, which started the first phase of his nearly three decades of almost uninterrupted dictatorship of Mexico, from 1876 to 1911. For more on Mexico during the presidency of Porfirio Díaz, see Friedrich Katz, "Mexico: Restored Republic and Porfiriato, 1867–1910," in *Cambridge History of Latin America*, vol. 5, ed. Leslie Bethell (Cambridge UP, 1986), 1–78. After his service in the Mexican Army was over in 1882, Rodríguez told Dodson: "I crossed the Río Grande, never again to set foot on Mexican soil." Although Rodríguez may have left the Mexican nation-state, he did not leave Mexico culturally, socially, or historically. In this, he was representative of Don Pedrito's patients in South Texas: they were of Mexican heritage, whether recently arrived or Tejanos like the Canales family who had lived in this region for decades. Américo Paredes has argued that the unnatural constructions of borders by nation-states often have little effect on the regions they bisect. He explains that the limits of cultural regions, such as the South Texas–Northeastern Mexico borderlands, "are not defined by the Customs and Immigration offices at the border. Parts of northern Mexico are included within the boundaries of each. These regional folk cultures thus include regions of two nations." The US-Mexico border is a construction, one that cuts across a geography, a history, and a culture that persists despite the creation of the border in 1848. Dionisio Rodríguez, a transnational migrant, is a part of a shared history between two nations, the one he left behind and the one where he would spend the rest of his life.

70. Dodson, *Don Pedrito Jaramillo, "Curandero,"* 22.

71. In the sample, 42.2 percent of the cures involved water, the most common material Don Pedrito used to heal. See table 3. Cenizo, or purple sage, is a plant common to the desert that stretches for hundreds of miles along the Texas-Mexico border and is known for its medicinal uses in healing colds, fever, and colic, and for its sedating quality while inducing perspiration to break a fever. Charles R. Hart, *Brush and Weeds of Texas Rangelands* (College Station: Texas A&M UP, 2008); http://www.cloverleaffarmherbs.com/sage/.

72. Dodson, *Don Pedrito Jaramillo, "Curandero,"* 21.

73. Paredes, *Folklore and Culture*, 51–52.

74. Paredes, 53.

75. Paredes, "Folk Medicine and the Intercultural Jest," in *Folklore and Culture*, 49–72.

76. Dodson, *Don Pedrito Jaramillo, "Curandero,"* 27–28.

77. Dodson, 27–28.

78. In the cure stories recounted in Dodson, there is some slippage between racial and national differences. Anglos are often identified as "Americans," including the Hernándezes' "American owner" of the ranch they worked for. It is possible that Manuel Hernández and his parents were American citizens as well as being ethnic Mexicans, but whether or not an ethnic Mexican was a US citizen, they would not be called "American," a term used only for Anglos. Dodson, *Don Pedrito Jaramillo, "Curandero,"* 27.

79. Dodson, 27.

80. Dodson, 27.

81. Henri Ellenberger, quoted in Harrington, *The Cure Within*, 42. Ellenberger, *The Discovery of the Unconscious: The History and Evolution of Dynamic Psychiatry* (New York: Basic Books, 1970), 57.

82. Dodson, *Don Pedrito Jaramillo, "Curandero,"* 28.

83. Torres, *Healing with Herbs and Rituals*; and Alberto Treviño-Hernández, *Curanderos: They Heal the Sick with Prayers and Herbs* (Tucson: Hats Off Books, 2005).

84. Dr. Robert Trotter, interview by author, Dallas, TX, Oct. 29, 2014.

85. Trotter interview.

86. In his study of Mexican border folk songs, Américo Paredes explains how "the inhabitants on both river banks continued to be the same people, with the same traditions, preserved in the same legends and the same songs." Paredes, *A Texas-Mexican Cancionero*, xvii.

87. For the Mexican–American War and the ways those who protested it in the United States shaped it, see Amy S. Greenberg, *A Wicked War: Polk, Lincoln, and the 1846 U.S. Invasion of Mexico* (New York: Alfred A. Knopf, 2012); for a northern Mexican perspective on the creation of the border after the war, see Juan Mora-Torres, *The Making of the Mexican Border: The State, Capitalism, and Society in Nuevo León, 1848–1910* (Austin: University of Texas Press, 2001).

88. For examples of the fluidity of the border in this period, see George Díaz, *Border Contraband: A History of Smuggling Across the Río Grande* (Austin: University of Texas Press, 2015); Paredes, *"With His Pistol in His Hand"*; and Elliot Young, *Caterino Garza's Revolution on the Texas-Mexico Border* (Durham: Duke UP, 2004).

89. One historian describes how Anglos became dominant in South Texas through intermarriage and *compadrazgo* (god-parentage) with elite Tejanos, and through outright violence and intimidation. David Montejano, *Anglos and Mexicans*, 34–36. The dispossession of Tejano landowners and the "proletarianization" of Tejano labor during this period have been covered by many historians, including Armando Alonzo, *Tejano Legacy: Rancheros and Settlers in South Texas, 1734–1900* (Albuquerque: University of New Mexico Press, 1998); Daniel D. Arreola, *A Mexican Cultural Province: Tejano South Texas* (Austin: University of Texas Press, 2002); Timothy P. Bowman, *Blood Oranges: Colonialism and Agriculture in the South Texas*

Borderlands (Texas A&M UP, 2016); De León, *The Tejano Community* and *They Called Them Greasers*; Jovita González, "Social Life in Cameron, Starr, and Zapata Counties," MA thesis, University of Texas at Austin, 1930; and Montejano, *Anglos and Mexicans*.

90. Rodolfo Acuña, *Occupied America: The Chicano Struggle for Liberation*; Albert Camarillo, *Chicanos in a Changing Society*, 143; and John R. Chávez, "Aliens in Their Native Lands: The Persistence of Internal Colonial Theory," *Journal of World History* 22, no. 4 (2011): 785–809. For the connection between intimacy and internal colonialism in the Southwest, see Linda Gordon, "Internal Colonialism and Gender," in *Haunted By Empire: Geographies of Intimacy in North American History*, ed. Ann Laura Stoler (Durham, NC: Duke UP, 2006), 427–451.

91. Montejano, *Anglos and Mexicans*, 50–68.

92. Montejano, 52.

93. Montejano, 52.

94. Quoted in Montejano, 32. Juan Cortina was a great-uncle to J. T. Canales, and Canales wrote two books about him: *Juan N. Cortina: Bandit or Patriot* (1951) and *Juan N. Cortina Presents His Motion for a New Trial* (1951). Evan Anders, "CANALES, JOSE TOMAS," Handbook of Texas Online, http://www.tshaonline.org /handbook/online/articles/fcaag (accessed June 11, 2015). Published by the Texas State Historical Association.

95. Montejano, *Anglos and Mexicans*, 32–33: Jerry Thompson, "CORTINA, JUAN NEPOMUCENO," Handbook of Texas Online, http://www.tshaonline.org /handbook/online/articles/fco73 (accessed June 2, 2015). For a biography of Cortina, see Jerry Thompson, *Cortina: Defending the Mexican Name in Texas* (College Station: Texas A&M UP, 2007).

96. Caterino Garza was a second cousin of J. T. Canales. Canales, "Personal Recollections," 7.

97. For an in-depth study of Caterino Garza's rebellion, see Elliot Young, *Caterino Garza's Revolution on the Texas-Mexico Border* (Durham. NC: Duke UP, 2004).

98. Information in this paragraph on the Garzas' and Don Pedrito's possible connection to the Garzistas comes from conversations with Homero Vero, the former editor and publisher of *El Mesteño* magazine and the South Texas field historian with Texas A&M University–Kingsville TAMUK Archives; and Young, *Caterino Garza's Revolution*, 52–54.

99. J. T. Canales, "Personal Recollections," 2. One historian of South Texas has pointed out that after the 1850s, "the management of the agrarian economy progressively fell into the hands of Anglo American Capitalists intent on using the labor of Mexicanos." De León, *Tejano Community*, 50.

100. Dodson, "Don Pedrito Jaramillo: The Curandero of Los Olmos," 9–10.

101. Dodson, 9–10.

102. Dodson, 9–10.

103. For use of water to cure a migraine, see Dodson, *Don Pedrito Jaramillo*, "Curandero," 21–22.

104. For the Panic of 1893 and the following years of depression, see Jackson Lears, *Rebirth of a Nation: The Making of Modern America, 1877–1920* (New York: HarperCollins, 2009), 169–195.

105. Lasater, *Falfurrias*, 38.

106. Montejano, *Anglos and Mexicans*, 67–69; for one example of a Tejano rancher who was forced to kill off his horses so that they would not eat the scarce grass or drink the water, see Montejano, 61.

107. Ramiro Rodríguez, conversation with the author at the Falfurrias Heritage Museum, Falfurrias, TX, February 18, 2014.

108. Quoted in Lasater, *Falfurrias*, 37.

109. Montejano, *Anglos and Mexicans*, 61–62. For a celebratory description of Anglo ranchers buying up land in South Texas during the Great Die-Up, see Lasater, *Falfurrias*, 37–53.

110. For Andrés Canales's land sales to King in 1892, 1895, and 1896, see Montejano, *Anglos and Mexicans*, 65–66.

111. "Terrible Tale of Torture, Slow Deaths by Starvation in Starr County, A Vision Seen in the Heavens That is Interpreted to Mean No More Rain Will Fall For a Year," *San Antonio Express*, April 15, 1894, 11.

112. "Terrible Tale of Torture," 11.

113. "Terrible Tale of Torture," 11.

114. Sixto García does not specify, but he may have been referring to prophesy in the Old Testament Book of Zechariah 13:8 (Apologetics Study Bible) that states: "In the whole land—the Lord's declaration—two-thirds will be cut off and die, but a third will be left in." He also may have been referring to the New Testament Book of Revelation 9:15 (Apologetics Study Bible): "So the four angels who were prepared for the hour, day, month, and year were released to kill a third of the human race."

115. "Terrible Tale of Torture," *San Antonio Express*, April 15, 1894, 11.

116. "Terrible Tale of Torture," 11. The miasma theory of disease, which was supported by the ancient Greek physician Hippocrates and prevailed from the fourth or fifth century BCE until the discovery of the germ theory of disease transmission in the late nineteenth century by Louis Pasteur and Robert Koch, proposed that the origin of epidemic diseases was "corrupt air" or "miasma" emanating from rotting organic matter (such as the dead cattle Sixto Garcia described). The popularity of this idea was slow to die, even when science had disproved it with the germ theory. John M. Last, "Miasma Theory," in *Encyclopedia of Public Health*, ed. Lester Breslow (New York: Macmillan Reference, 2001), 765.

117. Andrés Sáenz, *Early Tejano Ranching: Daily Life at Ranchos San José and El Fresnillo* (College Station: Texas A&M Press, 1999), 20–21, 42–43; and Lasater, *Falfurrias*, 73.

118. Lasater, *Falfurrias*, 73. Ruth Dodson describes how Don Pedrito bought sometimes four to five hundred dollars' worth of groceries at a time in Alice, and that he farmed a hundred acres of land (a gift from a grateful client), growing corn, watermelons, beans, peppers, and garlic to add to his food stores and to use in his cures. Dodson, "Don Pedrito Jaramillo: The Curandero of Los Olmos," 13–14.

119. For the Albino Canales quote, see Dodson, 14.

120. Dodson, *Don Pedrito Jaramillo, "Curandero,"* 14; Lasater, *Falfurrias*, 73.

121. Another example of Don Pedrito supporting this community is when he donated money for the purchase of a bell for the Catholic church in 1905. Although Don Pedrito did not attend church, he understood the importance of a church bell for this community as a means to communicate and draw people together. Ruth Dodson tells this story in "Don Pedrito Jaramillo: The Curandero of Los Olmos,"

and direct descendants of the man who approached Don Pedrito, Lino Treviño—Lourdes Treviño Cantu and her mother, Maria Lemus Treviño—relayed this story to me on March 2, 2019, in Falfurrias. Don Lino Olivares Treviño was a founder of Paisano (later Falfurrias) and the first justice of the peace of Starr County (later Brooks County).

122. This information comes from the author's conversations between July 2018 and July 2019 with Gonzo Flores, the current owner of the Don Pedrito Jaramillo Shrine. Mr. Flores, from George West, TX, has deep roots in the South Texas Río Grande Valley region. He is descended from Lipan Apache and Mexican parents and comes from a family with a long line of healers, some who knew Don Pedrito. His great-grandmother Petra Longoria was a healing curandera "assistant" to Don Pedrito as well as a leader of the Sun Otter Clan-Lipan Apache Tribe of Texas; his grandmother Grabiella Pena performed her first healing at the Don Pedrito Jaramillo Shrine in 1923, when she reset her mother's broken arm. Today Flores lives with his family in Portland, OR, and is an active Apache medicine man or, more accurately, a "carrier of traditional medicines"—particularly the "Ghost medicine" (peyote)—and a curandero, specifically a *yerbero* and a *peyotero*. Flores is a member of the Lipan Apache Tribe of Texas.

123. More work needs to be done on the exact numbers of Indigenous people that Don Pedrito healed. For ethnic Mexican numbers, one historian of the border presents population estimates for Cameron, Starr, and Webb Counties (the approximate area that Don Pedrito worked in) that claim 90 to 91 percent of the population in these counties identified as Mexican American. Valerio-Jiménez, *River of Hope*, 148. For the presence of ethnic Mexicans and the dominance of Mexican culture in South Texas at the turn of the twentieth century, see Jovita González, *Life Along the Border: A Landmark Tejana Thesis*, ed. María Eugenia Cotera (College Station: Texas A&M University, 2006); Paredes, *A Texas-Mexican Cancionero*, 153; and Benjamin Heber Johnson, *Revolution in Texas: How a Forgotten Battle and Its Bloody Suppression Turned Mexicans Into Americans* (New Haven, CT: Yale UP, 2003), 26–27.

Chapter 4. In the Clutches of Black Magic

1. For Fidencio, see Kay F. Turner, "'Because of This Photography': The Making of a Mexican Folk Saint," in Dore Gardner, *Niño Fidencio, A Heart Thrown Open* (Santa Fe: Museum of New Mexico Press, 1992), 120–134; and Antonio N. Zavaleta, "El Niño Fidencio and the *Fidencistas*," in *Sects, Cults, and Spiritual Communities: A Sociological Analysis*, ed. William W. Zellner and Marc Petrowsky (Westport, CT: Praeger, 1998), 95–115. For Calles's skin ailment, see Jürgen Buchenau, *Plutarco Elías Calles and the Mexican Revolution* (Lanham, MD: Rowman and Littlefield, 2007), 197; Zavaleta, "El Niño Fidencio," 103; Gardner, *Niño Fidencio*, 5, 124; and Paul J. Vanderwood, *Juan Soldado: Rapist, Murderer, Martyr, Saint* (Durham, NC: Duke UP, 2004), 216.

2. After healing Calles, Fidencio wrote letters to the president asking him to stop the Department of Health from closing down his healing practice because of alleged disease outbreaks. Calles intervened for Fidencio; he even ordered a pipeline built from a nearby spring to carry water to Espinazo, which to this day is the

only source of water for the town. Plutarco Elías Calles, *Plutarco Elías Calles: Correspondencia Personal, 1919–1945, Introducción, Selección y Notas de Carlos Macías* (Mexico City: Gobierno del Estado de Sonora: Instituto Sonorense de Cultura: Fideicomiso Archivos Plutarco Elías Calles y Fernando Torreblanco: Fondo de Cultura Económica, 1991), 342–343, 347–348. The pipeline is mentioned in Buchenau, *Plutarco Elías Calles and the Mexican Revolution*, 197; Zavaleta, "El Niño Fidencio and the Fidencistas," 103; and Zavaleta and Salinas, *Curandero Conversations*, 13.

3. "Calles Visitó al Famoso Fidencio," *La Prensa*, February 15, 1928, 1. Calles's visit to el Niño Fidencio is also discussed in Buchenau, *Plutarco Elías Calles*, 196; Gardner, *Niño Fidencio*, 124; Griffith, *Folk Saints of the Borderlands*, 123–133; Alan Knight, "The Mentality and Modus Operandi of Revolutionary Anticlericalism," in *Faith and Impiety in Revolutionary Mexico*, ed. Matthew Butler (New York: Palgrave Macmillan, 2007), 31, 42; Antonio N. Zavaleta and Alberto Salinas, *Curandero Conversations: El Niño Fidencio, Shamanism and Healing Traditions of the Borderlands* (Bloomington, IN: AuthorHouse, 2009), 13; and Zavaleta, "El Niño Fidencio," 103.

4. "Mexico en Las Garras de la Magia Negra," originally titled "Era Jaramillo el último de los alquimistas, y como tal, presidia ese mundo sobrenatural. En ruinosa cabaña contigua al Río Grande pasaba la noche en vela desentrañado secretos, urdeindo encantos, perfeccionando la ciencia oculta."

5. Even though Lozano was part of this "México de Afuera" group, he understood that others in his community did not identify this way. In fact, it appears that J. T. Canales and Lozano were friends. A letter from Carlos Castañeda to J. T. Canales closed with this remark: "I am looking forward to seeing you in San Antonio on Friday at the dinner in honor of our mutual friend, Don Ignacio Lozano." J. T. Canales Collection, Correspondence File, Box 436A, South Texas Archives, Texas A&M–Kingsville. Lozano was also the first to publish Ruth Dodson's book about Jaramillo through his press, Casa Editorial Lozano. Dodson, *Don Pedrito Jaramillo, "Curandero"* (1934).

6. For "México de Afuera," see Sánchez, "From Pocholandia to Aztlán," 28–60. Américo Paredes describes the complexity of "México de Afuera" by explaining that Mexicans in the United States are not a monolithic group, but composed of three strands: urban exiled elites, regional groups like Tejanos, and migratory laborers. Paredes, *Folklore and Culture*, 1–18.

7. One postcolonial scholar describes the way exiled elites create an idealized past for their national imaginary. Robert C. J. Young, *Postcolonialism: A Very Short Introduction* (Oxford: Oxford UP, 2003), 63.

8. Another *La Prensa* article described Calles's visit to El Niño Fidencio, suggesting that Calles secretly left the capital city, hiding from "las grandes eminencias médicas" (great eminent doctors) and "los políticos metropolitanos" (metropolitan politicians) in order to visit El Niño Fidencio. "Calles Visitó el Famoso Fidencio," *La Prensa*, February 15, 1928, 1.

9. For northern Mexico as a place of barbarism, superstition, and fierce independence, see Ana María Alonso, *Thread of Blood: Colonialism, Revolution, and Gender on Mexico's Northern Frontier* (Tucson: University of Arizona Press, 1995), esp. 15–17; and Friedrich Katz, *The Secret War in Mexico* (Chicago: University of Chicago Press, 1981). For late eighteenth-century enlightenment ideas about civili-

zation and barbarism on the Spanish frontier, see David J. Weber, *Bárbaros: Spaniards and Their Savages in the Age of Enlightenment* (New Haven: Yale UP, 2005).

10. "Mexico en las Garras de la Magia Negra" (Mexico in the Clutches of Black Magic), *La Prensa*, March 11, 1928, 15.

11. "Mexico en las Garras," 15. Original Spanish: "una especie de brujo y de curandero que la ciencia no puede tomar en serio," and "El último de los alquimistas, Pedro Jaramillo." All translations are by the author.

12. J. T. Canales, "Don Pedrito Jaramillo curaba a los enfermos pobres, desahuciados" (Don Pedrito Jaramillo cured poor, sick people and the terminally ill), *La Prensa*, March 21, 1928.

13. Canales, "Don Pedrito Jaramillo curaba a los enfermos."

14. In Canales, "Don Pedrito Jaramillo curaba los enfermos." Canales wrote: "Don Pedrito Jaramillo fue un poderoso sanador . . . un labrador humilde, y un hombre bueno, que practicaba las virtudes cristiansas: Muy compasivo y caritativo con la gente pobre."

15. For two mentions of Don Pedrito Jaramillo as the "Benefactor of Humanity," see Dodson, "Don Pedrito Jaramillo: The Curandero of Los Olmos," 11; and Romano, "Don Pedrito Jaramillo," 109.

16. For *brujería* and curanderismo as oppositional, see Perrone, Stockel, and Krueger, *Medicine Women*, 177–196. For a feminist non-oppositional interpretation of *brujas* and curanderas, see Ana Castillo, "Brujas and Curanderas," in *Massacre of the Dreamers*, 145–161, esp. 157.

17. J. T. Canales received his law degree from the University of Michigan Law School in 1899 and returned to South Texas to practice law in Corpus Christi, Laredo, and eventually Brownsville. Canales, "Personal Recollections," 10–11.

18. J. T. Canales editorial published in *La Prensa*, "Don Pedrito Jaramillo Curaba a los Enfermos," March 21, 1928; Lilia Aurora Cruz, "New Light On Pedro Jaramillo," 62; Dodson, "Don Pedrito Jaramillo: The Curandero of Los Olmos," 15; Garza, "En el Nombre de Dios," 12–14; and Lasater, *Falfurrias*, 7.

19. Garza, "En el Nombre de Dios," 11.

20. Ruth Dodson recounted that when the mail began to be delivered to Los Olmos by stagecoach rather than horseback, "much of Don Pedrito's work was done by mail, and he received as many as two hundred letters a week, often with money or stamps enclosed in them." Dodson, "Don Pedrito Jaramillo: The Curandero of Los Olmos," 15.

21. J. T. Canales, "Don Pedrito Jaramillo Curaba los Enfermos."

22. James Harvey Young, *The Medical Messiahs: A Social History of Health Quackery in Twentieth-Century America*, 66–87.

23. *Herald of Health*, published by Dr. William O. Bye Combination Oil Cure Co., 1901, in the American Medical Association Historic Health Fraud Collection, Box 106, Folder 6, "Bye Cancer Cures."

24. The "Bye Cancer Cures" file at the AMA Historic Health Fraud Collection reveals a long history of the issuance of fraud orders against Bye. Young, *Medical Messiahs*, 84–85.

25. Quoted in Dodson, "Don Pedrito Jaramillo: The Curandero of Los Olmos," 16. Dodson explains how scarce physicians were in the South Texas Valley at the time of Jaramillo: "At that time there was only one doctor between Corpus Christi

and Laredo, at San Diego." Dodson, "Don Pedrito Jaramillo: The Curandero of Los Olmos," 12. Dodson describes one rural doctor who healed over the same area as Don Pedrito: "The late Dr. J. S. Strickland, who knew Don Pedrito better than any other doctor in the country, who covered the same territory he did, and who no doubt treated the same patients at times when neither knew it, and that Don Pedrito was a smart but uneducated man, and that he did perform wonderful cures." Dodson, "Don Pedrito Jaramillo: The Curandero of Los Olmos," 16.

26. Dr. J. S. Strickland, quoted in Dodson, "Don Pedrito Jaramillo: The Curandero of Los Olmos," 16.

27. For professional medicine claiming cultural authority by invoking Protestant morality, see Timothy E. W. Gloege, "Faith Healing, Medical Regulation, and Public Religion in Progressive Era Chicago," *Religion and American Culture: A Journal of Interpretation* 23, no. 2: 185–231. For the "rise of the professions," see Robert M. Crunden, *Ministers of Reform: The Progressives' Achievement in American Civilization, 1889–1920* (New York: Basic Books, 1982).

28. For the enforcement of the professionalization of medicine in Texas in the nineteenth and twentieth centuries, see Calli Johnson Vaquera, "'If 3000 Men Were Unanimous On Any Subject, You Would Know At Once They Were Not Doctors': The Slow and Difficult Path To Professionalization of Medicine In Texas," MA thesis, University of Texas at Arlington, 2006. For the AMA's fight against medical fraud at the end of the century, see Young, *Medical Messiahs*.

29. "Does it Pay to Be a Doctor?," *JAMA* 42 (January 23, 1904): 247. Quoted in Paul Starr, *The Social Transformation of American Medicine* (New York: Basic Books, 1982), 85.

30. "Why Is the Profession Poor in the Purse?," in *Journal of the American Medical Association* (May 1899); "Causes of the Decline of Physicians' Income," in *Medical News* (October 1897).

31. Dean of Tulane, quoted in Vaquera, "'If 3000 Men Were Unanimous,'" 10.

32. Vaquera, 62–64.

33. See John B. Huber, *Faith Cures and the Law* (New York: Publishers' Printing Company, 1901), 3, in the American Medical Association Historic Health Fraud Collection, Box 142, Folder 23.

34. "Medicine Men in Council," *San Antonio Daily Express*, April 26, 1894.

35. Huber, *Faith Cures and the Law*, 6–9.

36. Huber, 6–9.

37. Francis Schlatter (1856–1897) was also called "the New Mexico Messiah" and "El Gran Hombre" (The Great Man). He died of unknown causes in Chihuahua, Mexico, in 1897. A German immigrant and a Catholic, Schlatter believed he had been given a gift from God to heal, and he traveled throughout the Southwest at the end of the nineteenth century healing Anglos, Hispanos, and ethnic Mexicans by touch and use of a "divine rod." Schlatter's adherents called him "El Sanador" (The Healer) because he drew on the curanderismo tradition prevalent in the Southwest. See Ada Morely Jarrett, *The Life of the Harp in the Hand of the Harper* (Denver: Privately printed, 1897); Norman Cleaveland, *The Healer: The Story of Francis Schlatter* (Santa Fe, NM: Sunstone, 1989); Ferenc M. Szasz, "Francis Schlatter: The Healer of the Southwest," in *Mystic Healers and Medicine Shows: Blazing Trails to Wellness in the Old West and Beyond*, ed. Gene Fowler (Santa Fe, NM: Ancient City, 1997), 15–

30. One journalist compared Teresa Urrea to Schlatter: "She has healed the sick in much the same way that Schlatter did in Colorado last year"; in "Mexican Jeanne D'Arc," *Los Angeles Herald*, September 18, 1896.

38. Don Pedrito became so popular that when he would leave for a healing trip to San Antonio, Corpus Christi, or Laredo, he would order a wagonful of groceries from a general store in the nearby town of Alice to be delivered to Los Olmos to feed as many as five hundred people who might be camped out in the Los Olmos arroyo awaiting his return. Dodson, *Don Pedrito Jaramillo*, "Curandero," 12–13.

39. "Saint Don Pedrito," *Dallas Morning News*, April 21, 1894.

40. "Saint Don Pedrito." Walter Prescott Webb argued that the "cruel streak" as well as the "ignorance and superstition" in Mexicans could be attributed to their "Indian Blood." Webb, *The Texas Rangers: A Century of Frontier Defense* (Austin: University of Texas Press, 1935), 13–14.

41. Hawkins, "She Is Not a Saint," *Los Angeles Times*, September 20, 1896, 19. For an examination of how twentieth- and twenty-first century curanderos claim ancient Aztec knowledge as the basis of their practice, see Hendrickson, *Border Medicine*, esp. chap. 6, "Reclaiming the Past and Redefining the Present," 100–171. For the various ways Aztec history has been interpreted to suit different nation-building projects, see Benjamin Keen, *The Aztec Image in Western Thought* (New Brunswick, NJ: Rutgers UP, 1990).

42. John G. Bourke, "The American Congo," *Scribner's* 25, no. 5 (1894). For a full-length biography of Bourke, see Joseph C. Porter, *Paper Medicine Man: John Gregory Bourke and His American West* (Norman: University of Oklahoma Press, 1986). For Caterino Garza's rebellion, see Young, *Caterino Garza's Revolution*.

43. Bourke, "The American Congo," 594; Joseph Conrad, *The Heart of Darkness: An Authoritative Text, Background and Sources Criticism* (New York: W. W. Norton, 1963).

44. An article that puts Bourke's "The American Congo" in conversation with Jovita Gonzaléz's 1930 University of Texas master's thesis is María Eugenia Cotera, "Refiguring 'The American Congo': Jovita González, John Gregory Bourke, and the Battle Over Ethno-Historical Representations of the Texas Mexican Border," *Western American Literature* 35, no. 1 (Spring 2000): 75–94.

45. In his publications and private journals, Bourke dedicated hundreds of pages to the cataloging of herbs and medicinal remedies of Apaches, Mexicans, and other groups. Other publications by Bourke include: "Superstition of the Río Grande: Popular Medicine, Customs, and Superstitions of the Río Grande," *Journal of American Folklore* 7, no. 25 (April–June 1894): 119–146; *The Medicine Men of the Apache, Ninth Annual Report of the Bureau of Ethnology, 1887–188* (Washington, DC: Government Printing Office, 1892); *The Snake Dance of the Moquis of Arizona* (New York: Charles Scribner's Sons, 1884); *Scatalogic Rites of All Nations* (Washington, DC: W. H. Lowdermilk, 1891); and *On the Border with Crook* (New York: Charles Scribner's Sons, 1891).

46. Bourke, quoted in Porter, *Paper Medicine Man*, 293.

47. Bourke, quoted in Porter, 293.

48. Adam Hochschild, *King Leopold's Ghost: A Story of Greed, Terror, and Heroism in Colonial Africa* (Boston: Houghton Mifflin, 1998); Kristin L. Hoganson, *Fighting for American Manhood: How Gender Politics Provoked the Spanish-American*

and Philippine-American Wars (New Haven: Yale UP, 1998); Alexandra Minna Stern, "Yellow Fever Crusade: U.S. Colonialism, Tropical Medicine and the International Politics of Mosquito Control, 1900-1920," in *Medicine at the Border: Disease, Globalization and Security, 1850 to the Present,* ed. Alison Bashford (London: Palgrave Macmillan, 2006), 41-59; and Mckiernan-Gonzalez, *Fevered Measures.*

49. Mckiernan-González, 33-35.

50. Quoted in Mckiernan-González, 49.

51. Espinosa, *Epidemic Invasions,* 31-32.

52. Mckiernan-González describes the racial politics of the quarantines involving both northern Mexico and South Texas during the outbreaks of yellow fever in 1882, 1889, and 1903. Mckiernan-González, *Fevered Measures,* 35-77.

53. Quoted in McKiernan-González, 57.

54. Espinosa, *Epidemic Invasions,* 4.

55. Mckiernan-González, *Fevered Measures,* 48-49.

56. Mckiernan-González, 21-58, esp. 39-40.

57. Mckiernan-González, 48.

58. Mckiernan-González, 49. The involvement of the state in public health measures and the establishment and growth of national health organizations were main features of tropical medicine. Institutions such as the London School of Tropical Medicine, the Royal Society of Tropical Medicine and Hygiene, the Pasteur Institute, the American Society of Tropical Medicine, the Johns Hopkins Rockefeller Institute, and the Harvard Department of Tropical Medicine all emerged at this time as places to research tropical diseases, train physicians in the unique field of tropical medicine, and to assist the state in areas where these diseases affected national and imperial interests. As the Brownsville Quarantine demonstrates, in the United States, the military played a significant role in enforcing public health measures connected with tropical disease through the United States Marine Hospital Service (USMHS).

59. Anthony J. Mazzaferri, "Public Health and Social Revolution in Mexico: 1877-1930," PhD diss., Kent State University, 1968, 48-55.

60. Mazzaferri, 46. Another factor that contributed to the initial lack of success in dealing with yellow fever outbreaks in Mexico was that during this period only the president of the republic, Porfirio Díaz, had power over quarantines, not state boards, as was the case in the United States and Canada. Yet Díaz's authoritarian style of rule eventually helped consolidate and centralize public health initiatives in Mexico, something that APHA members, as well as other figures in tropical medicine and advocates of public health, supported. In the case of yellow fever epidemics in Mexico, although the Consejo Superior de Salubridad was only empowered in Mexico City and had no authority to enforce the new 1891 Sanitary Code in the port cities and frontier districts, most of the states affected by yellow fever requested the federal government to direct the Consejo Superior de Salubridad to oversee the yellow fever campaign in their states. Through these state-supported efforts Mexico was able to suppress yellow fever throughout the nation by 1910. By the end of the Mexican Revolution and the passage of the 1917 Constitution, the Consejo Superior de Salubridad became the federal public health department with authority to respond to epidemics in all states of the Mexican Republic. Claudia Agostoni, *Monuments of Progress: Modernization and Public Health in Mexico City, 1876-1910* (Calgary

and Boulder, CO: University of Calgary Press and the University Press of Colorado, 2003); Claudia Agostoni, "Popular Health Education and Propaganda in Times of Peace and War in Mexico City, 1890s-1920s," *American Journal of Public Health* 96, no. 1 (2006); Claudia Agostini, "Estrategias, Actores, Promesas y Temores," *Ciência y Saúde Coletiva* 16, no. 2 (2011); Ana María Carrillo, "Economía, Política y Salud Pública en el México Porfiriano (1876-1910)," *Ciências, Saúde-Manguinhos* 9 (2002); Mariola Espinosa, *Epidemic Invasions: Yellow Fever and the Limits of Cuban Independence, 1878-1930* (Chicago: University of Chicago Press, 2009).

61. Two historians have examined the ways in which Mexicans in the United States, regardless of citizenship status, have come to be associated with illegality through immigration law and the creation of the Border Patrol. Kelly Lytle Hernández, *Migra! A History of the U.S. Border Patrol* (Berkeley: University of California Press, 2010); and Mae M. Ngai, *Impossible Subjects: Illegal Aliens and the Making of Modern America* (Princeton, NJ: Princeton UP, 2004).

62. Sierra, *Political Evolution of the Mexican People*, 62.

63. Justo Sierra, quoted in Alan Knight, "Racism, Revolution, and *Indigenismo*: Mexico, 1910-1094," in *The Idea of Race in Latin America, 1870-1940*, ed. Richard Graham (Austin: University of Texas Press, 1990), 78.

64. Francisco G. Cosmes, from *La Dominación Española y la Patria Mexicana* (Mexico City, 1896), quoted in Keen, *Aztec Image in Western Thought*, 435.

65. However, revolutionary *indigenismo* was a non-Indian construct forged by a group of elitist, Mestizo, nationalist intellectuals. Knight, "Racism, Revolution, and *Indigenismo*," 82.

66. Manuel Gamio, *Forjando Patria: Pro-nacionalismo* (Forging a Nation), trans. and ed. Fernando Armstrong-Fumero (Boulder: University Press of Colorado, 2010), 10-12 (originally published in Mexico City, 1916); Keen, *Aztec Image in Western Thought*, 470-471; Lesley Byrd Simpson, *Many Mexicos* (Berkeley: University of California Press, 1960).

67. Gamio, quoted in Knight, "Racism, Revolution, and *Indigenismo*," 77.

68. Gamio, *Forjando Patria*, 97.

69. Gamio, 97-99.

70. José Vasconcelos, *The Cosmic Race/La Raza Cósmica*, trans. Didier T. Jaén (Baltimore: Johns Hopkins UP, 1997). Although Vasconcelos presented a critique of 1920s US racism by celebrating *mestizaje* as opposed to the American embrace of white racial purity, he viewed the African race as inferior. One historian explains: "Mestizaje redeems blacks essentially by obliterating them." Neil Foley, *Quest For Equality: The Failed Promise of Black-Brown Solidarity* (Cambridge: Harvard UP, 2010), 8. For the positive aspects of Vasconcelos's racial theory, see Benjamin H. Johnson, "The Cosmic Race in Texas: Racial Fusion, White Supremacy, and Civil Rights Politics," *Journal of American History* (September 2011): 404-419.

71. Like Francisco Madero (who considered Vasconcelos a fellow *espiritista* and with whom he cofounded the Anti-Reelectionist Party that overthrew the Díaz regime), Vasconcelos was influenced by esoteric philosophies such as Theosophy and Spiritism. He invoked the language of *espiritismo* when he wrote of a "spiritual renaissance" of a new era he named the "Spiritual" or "Aesthetic" era. Vasconcelos, *Cosmic Race/La Raza Cósmica*, xxii, ix.

72. Johnson, *Revolution in Texas*, 411.

73. For the Plan de San Diego uprising, see Johnson, *Revolution in Texas*. For one example of the violence perpetrated by the Texas Rangers and their allies against ethnic Mexicans, see Johnson, 86.

74. Johnson, 171–176. For an in-depth examination of J. T. Canales's legal fight against the Texas Rangers, see Ribb, "José Tomás Canales and the Texas Rangers."

75. Foley, *Mexicans in the Making of America*, 49; Hernández, *Migra!*, 26–30; Ngai, *Impossible Subjects*, 17–20.

76. For Mexicans as a threat to national health in turn-of-the-century Los Angeles, see Abel, *Tuberculosis and the Politics of Exclusion*; for Mexican illegality, see Ngai, *Impossible Subjects*. For a history of the eugenics movement in the United States, see Alexandra Minna Stern, *Eugenic Nation: Faults and Frontiers of Better Breeding in Modern America* (Berkeley: University of California Press, 2005).

77. Lothrop Stoddard, *Reforging America: The Story of Our Nationhood* (1920; reprint, New York: Charles Scribner's Sons, 1925), 214–215. Stoddard's ideas filtered down to the popular press. The 1920s saw a proliferation of publications about the threat of Mexicans to American identity, including articles in the *Saturday Evening Post* with titles such as "The Mexican Invasion" (April 19, 1930): 43–44; "Wet and Other Mexicans" (February 4, 1928): 10–11; and "The Mexican Conquest" (June 22, 1929): 26. One racist novelist encouraged a Texas congressman to read Stoddard's *The Rising Tide of Color Against White World-Supremacy* to understand the urgent need for immigration restriction. Neil Foley, *The White Scourge: Mexicans, Blacks, and Poor Whites in Texas Cotton Culture* (Berkeley: University of California Press, 1997), 6.

78. Stoddard, *Rising Tide of Color*, 120.

79. In 1929, with the crash of the stock market and the onset of the Great Depression, a more virulent anti-Mexican sentiment would emerge alongside "Repatriation," the voluntary and forcible deportation of over half a million Mexicans that took place from 1929 to 1939. Francisco E. Balderrama and Raymond Rodríguez, *Decade of Betrayal: Mexican Repatriation in the 1930s* (Albuquerque: University of New Mexico Press, 1995); Camille Guerin-Gonzales, *Mexican Workers and the American Dream: Immigration, Repatriation, and California Farm Labor* (New Brunswick, NJ: Rutgers UP, 1994). For the overlooked history of vigilante and state-sanctioned violence against Mexicans in the United States, see William D. Carrigan and Clive Webb, *Forgotten Dead: Mob Violence against Mexicans in the United States, 1848–1928* (Oxford: Oxford UP, 2013).

80. Cynthia Orozco, *No Mexicans, Women, or Dogs Allowed*, 2. For more on J. T. Canales's involvement in LULAC, see Johnson, *Revolution in Texas*, 183–194.

81. "Una Importante Asemblea en Brownsville," *La Prensa*, October 26, 1927, 10. Article II of the LULAC constitution states that their primary goal was to "develop within the members of our race the best, purest, and most perfect type of a true and loyal citizen of the United States of America." A copy of the LULAC constitution is in the J. T. Canales Estate Collection, South Texas Archives at Texas A&M–Kingsville, Box 436B, "Correspondence-LULAC 1953–1954."

82. Orozco, *No Mexicans, Women, or Dogs Allowed*, 147. Orozco provides an overview of the Harlingen Convention and concludes that Mexican Americans who wanted to exclude Mexican citizens did not do so for lack of solidarity with ethnic Mexicans, but out of political necessity. Orozco, 120–150.

83. J. T. Canales, "The Romans of Today," *Lulac News* (February 1932): 5. Quoted in Ben Johnson, "Cosmic Race in Texas," 416. The biographical information in this paragraph comes from Canales, "Personal Recollections"; Ribb, "José Tomás Canales and the Texas Rangers"; and Evan Anders, "CANALES, JOSE TOMAS," Handbook of Texas Online, http://www.tshaonline.org/handbook/online/articles/feaag.

84. The J. T. Canales Estate Collection at the South Texas Library in the Jernigan Library at Texas A&M–Kingsville contains files filled with correspondence and essays demonstrating Canales's activism in defending the representations of Mexican Americans, the Spanish language, and Tejano culture. See letter from J. T. Canales to Mr. Clarence R. Wharton, June 12, 1935, J. T. Canales Estate Collection, Box 435, File "Correspondence."

85. Tomasita Canales died in December 1928, and it is likely that she was very ill in March when *La Prensa* published Canales's defense of Jaramillo, and the memory of Don Pedrito healing his mother must have been foremost in his mind. See Tomasita Canales's Death Certificate, dated December 26, 1928, and signed by J. T. Canales, www.ancestry.com.

86. Dodson, "Don Pedrito Jaramillo: The Curandero of Los Olmos," 10.

87. Quoted in Octavio Romano, "Don Pedrito Jaramillo: The Emergence of a Mexican American Folk Saint," 104. There is also a corrido about Don Pedrito that was written in the 1950s by Spiritualists in Mexico and Texas that channeled Don Pedrito. This is discussed and reprinted in Américo Paredes, *A Texas-Mexican Cancionero*, 114, 120–121.

Conclusion

1. Anzaldúa, *Borderlands/La Frontera*, 25.

2. Anzaldúa, *"La curandera,"* in *Borderlands/La Frontera*, 198–201. My interpretation of *"La curandera"* is informed by AnaLouise Keating, "Shifting Perspectives: Spiritual Activism, Social Transformation, and the Politics of Spirit," in *Entre Mundos/Among Worlds: New Perspectives on Gloria E. Anzaldúa*, ed. AnaLouise Keating (New York: Palgrave Macmillan, 2005), 241–252. Another reading of *"La curandera"* that focuses on its meaning connected to nature and the environment is Inés Hernández-Ávila, "Tierra Tremenda: The Earth's Agony and Ecstasy in the Work of Gloria Anzaldúa," in *Entre Mundos/Among Worlds*, 236–237.

3. The term *subaltern* refers to people outside of the hegemonic power structure who are culturally, socially, politically, and sometimes physically oppressed and marginalized, but who often subvert or strategically accommodate hegemonic authority. See Hommi Babha, *Location of Culture* (New York: Routledge, 1994); and Gayatri Chakravorty Spivak, "Can the Subaltern Speak?," in *Marxism and the Interpretation of Culture*, ed. Cary Nelson and Lawrence Grossberg (Chicago: University of Chicago Press, 1988), 271–313. For border knowledge as subaltern knowledge, see Ramón Saldívar, *The Borderlands of Culture: Américo Paredes and the Transnational Imaginary* (Durham: Duke UP, 2006), 32, 55.

4. In the 2017 fiscal year, 294 immigrants died along the US-Mexico border—104 of them in the Rio Grande Sector, the most among the Customs and Border Patrol's nine sectors. Silvia Foster-Frau, "The Brutal Border," *U.S. News and World Re-*

port, July 10, 2018, https://www.usnews.com/news/national-news/articles/2018–07 –10/brooks-county-in-south-texas-part-of-main-trek-by-immigrants. See also Karla Zabludovsky, "Hunting Humans: The Americans Taking Immigration Into Their Own Hands," in *Newsweek*, July 23, 2014, http://www.newsweek.com/2014/08/01 /hunting-humans-americans-go-war-migrants-260642.html.

5. Molly Hennessy-Fiske, "Skirting Checkpoint Often Deadly: Ranches of Brooks County Become Killing Field for Migrants," *Dallas Morning News*, July 23, 2014, 13.

6. One South Texas rancher interviewed in Zabludovsky, "Hunting Humans," contends that she has no sympathy for "illegals" and prefers to hunt these migrants like animals. In this same article, Zabludovsky discusses the work of Eduardo Canales, a resident of Corpus Christi and founder of the South Texas Human Rights Center, which places water stations on ranches for migrants and helps to identity dead bodies.

7. Debbie Nathan, "The Best Laid Plan," *Texas Monthly* (February 2013), http:// www.texasmonthly.com/articles/the-best-laid-plan/; and Joel Zapata, "Women's Grassroots Revitalization of South El Paso: La Mujer Obrera's Challenge to Gentrification and Urban Neglect," *Río Bravo* 231, no. 1 (Spring 2014): 24–67. Zapata states that 96 percent of the inhabitants of Segundo Barrio are of Mexican origin (50).

8. Zapata, "Women's Grassroots Revitalization of South El Paso," 51. See also "The Battle for El Paso's South Side," *Texas Monthly* (October 2017), https://www .texasmonthly.com/politics/battle-el-pasos-south-side/.

9. Zapata, "Women's Grassroots Revitalization of South El Paso," 52–57.

10. Senator Rodriguez, quoted in "The Battle for El Paso's South Side," *Texas Monthly* (October 2017).

11. Although El Museo Urbano is no longer situated in the former residence of Teresa Urrea, at 500 South Oregon Street in Segundo Barrio, the organization, formed and led by Dr. Yolanda Leyva and Dr. David Dorado Romo, continues the work started in 2011. See David Romo, "Uncaged Art: Finding Life and Light in Art from Detention," *Texas Observer*, April 22, 2019, https://www.texasobserver.org /uncaged-art/.

12. One historian predicts that by 2060, the Hispanic population in the United States will have doubled, and that nearly one in three US residents will be Hispanic by midcentury. Foley, *Mexicans in the Making of America*, 232.

Appendix. Don Pedrito Jaramillo Cure Sample

1. The sample was drawn from the following sources, with most cases (107) coming from Dodson, *Don Pedrito Jaramillo, "Curandero"* (1934) and "Don Pedrito Jaramillo: The Curandero of Los Olmos" (1951), 9–71. The two versions overlap, but there are cures in the 1934 original that are not included in the 1951 "updated" version, and conversely, Dodson added some cure stories to the 1951 version that are not in the original. In 1994, Henrietta Newbury, Ruth Dodson's niece, self-published a version with the same title of the 1934 version, *Don Pedrito Jaramillo, "Curandero."* Newbury's version is basically a word-for-word English translation alongside the Spanish text of the 1934 original, with the addition of a short pref-

ace by Newbury and a copy of two letters Dodson received from the Library of the College of Physicians in Philadelphia requesting copies of *Don Pedrito Jaramillo* for their collection. The additional twenty-eight cures come from the following sources (almost all of the sources listed below draw on Ruth Dodson for the basic contours of Jaramillo's life, and many repeat some of the healing cure accounts she presents; however, I have used only what is different from Dodson in the following sources to add to the cure sample): Arbuckle, "Don Jose and Don Pedrito," 84–86; Gene Fowler, *Mystic Healers and Medicine Shows*, 52; Garza, "En el Nombre de Dios," 18–27; Romano, "Don Pedrito Jaramillo," 89–99; Andrés Sáenz, *Early Tejano Ranching*, 66, 73; Sauvageau, *Stories That Must Not Die*, 13–15, 107–109, 139–142; "Saint Don Pedrito," *Dallas Morning News*, April 21, 1894; "Miracles of Don Pedrito," *San Antonio Express*, April 18, 1894; and "One of Don Pedrito's Cures," *San Antonio Express*, April 19, 1894.

2. One scholar analyzed Jaramillo's cures as presented in Dodson (*Don Pedrito Jaramillo, "Curandero"*) to demonstrate that his healing had appeal across cultures, in particular to Anglos. Hendrickson, *Border Medicine*, 69.

3. Dodson, "Don Pedrito Jaramillo: The Curandero of Los Olmos," 9.

4. Dodson, 7.

5. Dodson, 9–11; and "Folklore Writer Dies Here at 86," unidentified newspaper (probably the *Corpus Christi Caller*) from July 20, 1963, in Ruth Dodson Vertical File, Briscoe Center for American History, University of Texas at Austin.

6. Dobie also grew up on a ranch in South Texas less than fifteen miles from Dodson and read some of her work on folk medicine. He suggested that she write an article on faith healing among Mexicans, which eventually led her to write a whole book about Don Pedrito and his cures. Agnes G. Grimm, "DODSON, VIOLA RUTH," Handbook of Texas Online, http://www.tshaonline.org/handbook/online/articles/fdo06 (accessed November 20, 2014; uploaded June 12, 2010), published by the Texas State Historical Association. For J. Frank Dobie and his views of South Texas Mexicans, see Limón, *Dancing with the Devil*, 43–59; and María Eugenia Cotera, "A Woman of the Borderlands: 'Social Life in Cameron, Starr, and Zapata Counties' and the Origins of Borderlands Discourse," in *Life Along the Border: A Landmark Tejana Thesis* (College Station: Texas A&M UP, 2006), 12–25.

7. Dodson, "Don Pedrito Jaramillo: The Curandero of Los Olmos," 7.

Bibliography

Archival Sources

Arizona Historical Society, Tucson, AZ
    Arthur L. Peck Manuscript
    Albert S. Reynolds Photographic Collection
    Abijah Smith Photographic Collection
    "Out-of-State-Mexico-Soldier, Wars, and Revolutions—Part One" File
    Historic Arizona Newspapers Collection
American Medical Association, Chicago, IL
    Historical Health Fraud and Alternative Medicine Collection
Archivo Histórico, Secretaría del Estado y Despacho de Relaciones Exteriores, Mexico City
    Teresa Urrea, Tomás Urrea, and Lauro Aguirre Extradition Files
Border Heritage Center, El Paso Public Library, El Paso, TX
    Historic El Paso Newspapers
DeGolyer Library, Special Collections, Southern Methodist University, Dallas, TX
    Plutarco Elías Calles: Correspondencia personal, 1919–1945, Introducción, selección y notas de Carlos Macías. Mexico City: Gobierno del Estado de Sonora: Instituto Sonorense de Cultura: Fideicomiso Archivos Plutarco Elías Calles y Fernando Torreblanco: Fondo de Cultura Económica, 1991.
Dolph Briscoe Center for American History, University of Texas at Austin, Vertical Files
    J. T. Canales
    Viola Ruth Dodson
    Unpublished manuscript: José T. Canales, "Personal Recollections of J. T. Canales Written at the Request of and for Use by the Honorable Harbert Davenport in Preparing a Historical Sketch of the Lower Río Grande Valley for the Soil Conservation District, Recently Organized, in Cameron County, Texas," typescript, 1945.
Falfurrias Heritage Museum/Brooks County Historical Society
    Don Pedrito Jaramillo Photograph and Memorabilia Collection

Library of Congress
  *Chronicling America: Historic American Newspapers, Prints and Photographs
    Online Catalog* (PPOC)
National Archives at Fort Worth, Texas
  Records of the United States District Courts for the Southern District of Texas,
    RG 21.
National Archives of the United States, General Records of the US Department of
    State, RG 59
  Despatches From US Consuls in Ciudad Juárez (Paso Del Norte), 1850–1906
  US Department of State, Despatches from US Ministers to Mexico, 1823–1906
  US Department of State, Washington, DC, Consular Reports: Guaymas 1889–91;
    Nuevo Laredo 1871–1906
South Texas Archives, Texas A&M University–Kingsville
  J. T. Canales Estate Collection
  Joe Stanley Graham, Jr., Collection
  Regional Historical Resource Depository Collection
Texas Tech University, Lubbock, Southwest Collection/Special Collections Library
  W. C. Holden and Frances Mayhugh Holden Papers, 1836–1989
  W. C. Holden and Frances Mayhugh Holden Photograph Collection, 1933–1934
University of Texas at El Paso, University Library
  Amador Collection
  Silvestre Terrazas Papers
  Southwest and Border Studies Collection

Published Primary Sources

Aguirre, Lauro, and Teresa Urrea. *¡Tomóchic!* Published serially in *El Independiente*,
  an imprint of the *Evening Tribune*, El Paso, TX, 1896.
Annual Report on the National Board of Health. Washington, DC: Government
  Printing Office, 1881.
Bonney, Sherman J. *Pulmonary Tuberculosis and Its Complications: With Special
  Reference to Diagnosis and Treatment For General Practitioners and Students*.
  Philadelphia and London: W. B. Saunders Company, 1908.
Bourke, John G. "The American Congo." *Scribner's Magazine*, vol. 15, no. 5 (1894).
———. *The Medicine Men of the Apache*. Ninth Annual Report of the Bureau of
  Ethnology, 1887–1888. Washington, DC: Government Printing Office, 1892.
———. "Superstition of the Río Grande: Popular Medicine, Customs, and Supersti-
  tions of the Río Grande." *Journal of American Folklore*, vol. 7, no. 25 (April–June
  1894): 119–146.
Cabeza de Vaca, Álvar Núñez. *The Narrative of Cabeza De Vaca*. A translation of *La
  Relación* (1542) by Rolena Adorno and Patrick Charles Paultz. Lincoln: Univer-
  sity of Nebraska Press, 2003.
Conrad, Joseph. *The Heart of Darkness: An Authoritative Text; Backgrounds and
  Sources Criticism*. 1902. Reprint, New York and London: W. W. Norton, 1963.
Dodson, Ruth. *Don Pedrito Jaramillo, "Curandero."* San Antonio: Casa Editorial Lo-
  zano, 1934.

Frías, Heriberto. *Tomóchic*. 1893. Reprint, Mexico City: Consejo Nacional de la Cultura y las Artes, 1998.

Huber, John B., MD. *Faith Cures and the Law*. New York: Publishers' Printing Company, 1901.

Hunt, John. "National Register of Historic Places Inventory-Nomination: Los Angeles Plaza Historic District/El Pueblo de Los Angeles." US Department of the Interior, National Park Service, Aug. 14, 1982.

Kneipp, Sebastian. *My Water Cure, As Tested Through More Than Thirty Years, and Described for the Healing of Diseases and the Preservation of Health*. Edinburgh and London: William Blackwood and Sons, 1891.

Lowell, Francis C. *Joan of Arc*. Boston and New York: Houghton Mifflin Company, 1896.

Twain, Mark. *Personal Recollections of Joan of Arc by the Sieur Louis de Conte (Her Page and Secretary) Freely Translated Out of the Ancient French into Modern English from the Original Unpublished Manuscripts in the National Archives in France by Jean François Alden*. New York: Harper and Brothers, 1896 and 1899.

Walling, William English. *The Mexican Question: Mexico and American-Mexican Relations Under Calles and Obregon*. New York: Robins Press, 1927.

Newspapers

Arizona Daily Star (Tucson)
Dallas Morning News
DC Morning Times
Duluth (MN) News Tribune
El Estado de Sonora (Nogales, Sonora, Mexico)
El Fronterizo (Tucson, AZ)
El Independiente (El Paso)
El Monitor Republicano (Mexico City, 1889–1893)
El Paso Times
El Popular (Mexico City)
Evening Tribune (El Paso)
Kansas City (MO) Journal
La Ilustración Espírita (Mexico City)
La Prensa (San Antonio)
La Voz de México (Mexico City)
Los Angeles Herald
Los Angeles Record
Los Angeles Times
New York Journal
Omaha (NE) Daily Bee
Philadelphia Inquirer
San Antonio Express
San Antonio Daily Express
San Antonio Light
San Francisco Call

San Francisco Examiner
The Oasis (Nogales, AZ)
Tucson Citizen
Washington Post

Secondary Sources

Online Sources

The Handbook of Texas Online, http://www.tshaonline.org/handbook/online.
The Portal to Texas History, http://texashistory.unt.edu/.Texas State Historical
   Association.

Pamphlet

"The Faith Healer of Los Olmos: Biography of Don Pedrito Jaramillo." Compiled by
   Brooks County Historical Survey Committee, 1972.

Books

Abel, Emily. *Suffering in the Land of Sunshine*. New Brunswick, NJ, and London:
   Rutgers University Press, 2006.
———. *Tuberculosis and the Politics of Exclusion: A History of Public Health and
   Migration to Los Angeles*. New Brunswick, NJ, and London: Rutgers University
   Press, 2007.
Acosta, Teresa Palomo, and Ruthe Winegarten. *Las Tejanas: Three Hundred Years of
   History*. Austin: University of Texas Press, 2003.
Acuña, Rodolfo. *Occupied America: The Chicano Struggle for Liberation*. New York:
   Harper and Row, 1972.
Adams, David Wallace. *Education for Extinction: American Indians and the Board-
   ing School Experience, 1875–1928*. Lawrence: University of Kansas Press, 1995.
Agostoni, Claudia. *Curar, Sanar y Educar: Enfermedad y Sociedad en México, Siglos
   XIX y XX*. Mexico City: Universidad Nacional Autónoma de México, 2008.
———. *Monuments of Progress: Modernization and Public Health in Mexico City,
   1876–1910*. Latin American and Caribbean Series. Calgary: University of Calgary
   Press, and Boulder: University Press of Colorado, 2003.
Aguilar Camín, Héctor, and Lorenzo Meyer. *In the Shadow of the Mexican Revo-
   lution: Contemporary Mexican History, 1910–1989*. Austin: University of Texas
   Press, 1993.
Albanese, Catherine L. *A Republic of Mind and Spirit: A Cultural History of Ameri-
   can Metaphysical Religion*. New Haven and London: Yale University Press, 2007.
Alexander, Benjamin F. *Coxey's Army: Popular Protest in the Gilded Age*. Baltimore:
   Johns Hopkins University Press, 2015.
Almada, Francisco R. *La Rebelión de Tomóchic*. Chihuahua: Talleres Linotipográfi-
   cos del Gobierno del Estado, 1938.
Alonso, Ana María. *Thread of Blood: Colonialism, Revolution, and Gender on Mex-
   ico's Northern Frontier*. Tucson: University of Arizona Press, 1995.
Alonzo, Armando. *Tejano Legacy: Rancheros and Settlers in South Texas, 1734–1900*.
   Albuquerque: University of New Mexico Press, 1998.

Anderson, John Q. *Texas Folk Medicine: 1,333 Cures, Remedies, Preventives and Health Practices*. Austin, TX: Encino Press, 1970.

Andersson, Rani-Herik. *The Lakota Ghost Dance of 1890*. Lincoln: University of Nebraska Press, 2008.

Anzaldúa, Gloria. *Borderlands/La Frontera: The New Mestiza*. San Francisco: Aunt Lute Books, 1987.

Arreola, Daniel D. *A Mexican Cultural Province: Tejano South Texas*. Austin: University of Texas Press, 2002.

Avila, Elena, with Joy Parker. *Woman Who Glows in the Dark: A Curandera Reveals Traditional Aztec Secrets of Physical and Spiritual Health*. New York: Tarcher/Putnam, 1999.

Babha, Hommi. *Location of Culture*. New York: Routledge, 1994.

Balderrama, Francisco E., and Raymond Rodríguez. *Decade of Betrayal: Mexican Repatriation in the 1930s*. Albuquerque: University of New Mexico Press, 1995.

Barr, Juliana. *Peace Came in the Form of a Woman: Indians and Spaniards in the Texas Borderlands*. Chapel Hill: University of North Carolina Press, 2007.

Barstow, Anne Llewellyn. *Heretic, Mystic, Shaman*. Lewiston/Queenston: Edwin Mellen, 1986.

Bay, Ignacio Almada. *Sonora: Historia Breve*. Mexico City: El Colegio de México, Fondo de Cultura Económico, 2010.

Bazant, Jan. *Alienation of Church Wealth in Mexico: Social and Economic Aspects of the Liberal Revolution, 1856–1875*. Cambridge and New York: Cambridge University Press, 1971.

Becker, Marjorie. *Setting the Virgin on Fire: Lázaro Cárdenas, Michoacán Peasants, and the Redemption of the Mexican Revolution*. Berkeley: University of California Press, 1996.

Bederman, Gail. *Manliness and Civilization: A Cultural History of Gender and Race in the United States, 1880–1917*. Chicago: University of Chicago Press, 1995.

Beezley, William H. *Mexican National Identity: Memory, Innuendo, and Popular Culture*. Tucson: University of Arizona Press, 2008.

Bell, Catherine. *Ritual: Perspectives and Dimensions*. Oxford: Oxford University Press, 1997.

Benton-Cohen, Katerine. *Borderline Americans: Racial Division and Labor War in the Arizona Borderland*. Cambridge and London: Harvard University Press, 2009.

Berkhofer, Robert F., Jr. *The White Man's Indians: Images of American Indians from Columbus to the Present*. New York: Alfred A. Knopf, 1978.

Blauner, Robert. *Racial Oppression in America*. New York: Harper and Row, 1972.

Bourke, John G. *The Medicine Men of the Apache*. Ninth Annual Report of the Bureau of Ethnology, 1887–1888. Washington, DC: Government Printing Office, 1892.

———. *On the Border with Crook*. New York: Charles Scribner's Sons, 1891.

———. *Scatalogic Rites of All Nations: A Dissertation upon the Employment of Excrementious Remedial Agents in Religion, Therapuetics, Divination, Witchcraft, Love Philters, etc., in All Parts of the Globe*. Washington DC: W. H. Lowdermilk, 1891.

———. *The Snake Dance of the Moquis of Arizona*. New York: Charles Scribner's Sons, 1884.

Brading, David A. *Church and State in Bourbon Mexico*. New York: Cambridge University Press, 2002.

———. *Mexican Phoenix: Our Lady of Guadalupe: Image and Tradition Across Five Centuries*. Cambridge: Cambridge University Press, 2001.

———. *Miners and Merchants in Bourbon Mexico, 1763–1810*. New York: Cambridge University Press, 2008.

Braude, Anne. *Radical Spirits: Spiritualism and Women's Rights in Nineteenth Century America*. Bloomington and Indianapolis: Indiana University Press, 1989.

Brodsky, Alyvn. *Benjamin Rush: Patriot and Physician*. New York: Truman Talley Books/St. Martin's Press, 2004.

Brooks, James F., Christopher R. N. DeCorse, and John Walton, eds. *Small Worlds: Method, Meaning, and Narrative in Microhistory*. Santa Fe, NM: School for Advanced Research Press, 2008.

Buchenau, Jürgen. *Plutarco Elías Calles and the Mexican Revolution*. Lanham, MD: Rowman and Littlefield, 2007.

Buitron, Richard A., Jr. *The Quest for Tejano Identity in San Antonio, Texas, 1913–2000*. New York: Routledge, 2004.

Butler, Matthew, ed. *Faith and Impiety in Revolutionary Mexico*. New York: Palgrave MacMillan, 2007.

Bynum, Caroline Walker. *Holy Feast and Holy Fast: The Religious Significance of Food to Medieval Women*. Berkeley: University of California Press, 1987.

Bynum, William. *The History of Medicine: A Very Short Introduction*. Oxford: Oxford University Press, 2008.

Cady Stanton, Elizabeth, and Ida Husted Harper, eds. *The History of Woman Suffrage, 1883–1900*. Indianapolis: Hollenbeck, 1902.

Calloway, Colin G. *New Worlds for All: Indians, Europeans, and the Remaking of Early America*. Baltimore: Johns Hopkins University Press, 1997.

Camarillo, Alberto. *Chicanos in a Changing Society: From Mexican Pueblos to American Barrios in Santa Barbara and Southern California*. 1979. Reprint, Dallas: Southern Methodist University Press, 2005.

Camín, Héctor Aguilar. *La Frontera Nómada: Sonora y la Revolución Mexicana*. Mexico City: Ediciones Cal Y Arena, 1971.

Campbell, Randolph B. *Gone to Texas: A History of the Lone Star State*. Oxford: Oxford University Press, 2003.

Carrasco, Davíd. *City of Sacrifice: The Aztec Empire and the Role of Violence in Civilization*. Boston: Beacon, 2000.

Carrigan, William D., and Clive Webb. *Forgotten Dead: Mob Violence against Mexicans in the United States, 1848–1928*. Oxford: Oxford University Press, 2013.

Carrillo, Ricardo A., et al. *Cultura y Bienestar: MesoAmerican Based Healing and Mental Health Practice Based Evidence*. CreateSpace Independent Publishing Platform, 2017.

Cassedy, James H. *Medicine in America: A Short History*. Baltimore: Johns Hopkins University Press, 1991.

Castillo, Ana. *Massacre of the Dreamers: Essays on Xicanisma*. Albuquerque: University of New Mexico Press, 1994.

Chávez, John R. *The Lost Land: The Chicano Image of the Southwest*. Albuquerque: University of New Mexico Press, 1984.

Chavez, Jose Carlos. *Peleando en Tomóchic*. Ciudad Juárez: Imprenta Moderna, 1957.

Chávez Calderón, Plácido. *La Defensa de Tomochi*. Mexico City: Editorial Jus, 1964.

Chestnut, R. Andrew. *Devoted to Death: Santa Muerte, the Skeleton Saint*. Oxford: Oxford University Press, 2012.

Chipman, Donald E. *Álvar Núñez Cabeza de Vaca: The Great Pedestrian of North and South America*. Denton: Texas State Historical Association, 2012.

Christian, William. *Local Religion in Sixteenth Century Spain*. Princeton, NJ: Princeton University Press, 1981.

Cleaveland, Norman. *The Healer: The Story of Francis Schlatter*. Santa Fe, NM: Sunstone, 1989.

Cockcroft, James D. *Intellectual Precursors to the Mexican Revolution, 1900–1913*. Austin and London: University of Texas Press, 1968.

Cohen, I. Bernard. *The Birth of a New Physics*. Rev. ed. New York: W. W. Norton, 1985.

Córdova, James M. *The Art of Professing in Bourbon Mexico: Crowned Nun Portraits and Reform in the Convent*. Austin: University of Texas Press, 2014.

Cortez, Constance. *Carmen Lomas Garza*. Los Angeles: UCLA Chicano Studies Research Press, 2010.

Cosío Villegas, Daniel. *La Constitución de 1857 y Sus Críticos*. Mexico City: Editorial Hérmes, 1957.

Covey, Stephen A. *Early Escondido: The Louis A. Havens Collection*. Charleston, SC: Arcadia, 2008.

Crosby, Molly Caldwell. *The American Plague: The Untold Story of Yellow Fever, the Epidemic that Shaped Our History*. New York: Penguin, 2006.

Crumrine, N. Ross. *The Mayo Indians of Sonora: A People Who Refuse to Die*. Tucson: University of Arizona Press, 1977.

Crunden, Robert M. *Ministers of Reform: The Progressives' Achievement in American Civilization, 1889–1920*. New York: Basic Books, 1982.

Curtis, Heather D. *Faith in the Great Physician: Suffering and Divine Healing in American Culture, 1860–1900*. Baltimore: Johns Hopkins University Press, 2007.

Darnton, Robert. *Mesmerism and the End of the Enlightenment in France*. Cambridge, MA: Harvard University Press, 1968.

Daudistel, Marcia Hatfield, ed. *Grace and Gumption: The Women of El Paso*. Fort Worth: Texas Christian University Press, 2011.

Delay, Brian. *War of a Thousand Deserts: Indian Raids and the U.S.-Mexican War*. New Haven and London: Yale University Press, 2008.

De León, Arnoldo. *The Tejano Community, 1836–1900*. Dallas: Southern Methodist University Press, 1997.

———. *They Called Them Greasers: Anglo Attitudes Toward Mexicans in Texas, 1821–1900*. Austin: University of Texas Press, 1983.

DeLuzio, Crista. *Female Adolescence in American Scientific Thought, 1830–1930*. Baltimore: Johns Hopkins University Press, 2007.

Deutsch, Sarah. *No Separate Refuge: Culture, Class, and Gender on an Anglo-Hispanic Frontier in the American Southwest*. New York: Oxford University Press, 1987.

Dewhurst, Kenneth. *Dr. Thomas Sydenham (1624–1689): His Life and Original Writings*. Berkeley: University of California Press, 1966.

Díaz, George. *Border Contraband: A History of Smuggling across the Río Grande.* Austin: University of Texas Press, 2015.

Dippie, B. W. *The Vanishing American: White Attitudes and U.S. Indian Policy.* Middletown, CT: Wesleyan University Press, 1982.

Dolgin, Ellen Ecker. *Modernizing Joan of Arc: Conceptions, Costumes, and Canonizations.* Jefferson, NC, and London: McFarland, 2008.

Domecq, Brianda. *La Insólita Historia de la Santa de Cabora.* Mexico City: Plantea, 1990.

DuBois, Ellen Carol, and Lynn Dumenil. *Through Women's Eyes: An American History with Documents.* Vol. 1, *To 1900.* 3rd ed. Boston and New York: Bedford/St. Martins, 2012.

DuBois, Ellen Carol, and Richard Cándida Smith, eds. *Elizabeth Cady Stanton, Feminist as Thinker: A Reader in Documents and Essays.* New York: NYU Press, 2007.

Duncan, James S. *In the Shadows of the Tropics: Climate, Race, and Biopower in Nineteenth Century Ceylon.* Hampshire, UK: Ashgate, 2007.

Ebright, Malcolm, and Rick Hendricks. *The Witches of Abiquiu: The Governor, the Priest, the Genízaro Indians, and the Devil.* Albuquerque: University of New Mexico Press, 2006.

Ehrenreich, Barbara, and Deidre English. *Witches, Midwives, and Nurses: A History of Women Healers.* New York: Feminist Press, 1973.

Elias, Norbert. *The Civilizing Process: The History of Manners.* New York: Pantheon Books, 1982.

Ellinghaus, Katherine. *Blood Will Tell: Native Americans and the Assimilation Policy.* Lincoln: University of Nebraska Press, 2017.

Enstad, Nan. *Ladies of Labor, Girls of Adventure: Working Women, Popular Culture, and Labor Politics at the Turn of the Twentieth Century.* New York: Columbia University Press, 1999.

Espinosa, Gastón, and Mario T. García, eds. *Mexican American Religions: Spirituality, Activism, and Culture.* Durham, NC, and London: Duke University Press, 2008.

Espinosa, Mariola. *Epidemic Invasions: Yellow Fever and the Limits of Cuban Independence, 1878–1930.* Chicago and London: University of Chicago Press, 2009.

Fadiman, Anne. *The Spirit Catches You and You Fall Down: A Hmong Child, Her American Doctors, and the Collision of Two Cultures.* New York: Farrar, Straus, Giroux, 1997.

Farge, Emile J. *La Vida Chicana: Health Care Attitudes and Behaviors of Houston Chicanos.* San Francisco: R and E Research Associates, 1975.

Ferris, Sylvia Van Voast, and Eleanor Sellars Hoppe. *Scalpels and Sabers: Nineteenth Century Medicine in Texas.* Austin: Eakin, 1985.

Finkler, Kaja. *Spiritualist Healers in Mexico: Successes and Failures of Alternative Therapeutics.* South Hadley, MA: Bergin and Garvey, 1985.

Flint, Karen E. *Healing Traditions: African Medicine, Cultural Exchange, and Competition in South Africa, 1820–1948.* Athens: Ohio University Press, 2008.

Fogarty, Robert S. *All Things New: American Communes and Utopian Movements, 1860–1914.* Lanham, MD: Lexington Books, 2013.

Foley, Neil. *Mexicans in the Making of America.* Cambridge, MA, and London: Belknap Press of Harvard University, 2014.

———. *Quest for Equality: The Failed Promise of Black-Brown Solidarity.* Cambridge, MA, and London: Harvard University Press, 2010.

———. *The White Scourge: Mexicans, Blacks, and Poor Whites in Texas Cotton Culture.* Berkeley: University of California Press, 1997.

Foster, George M. *Hippocrates' Latin American Legacy: Humoral Medicine in the New World.* Amsterdam: Gordon and Breach Science Publishers, 1994.

Foucault, Michel. *The Birth of the Clinic: An Archaeology of Medical Perception.* New York: Pantheon Books, 1973.

———. *The History of Sexuality.* New York: Random House, 1990.

Fowler, Gene. *Mystic Healers and Medicine Shows: Blazing Trails to Wellness in the Old West and Beyond.* Santa Fe, NM: Ancient City, 1997.

Fowler-Salamini, Heather. *Women of the Mexican Countryside, 1850–1990.* Tucson: University of Arizona Press, 1994.

Gamio, Manuel. *Forjando Patria: Pro-nacionalismo.* Mexico City, 1916. Translated and edited by Fernando Armstrong-Fumero as *Forging a Nation* (Boulder: University Press of Colorado, 2010).

Garcia, Richard A. *Rise of the Mexican American Middle Class, San Antonio, 1929–1941.* College Station: Texas A&M University Press, 1991.

Garcilazo, Jeffrey Marcos. *Traqueros: Mexican Railroad Workers in the United States, 1870–1930.* Denton: University of North Texas Press, 2012.

Gardner, Dore. *Niño Fidencio: A Heart Thrown Open.* Santa Fe: Museum of New Mexico Press, 1992.

Garner, Paul. *Porfirio Díaz: Profiles in Power.* London and New York: Longman, 2001.

Gilmore, Glenda Elizabeth. *Gender and Jim Crow: Women and the Politics of White Supremacy in North Carolina, 1896–1920.* Chapel Hill and London: University of North Carolina Press, 1996.

Ginzberg, Lori D. *Elizabeth Cady Stanton: An American Life.* New York: Hill and Wang, 2009.

Ginzburg, Carlo. *The Cheese and the Worms: The Cosmos of a Sixteenth-Century Miller.* Baltimore: Johns Hopkins University Press, 1992.

Goldberg, Mark. *Conquering Sickness: Race, Health, and Colonization in the Texas Borderlands.* Lincoln and London: University of Nebraska Press, 2016.

Goldsmith, Barbara. *Other Powers: The Age of Suffrage, Spiritualism, and the Scandalous Victoria Woodhull.* New York: Alfred A. Knopf, 1998.

Gómez, Laura E. *Manifest Destinies: The Making of the Mexican American Race.* New York and London: New York University Press, 2007.

Gonzales, Patrisia. *Red Medicine: Traditional Indigenous Rites of Birthing and Healing.* Tucson: University of Arizona Press, 2012.

González, Jovita. *Life Along the Border: A Landmark Tejana Thesis.* Edited and with an introduction by María Eugenia Cotera. College Station: Texas A&M University Press, 2006.

Gordon, Linda. *The Great Arizona Orphan Abduction.* Cambridge, MA: Harvard University Press, 1999.

———. *The Moral Property of Women: A History of Birth Control Politics in America.* Urbana and Chicago: University of Illinois Press, 2002.

Graziano, Frank. *Cultures of Devotion.* Oxford: Oxford University Press, 2007.

Graybill, Andrew, and Ben Johnson. *Bridging National Borders in North America:*

Transnational and Comparative Histories. Durham, NC, and London: Duke University Press, 2010.

Greenberg, Amy S. *Manifest Manhood and the Antebellum American Empire.* Cambridge: Cambridge University Press, 2005.

———. *A Wicked War: Polk, Lincoln, and the 1846 U.S. Invasion of Mexico.* New York: Alfred A. Knopf, 2012.

Greene, Jerome A. *American Carnage: Wounded Knee.* Norman: University of Oklahoma Press, 2014.

Griffith, James S. *Folk Saints of the Borderlands: Victims, Bandits, and Healers.* Tucson: Río Nuevo, 2003.

Griswold del Castillo, Richard. *The Los Angeles Barrio, 1850–1890: A Social History.* Berkeley: University of California Press, 1979.

———. *The Treaty of Guadalupe Hidalgo: A Legacy of Conflict.* Norman and London: University of Oklahoma Press, 1992.

Guerin-Gonzales, Camille. *Mexican Workers and the American Dream: Immigration, Repatriation, and California Farm Labor.* New Brunswick, NJ: Rutgers University Press, 1994.

Guidotti-Hernández, Nicole M. *Unspeakable Violence: Remapping U.S. and Mexican National Imaginaries.* Durham, NC, and London: Duke University Press, 2011.

Haake, Claudia B. *The State, Removal, and Indigenous Peoples in the United States and Mexico, 1620–2000.* New York: Routledge, 2007.

Haber, Stephan. *Industry and Underdevelopment: The Industrialization of Mexico, 1890–1940.* Stanford, CA: Stanford University Press, 1995.

Hahn, Steven. *A Nation Under Our Feet: Black Political Struggles in the Rural South from Slavery to the Great Migration.* Cambridge, MA, and London: Belknap Press of Harvard University, 2003.

———. *The Roots of Southern Populism: Yeoman Farmers and the Transformation of the Georgia Upcountry, 1850–1890.* Oxford: Oxford University Press, 2006.

Hale, Charles. *The Transformation of Liberalism in Late Nineteenth Century Mexico.* Princeton, NJ: Princeton University Press, 1990.

Haller, John S., Jr. *The History of American Homeopathy: From Rational Medicine to Holistic Health Care.* New Brunswick, NJ: Rutgers University Press, 2009.

———. *The History of American Homeopathy: The Academic Years, 1820–1935.* New York: Pharmaceutical Products Press, 2005.

———. *Kindly Medicine: Physio-Medicalism in America, 1836–1911.* Kent, OH, and London: Kent State University Press, 1997.

Hämäläinen, Pekka. *Comanche Empire.* New Haven and London: Yale University Press, 2008.

Hamnett, Brian R. *A Concise History of Mexico.* 2nd ed. Cambridge: Cambridge University Press, 2006.

———. *Juarez.* London and New York: Longman, 1994.

Hardin, Stephen L. *Texian Iliad: A Military History of the Texas Revolution.* Austin: University of Texas Press, 1994.

Harrington, Anne. *The Cure Within: A History of Mind-Body Medicine.* New York and London: W. W. Norton, 2008.

Harris, Ruth. *Lourdes: Body and Spirit in the Secular Age.* New York: Viking, 1999.

Hart, Charles R. *Brush and Weeds of Texas Rangelands*. College Station: Texas A&M University Press, 2008.

Harwell, Thomas Meade. *Studies in Texan Folklore—Rio Grande Valley*, Lore I: *Twelve Folklore Studies with Introductions, Commentaries & a Bounty of Notes*. Lewiston/Queenstown/Lampeter: Edwin Mellen, 1997.

Henderson, Timothy J. *A Glorious Defeat: Mexico and Its War with the United States*. New York: Hill and Wang, 2007.

Hendrickson, Brett. *Border Medicine: A Transcultural History of Mexican American Curanderismo*. New York: NYU Press, 2015.

Herrera-Sobek, María, ed. *Santa Barraza, Artist of the Borderlands*. College Station: Texas A&M University Press, 2001.

Hochschild, Adam. *King Leopold's Ghost: A Story of Greed, Terror, and Heroism in Colonial Africa*. Boston and New York: Houghton Mifflin, 1998.

Hoffman, Charles. *The Depression of the Nineties: An Economic History*. Westport, CT: Greenwood, 1970.

Hoganson, Kristin. *Fighting for American Manhood: How Gender Politics Provoked the Spanish-American and Philippine-American Wars*. New Haven and London: Yale University Press, 1998.

Holden, William Curry. *Teresita*. Owning Mills, MD: Stemmer House, 1978.

Hopgood, James P. *The Making of Saints: Contesting Sacred Ground*. Tuscaloosa: University of Alabama Press, 2005.

Howe, Daniel Walker. *What Hath God Wrought? The Transformation of America, 1815–1848*. Oxford: Oxford University Press, 2007.

Hu-Dehart, Evelyn. *Missionaries, Miners, and Indians: History of Spanish Contact with the Yaqui Indians of Northwestern New Spain, 1533–1830*. Tucson: University of Arizona Press, 1981.

———. *Yaqui Resistance and Survival: The Struggle for Land and Autonomy, 1821–1910*. Madison: University of Wisconsin Press, 1984.

Humphreys, Margaret. *Yellow Fever and the South*. Baltimore: Johns Hopkins University Press, 1999.

Hurtado, Albert L. *Intimate Frontiers: Sex, Gender, and Culture in Old California*. Albuquerque: University of New Mexico Press, 1999.

Illades Aguilar, Lillián. *La Rebelión de Tomóchic*. Mexico City: Instituto Nacional de Antropología y Historia, 1993.

Irwin, Robert McKee. *Bandits, Captives, Heroines, and Saints: Cultural Icons of Mexico's Northwest Borderlands*. Minneapolis: University of Minnesota Press, 2007.

Jarrett, Ada Morely. *The Life of the Harp in the Hand of the Harper*. Privately printed, Denver, 1897.

Johnson, Benjamin Heber. *Revolution in Texas: How a Forgotten Battle and Its Bloody Suppression Turned Mexicans into Americans*. New Haven and London: Yale University Press, 2003.

Johnson, Susan Lee. *Roaring Camp: The Social World of the California Gold Rush*. New York and London: W. W. Norton, 2000.

Joseph, Gilbert, and Jürgen Buchenau. *Mexico's Once and Future Revolution: Social Upheaval and the Challenge of Rule Since the Late Nineteenth Century*. Durham, NC, and London: Duke University Press, 2013.

Katz, Friedrich. *The Life and Times of Pancho Villa*. Stanford, CA: Stanford University Press, 1998.

———. *The Secret War in Mexico: Europe, the United States, and the Mexican Revolution*. Chicago: University of Chicago Press, 1981.

Kaufman, Martin. *Homeopathy in America: The Rise and Fall of a Medical Heresy*. Baltimore: Johns Hopkins Press, 1971.

Keating, AnaLouise, ed. *Entre Mundos/Among Worlds: New Perspectives on Gloria E. Anzaldúa*. New York: Palgrave Macmillan, 2005.

Keen, Benjamin. *The Aztec Image in Western Thought*. New Brunswick, NJ: Rutgers University Press, 1990.

Kehoe, Alice. *The Ghost Dance: Ethnohistory and Revitalization*. Long Grove, IL: Waveland, 2006.

Kiev, Ari. *Curanderismo: Mexican-American Folk Psychiatry*. New York: Free Press, 1968.

Kinkler, Kaja. *Spiritualist Healers in Mexico*. South Hadley, MA: Bergin and Garvey, 1985.

Kiple, Kenneth F., ed. *The Cambridge World History of Human Diseases*. Cambridge: Cambridge University Press, 1993.

Kirschmann, Anne Taylor. *A Vital Force: Women in American Homeopathy*. New Brunswick, NJ: Rutgers University Press, 2004.

Knight, Alan. *The Mexican Revolution*. Cambridge: Cambridge University Press, 1986.

Koyré, Alexandre. *From the Closed World to the Infinite Universe*. Baltimore: Johns Hopkins University Press, 1968.

Kraut, Alan M. *Silent Travelers: Germs, Genes, and the Immigrant Menace*. Baltimore: Johns Hopkins University Press, 1995.

Krauze, Enrique. *Francisco I. Madero: Místico de la Libertad*. Mexico City: Fondo de Cultura Económica, 1987.

———. *Mexico: Biography of Power; A History of Modern Mexico 1810–1996*. Translated by Hank Heifetz. New York: HarperCollins, 1998.

Kuethe, Allan J., and Kenneth J. Andrien. *The Spanish Atlantic World in the Eighteenth Century: War and the Bourbon Reforms, 1713–1796*. New York: Cambridge University Press, 2014.

Lack, Paul D. *The Texas Revolutionary Experience: A Political and Social History*. College Station: Texas A&M University Press, 1992.

Lanning, John T. *The Royal Protomedicato: The Regulation of the Medical Professions in the Spanish Empire*. Durham, NC: Duke University Press, 1985.

Larkin, Brian. *The Very Nature of God: Baroque Catholicism and Religious Reform in Bourbon Mexico City*. Albuquerque: University of New Mexico Press, 2010.

Larralde, Carlos. *Mexican-American Movements and Leaders*. Los Alamitos, CA: Hwong, 1976.

Lasater, Dale. *Falfurrias: Ed C. Lasater and the Development of South Texas*. College Station: Texas A&M University Press, 1985.

Lears, T. J. Jackson. *No Place of Grace: Antimodernism and the Transformation of American Culture, 1880–1920*. New York: Pantheon, 1981.

———. *Rebirth of a Nation: The Making of Modern America, 1877–1920*. New York: HarperCollins, 2009.

Leavitt, Judith Walzer. *Brought to Bed: Childbearing in America 1750 to 1950*. New York and Oxford: Oxford University Press, 1986.

León, Luis. *La Llorona's Children: Religion, Life, and Death in the U.S.-Mexico Borderlands*. Berkeley and Los Angeles: University of California Press, 2004.

Lerner, Gerda. *The Creation of a Feminist Consciousness: From the Middle Ages to Eighteen-seventy*. Vol. 2 of *Women in History*. Oxford: Oxford University Press, 1993.

Limón, José E. *Dancing with the Devil: Society and Cultural Poetics in Mexican-American South Texas*. Madison: University of Wisconsin Press, 1994.

Litwack, Leon. *Been in the Storm So Long: The Aftermath of Slavery*. New York: Vintage Books, 1980.

Long, Haniel. *Interlinear to Cabeza de Vaca: His Relation of the Journey, Florida to the Pacific, 1528–1536*. New York: Frontier Press, 1969.

Lytle Hernández, Kelly. *Migra: A History of the U.S. Border Patrol*. Berkeley: University of California Press, 2010.

Madsen, William. *The Mexican-Americans of South Texas*. New York: Holt, Rinehart and Winston, 1964.

———. *Society and Health in the Lower Río Grande Valley: Based Upon the Findings of the Hidalgo Project on Differential Culture Change and Mental Health*. Austin: University of Texas Press, 1961.

Maines, Rachel P. *The Technology of Orgasm: Hysteria, the Vibrator, and Women's Sexual Satisfaction*. Baltimore: Johns Hopkins University Press, 2001.

Margolis, Nadia. *Joan of Arc in History, Literature and Film*. New York and London: Garland, 1990.

Martin, Desirée A. *Borderlands Saints: Secular Sanctity in Chicano/a and Mexican Culture*. New Brunswick: Rutgers University Press, 2014.

Martinello, Marian L. *Don Pedrito Jaramillo: Folk Healer*. San Antonio: University of Texas Institute for Texan Cultures, 1982.

McClintock, Anne. *Imperial Leather: Race, Gender, and Sexuality in the Colonial Context*. New York: Routledge, 1995.

McCrossen, Alexis, ed. *Land of Necessity: Consumer Culture in the United States-Mexico Borderlands*. Durham, NC, and London: Duke University Press, 2009.

McGarry, Molly. *Ghosts of Futures Past: Spiritualism and the Cultural Politics of Nineteenth-Century America*. Berkeley: University of California Press, 2008.

Mckiernan-González, John. *Fevered Measures: Public Health and Race at the Texas-Mexico Border, 1848–1942*. Durham, NC, and London: Duke University Press, 2012.

McNeill, J. R. *Mosquito Empires: Ecology and War in the Greater Caribbean, 1620–1914*. Cambridge and New York: Cambridge University Press, 2010.

McWilliams, Carey. *North From Mexico: The Spanish-Speaking People of the United States*. New York, Westport (CT), and London: Praeger, 1948.

Melosi, Martin V. *The Sanitary City: Urban Infrastructure in America from Colonial Times to the Present*. Baltimore and London: Johns Hopkins University Press, 2000.

Meyer, Jean. *La Cristiada*. Mexico City: Siglo XXI, 1973–74.

Mirandé, Alfredo, and Evangelina Enríquez. *La Chicana: The Mexican-American Woman*. Chicago: University of Chicago Press, 1981.

Molina, Natalia. *Fit to Be Citizens? Public Health and Race in Los Angeles, 1879–1939*. Berkeley: University of California Press, 2006.

Monroe, John Warner. *Laboratories of Faith: Mesmerism, Spiritism, and Occultism in Modern France*. Ithaca, NY: Cornell University Press, 2008.

Montejano, David. *Anglos and Mexicans in the Making of Texas, 1836–1986*. Austin: University of Texas Press, 1987.

Mooney, James. *The Ghost Dance Religion and the Sioux Outbreak of 1890*. Chicago: University of Chicago Press, 1965.

Morantz-Sanchez, Regina Markell. *Sympathy and Science: Women Physicians in American Medicine*. New York and Oxford: Oxford University Press, 1985.

Mora-Torres, Juan. *The Making of the Mexican Border: The State, Capitalism, and Society in Nuevo León, 1848–1910*. Austin: University of Texas Press, 2001.

Neill, Deborah J. *Networks in Tropical Medicine: Internationalism, Colonialism, and the Rise of a Medical Specialty, 1890–1930*. Stanford, CA: Stanford University Press, 2012.

Ngai, Mae M. *Impossible Subjects: Illegal Aliens and the Making of Modern America*. Princeton, NJ, and Oxford: Princeton University Press, 2004.

Nye, David E. *Electrifying America: Social Meanings of a New Technology, 1880–1940*. Cambridge and London: MIT Press, 1990.

O'Connor, Mary I. *Descendants of Totoliquoqui: Ethnicity and Economics in the Mayo Valley*. Berkeley: University of California Press, 1989.

Opp, James. *The Lord for the Body: Religion, Medicine, and Protestant Faith Healing in Canada, 1880–1930*. Montreal and Kingston: McGill-Queen's University Press, 2005.

Orozco, Cynthia. *No Mexicans, Women, or Dogs Allowed: The Rise of the Mexican American Civil Rights Movement*. Austin: University of Texas Press, 2009.

Osorio, Rubén. *Tomóchic en Llamas*. Mexico City: Consejo Nacional para la Cultura y las Artes, 1995.

Ostler, Jeffrey. *The Plains Sioux and U.S. Colonialism from Lewis and Clark to Wounded Knee*. New York: Cambridge University Press, 2004.

Painter, Muriel Thayer. *With Good Heart: Yaqui Beliefs and Ceremonies in a Pasqua Village*. Tucson: University of Arizona Press, 1986.

Painter, Nell Irvin. *Sojourner Truth: A Life, A Symbol*. New York and London: W. W. Norton, 1996.

Paredes, Américo. *Folklore and Culture on the Texas-Mexican Border*. Austin: Center for Mexican American Studies, University of Texas at Austin, 1993.

———. *Folk Medicine and the Intercultural Jest*. Austin: Institute of Latin American Studies, University of Texas at Austin, 1969.

———. *A Texas-Mexican Cancionero: Folksongs of the Lower Border*. Austin: University of Texas Press, 1976.

———. *"With His Pistol in His Hand": A Border Ballad and Its Hero*. Austin: University of Texas Press, 1958.

Perales, Monica. *Smeltertown: Making and Remembering a Southwest Borderlands Community*. Chapel Hill: University of North Carolina Press, 2010.

Pérez, Emma. *The Decolonial Imaginary: Writing Chicanas Into History*. Bloomington and Indianapolis: Indiana University Press, 1999.

Perrone, Bobette H., Henrietta Stockel, and Victoria Krueger. *Medicine Women,*

Curanderas, and Women Doctors. Norman and London: University of Oklahoma Press, 1989.

Pohl, James W. *The Battle of San Jacinto*. Austin: Texas State Historical Association, 1989.

Porter, Joseph C. *Paper Medicine Man: John Gregory Bourke and His American West*. Norman and London: University of Oklahoma Press, 1986.

Porterfield, Amanda. *Healing in the History of Christianity*. Oxford: Oxford University Press, 2005.

Portilla, Elizabeth de la. *They All Want Magic: Curanderas and Folk Healing*. College Station: Texas A&M University Press, 2009.

Quirarte, Jacinto, and Carey Clements Rote. *César A. Martínez: A Retrospective*. Austin: University of Texas Press, 1999.

Raat, Dirk W. *Revoltosos: Mexico's Rebels in the United States, 1903–1923*. College Station: Texas A&M Press, 1981.

Ramaswamy, Sumathi. *The Goddess and the Nation: Mapping Mother India*. Durham, NC, and London: Duke University Press, 2010.

Ramos, Raquel Padilla. *Yucatán, Fin del Sueño Yaqui: El Tráfico de los Yaquis y el Otro Triunvirato*. Hermosillo: Gobierno del Estado de Sonora, 1995.

———. *Progreso y Libertad: Los Yaquis en la Víspera de la Repatriación*. Hermosillo: Programa Editorial de Sonora/Instituto Sonorense de Cultura, 2006.

Rasmussen, R. Kent. *Mark Twain A-Z: The Essential Reference to His Life and Writings*. New York and Oxford: Oxford University Press, 1995.

Remensnyder, Amy G. *La Conquistadora: The Virgin Mary at War and Peace in the Old and New Worlds*. Oxford: Oxford University Press, 2014.

Reséndez, Andrés. *Changing National Identities at the Frontier: Texas and New Mexico, 1800–1850*. Cambridge: Cambridge University Press, 2004.

———. *A Land So Strange: The Epic Journey of Cabeza de Vaca*. New York: Basic Books, 2007.

Reynolds, Ray. *Catspaw Utopia: Alfred K. Owen, the Adventurer of Topolobampo Bay, and the Last Great Utopian Scheme*. San Bernardino, CA: Borgo, 1996.

Richardson, Heather Cox. *Wounded Knee: Party Politics and the Road to an American Massacre*. New York: Basic Books, 2011.

Roeder, Beatrice A. *Chicano Folk Medicine from Los Angeles, California*. Berkeley: University of California Press, 1988.

Romo, David Dorado. *Ringside Seat to a Revolution: An Underground Cultural History of El Paso and Juárez: 1893–1923*. El Paso: Cinco Puntos, 2005.

Rothman, Shelia M. *Living in the Shadow of Death: Tuberculosis and the Social Experience of Illness in American History*. New York: Basic Books, 1994.

Royster, Jacqueline Joyce. *Southern Horrors and Other Writings: The Anti-Lynching Campaign of Ida B. Wells, 1892–1900*. Boston and New York: Bedford Books, 1997.

Ruíz, Ramón Eduardo. *The People of Sonora and Yankee Capitalists*. Tucson: University of Arizona Press, 1988.

Ruiz, Vicki L. *From Out of the Shadows: Mexican Women in Twentieth Century America*. Oxford: Oxford University Press, 1998.

Saborit, Antonio. *Los Doblados de Tomóchic: Un Episodio de Historia y Literatura*. Mexico City: Cal y Arena, 1994.

Sáenz, Andrés. *Early Tejano Ranching: Daily Life at Ranchos San José and El Fresni-*

llo. San Antonio: Institute for Texan Cultures, University of Texas at San Antonio, 1999.

Salas, Miguel Tinker. *In the Shadow of the Eagles: Sonora and the Transformation of the Border during the Porfiriato*. Berkeley: University of California Press, 1997.

Saldívar, Ramón. *The Borderlands of Culture: Américo Paredes and the Transnational Imaginary*. Durham, NC, and London: Duke UP, 2006.

Saldívar-Hull, Sonia. *Feminism on the Border: Chicana Gender Politics and Literature*. Berkeley: University of California Press, 2000.

Salomon, Carlos Manuel. *Pio Pico: The Last Governor of Mexican California*. Norman: University of Oklahoma Press, 2010.

Satter, Beryl. *Each Mind a Kingdom: American Women, Sexual Purity, and the New Thought Movement, 1875–1920*. Berkeley: University of California Press, 1999.

Sauvageau, Juan. *Stories That Must Not Die*. Los Angeles: Pan American, 1989.

Scheer, Mary L., ed. *Women and the Texas Revolution*. Denton: University of North Texas Press, 2012.

Schendel, Gordon. *Medicine in Mexico: From Aztec Herbs to Betatrons*. Austin and London: University of Texas Press, 1968.

Sedgwick, Eve Kosofsky. *Between Men: English Literature and Male Homosocial Desire*. New York: Columbia University Press, 1985.

Shah, Nayan. *Contagious Divides: Epidemics and Race in San Francisco's Chinatown*. Berkeley: University of California Press, 2001.

Shapin, Steven. *The Scientific Revolution*. Chicago: University of Chicago Press, 1998.

Sharp, Lynn L. *Secular Spirituality: Reincarnation and Spiritism in Nineteenth-Century France*. Lanham, MD: Lexington Books, 2006.

Shoemaker, Nancy. *Negotiators of Change: Historical Perspectives on Native American Women*. New York and London: Routledge, 1995.

Shorter, David Delgado. *We Will Dance Our Truth: Yaqui History in Yoeme Performances*. Lincoln and London: University of Nebraska Press, 2009.

Sierra, Justo. *The Political Evolution of the Mexican People*. Translated by Charles Ramsdell. Austin: University of Texas Press, 1969.

Simmons, Marc. *Witchcraft in the Southwest: Spanish and Indian Supernaturalism on the Río Grande*. Flagstaff, AZ: Northland, 1974.

Simpson, Lesley Byrd. *Many Mexicos*. Berkeley: University of California Press, 1960.

Smith, Sherry. *Reimagining Indians: Native Americans Through Anglo Eyes, 1880–1940*. Oxford: Oxford University Press, 2000.

Snowden, Frank M. *Naples in the Time of Cholera, 1884–1911*. Cambridge: Cambridge University Press, 1995.

Sontag, Susan. *Illness As Metaphor*. New York: Doubleday, 1977.

Spicer, Edward H. *Cycles of Conquest: The Impact of Spain, Mexico, and the United States on the Indians of the Southwest, 1533–1960*. Tucson: University of Arizona Press, 1962.

———. *People of Pascua*. Tucson: University of Arizona Press, 1988.

———. *The Yaquis: A Cultural History*. Tucson: University of Arizona Press, 1980.

Stage, Sarah. *Female Complaints: Lydia Pinkham and the Business of Women's Medicine*. New York and London: W. W. Norton, 1979.

Starr, Paul. *The Social Transformation of American Medicine*. New York: Basic Books, 1982.

Stavans, Ilan. *José Vasconcelos: The Prophet of Race*. New Brunswick, NJ: Rutgers University Press, 2011.

Steele, Volney. *Bleed, Blister, and Purge: A History of Medicine on the American Frontier*. Missoula, MT: Mountain Press, 2005.

Stepan, Nancy Leys. *"The Hour of Eugenics": Race, Gender, and Nation in Latin America*. Ithaca, NY, and London: University of Cornell Press, 1991.

St. John, Rachel. *Line in the Sand: A History of the Western U.S.–Mexico Border*. Princeton, NJ, and Oxford: Princeton University Press, 2011.

Stern, Alexandra Minna. *Eugenic Nation: Faults and Frontiers of Better Breeding in Modern America*. Berkeley: University of California Press, 2005.

Stoddard, Lothrop. *Reforging America: The Story of Our Nationhood*. New York and London: Charles Scribner's Sons, 1925.

———. *The Rising Tide of Color Against White World-Supremacy*. New York: Charles Scribner's Sons, 1925.

Stoler, Ann Laura. *Carnal Knowledge and Imperial Power: Race and the Intimate in Colonial Rule*. Berkeley: University of California Press, 2002.

Taves, Anne. *Fits, Trances, and Visions: Experiencing Religion from Wesley to James*. Princeton, NJ: Princeton University Press, 1999.

Taylor, William B. *Magistrates of the Sacred: Priests and Parishioners in Eighteenth Century Mexico*. Stanford, CA: Stanford University Press, 1998.

Tenorio-Trillo, Mauricio. *Mexico at the World's Fairs: Crafting a Modern Nation*. Berkeley and London: University of California Press, 1996.

Thompson, Jerry. *Cortina: Defending the Mexican Name in Texas*. College Station: Texas A&M University Press, 2007.

Tijerina, Andrés. *Tejano Empire: Life on the South Texas Ranchos*. College Station: Texas A&M University Press, 1998.

Torres, Eliseo, with Timothy L. Sawyer, Jr. *Curandero: A Life in Mexican Folk Healing*. Albuquerque: University of New Mexico Press, 2005.

———. *Healing with Herbs and Rituals: A Mexican Tradition*. Albuquerque: University of New Mexico Press, 2006.

Treviño-Hernández, Alberto. *Curanderos: They Heal the Sick with Prayers and Herbs*. Tucson: Hats Off Books, 2005.

Trotter, Robert T., II, and Juan Antonio Chavira. *Curanderismo: Mexican American Folk Healing*. Athens: University of Georgia Press, 1981.

Truett, Samuel, and Elliot Young. *Continental Crossroads: Remapping U.S.-Mexico Borderlands History*. Durham, NC, and London: Duke University Press, 2004.

Tucker, Catherine M. *Nature, Science, and Religion: Intersections Shaping Society and the Environment*. Santa Fe, NM: School For Advanced Research Press, 2012.

Turner, John Kenneth. *Barbarous Mexico*. 1910. Reprint, Austin: University of Texas Press, 1969.

Turner, Victor. *Dramas, Fields, and Metaphors: Symbolic Action in Human Society*. Ithaca, NY: Cornell University Press, 1974.

———. *The Ritual Process: Structure and Anti-Structure*. Ithaca, NY: Cornell University Press, 1969.

Tutino, John. *From Insurrection to Revolution in Mexico: Social Bases of Agrarian Violence, 1750–1940*. Princeton, NJ: Princeton University Press, 1986.

Ulrich, Laurel Thatcher. *A Midwife's Tale: The Life of Martha Ballard, Based on Her Diary, 1785–1812*. New York: Vintage Books, 1990.

Urrea, Luis Alberto. *The Hummingbird's Daughter*. New York: Little, Brown, 2005.
———. *The Queen of America*. New York: Little, Brown, 2011.
Utley, Robert M. *The Last Days of the Sioux Nation*. 2nd ed. New Haven: Yale University Press, 2004.
Valadés, José C. *Porfirio Díaz contra el Gran Poder de Dios: Las Rebeliones de Tomochic y Temósachic*. Mexico City: Ediciones Leega Júcar, 1985.
Valerio-Jiménez, Omar S. *River of Hope: Forging Identity and Nation in the Río Grande Borderlands*. Durham, NC, and London: Duke University Press, 2013.
Vanderwood, Paul J. *Disorder and Progress: Bandits, Police, and Mexican Development*. Lincoln and London: University of Nebraska Press, 1981.
———. *Juan Soldado: Rapist, Murderer, Martyr, Saint*. Durham, NC, and London: Duke University Press, 2004.
———. *The Power of God Against the Guns of Government: Religious Upheaval in Mexico at the Turn of the Nineteenth Century*. Stanford, CA: Stanford University Press, 1998.
Vargas Valdez, Jesús, ed. *Tomóchic: La Revolución Adelantada: Resistencia y Lucha de un Pueblo de Chihuahua contra el Sistema Porfirista (1891–1892)*. 2 vols. Juárez: Universidad Autónoma de Ciudad Juárez, 1994.
Vasconcelos, José. *The Cosmic Race/La Raza Cósmica*. Translated by Didier T. Jaén. Baltimore: Johns Hopkins University Press, 1997.
Vogel, Virgil J. *American Indian Medicine*. Norman and London: University of Oklahoma Press, 1970.
Warner, John Harley. *The Therapeutic Perspective: Medical Practice, Knowledge, and Identity in America, 1820–1895*. Cambridge. MA: Harvard University Press, 1986.
Weber, David. *Bárbaros: Spaniards and Their Savages in the Age of Enlightenment*. New Haven and London: Yale University Press, 2005.
———. *The Mexican Frontier, 1821–1846: The American Southwest Under Mexico*. Albuquerque: University of New Mexico Press, 1982.
———. *The Spanish Frontier in North America*. New Haven and London: Yale University Press, 1992.
Weiss, Harry B., and Howard K. Kemble. *The Great American Water Cure Craze: A History of Hydrotherapy in the United States*. Trenton: Past Times, 1967.
Welke, Barbara Young. *Recasting American Liberty: Gender, Race, Law, and the Railroad Revolution, 1865–1920*. Cambridge and New York: Cambridge University Press, 2001.
Werner, Michael S., ed. *Encyclopedia of Mexico: History, Society and Culture*. London: Routledge, 1998.
Wexler, Laura. *Tender Violence: Domestic Visions in an Age of U.S. Imperialism*. Chapel Hill: University of North Carolina Press, 2000.
Whissel, Kristin. *Picturing American Modernity: Traffic, Technology, and the Silent Cinema*. Durham, NC, and London: Duke University Press, 2008.
Wilentz, Sean. *The Rise of American Democracy: Jefferson to Lincoln*. New York: W. W. Norton, 2006.
Wilkinson, Charles. *Blood Struggle: The Rise of the Modern Indian Nation*. New York and London: W. W. Norton, 2005.
Wilson, Brian C. *Dr. John Harvey Kellogg and the Religion of Biologic Living*. Bloomington: Indiana University Press, 2014.

Womack, John, Jr. *Zapata and the Mexican Revolution*. New York: Knopf, 1969.

Wyckoff, James. *Franz Anton Mesmer: Between God and the Devil*. Englewood Cliffs, NJ: Prentice Hall, 1975.

Yetman, David, and Thomas Van Devender. *Mayo Ethnobotany: Land, History, and Traditional Knowledge in Northwest Mexico*. Berkeley: University of California Press, 2002.

Young, Elliot. *Caterino Garza's Revolution on the Texas-Mexico Border*. Durham, NC, and London: Duke University Press, 2004.

Young, James Harvey. *The Medical Messiahs: A Social History of Health Quackery in Twentieth-Century America*. Princeton, NJ: Princeton University Press, 1967.

Young, Robert J. C. *Postcolonialism: A Very Short Introduction*. Oxford: Oxford University Press, 2003.

Young, Sera L. *Craving Earth: Understanding Pica, the Urge to Eat Clay, Starch, Ice, and Chalk*. New York: Columbia University Press, 2011.

Zavaleta, Antonio N., and Alberto Salinas, Jr. *Curandero Conversations: El Niño Fidencio, Shamanism and Healing Traditions of the Borderlands*. Bloomington, IN: Author House, 2009.

Zellner, William W., and Marc Petrowsky, eds. *Sects, Cults, and Spiritual Communities: A Sociological Analysis*. Westport, CT: Praeger, 1998.

Chapters in Books

Agostini, Claudia. "Estrategias, Actores, Promesas y Temores en las Campañas de Vacunación Antivariolosa en México: Del Porfiriato a la Posrevolución (1880–1940)." *Ciência y Saúde Coletiva* 16, no. 2 (2011).

Arbuckle, H. C., III. "Don José and Don Pedrito." In *The Folklore of Texan Cultures*, edited by Francis Edward Abernethy and Dan Beaty, 84–87. Austin: Encino, 1974.

Avalos, Natalie. "Latinx Indigeneities and Christianity." In *The Oxford Handbook of Latino/a Christianities in the United States*. Oxford: Oxford University Press, forthcoming 2020.

Barrera, Mario, Carlos Muñoz, and Charles Ornelas. "The Barrio as Internal Colony." In *People and Politics in Urban Society*, edited by Harlan Hahn. Beverly Hills: Sage, 1972.

Blaetz, Robin. "Joan of Arc and the Cinema." In *Joan of Arc, A Saint for All Reasons: Studies in Myth and Politics*, edited by Dominique Goy-Blanquet, 143–144. Burlington, VT, and Hampshire: Ashgate, 2003.

Brewster, Keith, and Claire Brewster. "Ethereal Allies: Spiritism and the Revolutionary Struggle in Hidalgo." In *Faith and Impiety in Revolutionary Mexico*, edited by Matthew Butler, 93–110. New York: Palgrave Macmillan, 2007.

Broyles-Gonzáles, Yolanda. "Indianizing Catholicism: Chicana/India/Mexicana Indigenous Spiritual Practices in Our Image." In *Chicana Traditions: Continuity and Change*, edited by Norma Cantú and Olga Nájera-Ramírez, 117–133. Urbana and Chicago: University of Illinois Press, 2002.

Butler, Matthew. "Trouble Afoot? Pilgrimage in Cristero Mexico City." In *Faith and Impiety in Revolutionary Mexico*, edited by Matthew Butler, 149–167. New York: Palgrave Macmillan, 2007.

Carrillo, Ana María. "¿Indivisibilidad o Bifuración de la Ciencia?: La Instituciona-lización de la Homeopatía en México." In *Continuidades y Rupturas: Una Historia Tensa de la Ciencia en México*, edited by Francisco Javier Dosil Mancilla and Gerardo Sánchez Díaz. Morelia, Michoacán: Instituto de Investigaciones Históricas, Universidad Michoacana de San Nicolás de Hidalgo, Facultad de Ciencias, Universidad Nacional Autónoma de México, 2010.

Castañeda, Antonio I. "Engendering the History of Alta California, 1769–1848." In *Contested Eden: California Before the Gold Rush*, edited by Ramón Gutiérrez and Richard J. Orsi, 230–260. Berkeley: University of California Press, 1998.

Cruz, Lilia Aurora. "New Light on Pedro Jaramillo." In *Studies in Texan Folklore—Rio Grande Valley, Lore I: Twelve Folklore Studies with Introductions, Commentaries and a Bounty of Notes*, edited by Thomas Meade Harwell, 59–89. Lewiston/Queenstown/Lampeter: Edwin Mellen, 1997.

Dodson, Ruth. "Don Pedrito Jaramillo: The Curandero of Los Olmos." In *The Healer of Los Olmos and Other Mexican Lore*, edited by Wilson Hudson, 9–70. Dallas: Southern Methodist University Press and the Texas Folklore Society, 1951.

Domecq de Rodriguez, Brianda. "Teresa Urrea: La Santa de Cabora." In *Memoria del VII Simposio de Historia y Antropología*, 214–251. Hermosillo, Sonora, Mexico: Universidad de Sonora, Departamento de Historia y Antropología, 1982.

Fowler, Gene. "Don Pedrito and Dr. Mudd." In *Mystic Healers and Medicine Shows: Blazing Trails to Wellness in the Old West and Beyond*, edited by Gene Fowler, 51–60. Santa Fe, NM: Ancient City, 1997.

Fregoso, Rosa Linda. "Re-Imagining Chicana Urban Identities in the Public Sphere, Cool Chuca Style." In *Between Woman and Nation: Nationalisms, Transnational Feminisms, and the State*, edited by Caren Kaplan, Norma Alarcón, and Monoo Moallem, 72–91. Durham, NC, and London: Duke University Press, 1999.

González, Luis. "El Liberalism Triunfante." In *Historia General de México*, 2:897–925. Mexico City: El Colegio de México, 2007.

Gordon, Linda. "Internal Colonialism and Gender." In *Haunted by Empire: Geographies of Intimacy in North American History*, edited by Ann Laura Stoler, 427–451. Durham, NC, and London: Duke University Press, 2006.

Hernández-Ávila, Inés. "Tierra Tremenda: The Earth's Agony and Ecstasy in the Work of Gloria Anzaldúa." In *Entre Mundos/Among Worlds: New Perspectives on Gloria E. Anzaldúa*, edited by AnaLouise Keating, 233–240. New York: Palgrave Macmillan, 2005.

Johnston, William D. "Tuberculosis." In *The Cambridge World History of Human Diseases*, edited by Kenneth F. Kiple, 1059–1068. Cambridge: Cambridge University Press, 1993.

Kanellos, Nicolás. "Exiles, Immigrants, and Natives: Hispanic Print Culture in What Became the Mainland of the United States." In *Print in Motion: The Expansion of Publishing and Reading in the United States, 1880–1940*, edited by Carl F. Kaestle and Janice A. Radway, 312–338. Chapel Hill: University of North Carolina Press, 2009.

Katz, Friedrich. "Mexico: Restored Republic and Porfiriato, 1867–1910." In *Cambridge History of Latin America*, vol. 5, edited by Leslie Bethell, 3–79. Cambridge: Cambridge University Press, 1986.

Knight, Alan. "The Mentality and Modus Operandi of Revolutionary Anticlerical-ism." In *Faith and Impiety in Revolutionary Mexico*, edited by Matthew Butler, 21–57. New York: Palgrave Macmillan, 2007.

———. "Racism, Revolution, and Indigenismo: Mexico, 1910–1940." In *The Idea of Race in Latin America, 1870–1940*, edited by Richard Graham, 71–113. Austin: University of Texas Press, 1990.

Last, John M. "Miasma Theory." *Encyclopedia of Public Health*, edited by Lester Breslow. New York: Macmillan Reference, 2001.

León, Luis D. "Borderlands Bodies and Souls: Mexican Religious Healing Practices in East Los Angeles." In *Mexican American Religions: Spirituality, Activism, and Culture*, edited by Gastón Espinosa and Mario T. García, 296–325. Durham, NC, and London: Duke University Press, 2008.

Leyva, Yolanda Chávez. "Healing the Borderlands Across the Centuries." In *Grace and Gumption: The Women of El Paso*, edited by Marcia Hatfield Daudistel. Fort Worth: Texas Christian University Press, 2011.

Malagamba, Amelia. "Don Pedrito Jaramillo, una Leyenda Mexicana en el Sur de Texas." In *Entre la Magia y la Historia: Tradiciones, Mitos y Leyendas de La Frontera*, edited by José Manuel Valenzuela Arce, 63–75. Mexico City: El Colegio de La Frontera Norte, 1992.

Marx, Karl, and Friedrich Engels. "Manifesto of the Communist Party." In *The Marx-Engels Reader*, 2nd ed., edited by Robert C. Tucker, 473–500. New York and London: W. W. Norton, 1978.

McNeil, Brownie. "Curanderos in South Texas." In *And Horns on the Toads*, edited by Mody Coggin Boatright, 32–45. Texas Folklore Society. Denton: University of North Texas Press, 1959.

Meyer, Jean. "Mexico: Revolution and Reconstruction in the 1920s." In *The Cambridge History of Latin America*, vol. 5: *1870–1930*, edited by Leslie Bethell, 144–194. Cambridge: Cambridge University Press, 1986.

Morales Sarabia, Angelica. "The Culture of Peyote: Between Divination and Disease in Early Modern New Spain." In *Medical Cultures of the Early Modern Spanish Empire*, edited by John Slater, MariaLuz Lopez-Terrada, and Jose Pardo-Tomas, 21–39. Burlington, VT: Ashgate, 2014.

Moulin, Anne Marie. "The Pasteur Institute's International Network: Scientific Innovations and French Tropisms." In *Transnational Intellectual Networks: Forms of Academic Knowledge and the Search for Cultural Identities*, edited by Christophe Charle, Jürgen Schriewer, and Peter Wagner. Frankfurt: Campus Verlag, 2004.

Newell, Gillian E. "Teresa Urrea, Santa de Cabora and Early Chicana? The Politics of Representation, Identity, and Social Memory." In *The Making of Saints: Contesting Sacred Ground*, edited by James Hopgood, 90–106. Tuscaloosa: University of Alabama Press, 2005.

Norget, Kristin. "La Madre Tierra and Indigenous Moral Ecologies in Oaxaca, Mexico." In *Nature, Science, and Religion: Intersections Shaping Society and the Environment*, edited by Catherine M. Tucker, 85–105. Santa Fe, NM: School For Advanced Research Press, 2012.

Olds, Katrina. "Visions of the Holy in Counter-Reformation Spain: The Discovery and Creation of Relics in Arjona, c. 1628." In *The "Vision Thing": Studying Divine*

Intervention, edited by William A. Christman, Jr., and Gábor Klaniczay, 137–155. Budapest: Collegium Budapest, 2009.

Patterson, K. David. "Meningitis." In *The Cambridge World History of Human Disease*, edited by Kenneth F. Kiple, 877–878. Cambridge: Cambridge University Press, 1993.

Perales, Marian. "Teresa Urrea: Curandera and Folk Saint." In *Latina Legacies: Identity, Biography, and Community*, edited by Vikki Ruiz and Virginia Sánchez Korrol, 97–119. New York: Oxford University Press, 1998.

Quezada, Noemí. "The Inquisition's Repression of Curanderos." In *Cultural Encounters: The Impact of the Inquisition in Spain and the New World*, edited by Mary Elizabeth Perry and Anne J. Cruz, 36–54. Berkeley: University of California Press, 1991.

Ramos Escandón, Carmen. "Señoritas Porfirianas: Mujer e Ideología en el México Progresista, 1880–1910." In *Presencia y Transparencia: La Mujer en la Historia de México*, edited by Carmen Ramos et al. Mexico City: El Colegio de México, 1987.

Rasmussen, Kent R. *Mark Twain A-Z: The Essential Reference to His Life and Writings*. New York and Oxford: Oxford University Press, 1995.

Recorder, Cynthia Monter. "'Vieja a los Treinta Años': El Proceso de Enejecimiento Segun Algunas Revistas Mexicanas de Fines del Siglo XIX." In *Enjaular los Cuerpos*, edited by Julia Turñon, 281–323. Mexico City: El Colegio de México, 2008.

Smith-Rosenberg, Carroll. "The Woman as Androgyne: Social Disorder and Gender Crisis, 1870–1936." In *Disorderly Conduct: Visions of Gender in Victorian America*, 245–297. New York: Alfred A. Knopf, 1985.

Spivak, Gayatri Chakravorty. "Can the Subaltern Speak?" In *Marxism and the Interpretation of Culture*, edited by Cary Nelson and Lawrence Grossberg, 271–313. Chicago: University of Chicago Press, 1988.

Stern, Alexandra Minna. "Yellow Fever Crusade: U.S. Colonialism, Tropical Medicine and the International Politics of Mosquito Control, 1900–1920." In *Medicine at the Border: Disease, Globalization and Security, 1850 to the Present*, edited by Alison Bashford, 41–59. London: Palgrave, 2006.

Szasz, Ferenc M. "Francis Schlatter: The Healer of the Southwest." In *Mystic Healers and Medicine Shows: Blazing Trails to Wellness in the Old West and Beyond*, edited by Gene Fowler, 15–30. Santa Fe, NM: Ancient City, 1997.

Tadie, Andrew. "Introduction." In *Joan of Arc*, by Mark Twain, 9–17. San Francisco: Ignatius, 1989.

Turner, Kay F. "'Because of This Photography': The Making of a Mexican Folk Saint." In *Niño Fidencio: A Heart Thrown Open*, edited by Dore Gardner, 120–134. Santa Fe: Museum of New Mexico Press, 1992.

Washington, Ann Reed. "South Texas' Greatest Folk Healer." In *Roots by the River: A Story of Texas Tropical Borderlands*, edited by Valley By-Liners, 94–98. Mission, TX: Border Kingdom, 1978.

Worboys, Michael. "Tropical Diseases." In *Companion Encyclopedia of the History of Medicine*, vol. 1, edited by W. F. Bynum and Roy Porter. New York: Routledge, 1993.

Zavaleta, Antonio N. "El Niño Fidencio and the *Fidencistas*." In *Sects, Cults, and Spiritual Communities: A Sociological Analysis*, edited by William W. Zellner and Marc Petrowsky, 95–115. Westport, CT: Praeger, 1998.

Journal Articles and Presented Papers

Adorno, Rolena. "The Negotiation of Fear in Cabeza de Vaca's *Naufragios.*" *Representations*, no. 33 (Winter 1991). Special Issue: *The New World.*

Agostoni, Claudia. "Estrategias, Actores, Promesas y Temores en las Campañas de Vacunación Antivariolosa en México: Del Porfiriato a la Posrevolución (1880–1940)." *Ciência y Saúde Coletiva* 16, no. 2 (2011).

———. "Popular Health Education and Propaganda in Times of Peace and War in Mexico City, 1890s–1920s." *American Journal of Public Health* 96, no. 1 (2006).

Almaguer, Tomas. "Toward the Study of Chicano Colonialism." *Aztlán* 2 (Spring 1971).

Appleby, Joyce. "Commercial Farming and the Agrarian Myth in the Early Republic." *Journal of American History* 68 (March 1982): 833–849.

Arnold, Watson C. "Home Remedies, Folk Medicine, and Mad Stones." *Southwestern Historical Quarterly* 117, no. 2 (October 2013): 132–142.

Baud, Michiel, and Willem Van Shendel. "Toward a Comparative History of Borderlands." *Journal of World History* 8, no. 2 (Fall 1997): 211–242.

Baumgartner, Alice L. "The Line of Positive Safety: Borders and Boundaries in the Río Grande Valley, 1848–1880." *Journal of American History* 101, no. 4 (March 2015): 1106–1122.

Bayne, Brandon. "From Saint to Seeker: Teresa Urrea's Search for a Place of Her Own." *Church History* 75, no. 3 (September 2006): 594–597.

Bockarie, M. J., A. A. Gbakaima, and G. Barnish. "It All Began with Ronald Ross: One Hundred Years of Malaria Research and Control in Sierra Leonne (1899–1999)." *Annals of Tropical Medicine and Parasitology* 93, no. 3 (April 1999): 213–224.

Briggs, Laura. "The Race of Hysteria: 'Overcivilization' and the 'Savage' Women in Late Nineteenth Century Obstetrics and Gynecology." *American Quarterly* 52, no. 2 (June 2000): 246–273.

Campagne, Fabián Alejandro. "Charismatic Healers on Iberian Soil: An Autopsy of a Mythical Complex of Early Modern Spain." *Folklore* 118, no. 1 (2007): 44–64.

Carlson, Hannah. "Vulgar Things: James Fenimore Cooper's 'Clairvoyant' Pocket Handkerchief." *CommonPlace* 7, no. 2 (January 2007). www.commonplace.org.

Carrillo, Ana Maria. "Economía, Política y Salud Pública en el México Porfiriano (1876–1910)." *História, Ciências, Saúde-Manguinhos* 9 (2002).

———. "Médicos del México Decimonónico: Entre el Control Estatal y la Autonomía Professional." *Dynamis* 22 (2000): 351–375.

———. "Profesiones Sanitarias y Lucha de Poderes en el México del Siglo XIX." *Asclepio* 50, no. 2 (1998).

Carrillo, Ana Maria, and Anne-Emanuelle Birn. "Neighbors on Notice: National and Imperialist Interests in the American Public Health Association, 1872–1921." *CBMF/BCHM* 25, no. 1 (2008).

Carrier, John P. "Medicine in Texas: The Struggle with Yellow Fever, 1839–1903." *Texas Medicine* 82, no. 11 (November 1996): 62–65.

Chávez, John R. "Aliens in Their Native Lands: The Persistence of Internal Colonial Theory." *Journal of World History* 22, no. 4 (December 2011): 785–809.

Coatsworth, John. "Obstacles to Economic Growth in Nineteenth-Century Mexico." *American Historical Review* 83, no. 1 (February 1978): 80–100.

Cotera, María Eugenia. "Refiguring 'The American Congo': Jovita González, John Gregory Bourke, and the Battle Over Ethno-Historical Representations of the Texas Mexican Border." *Western American Literature* 35, no. 1 (Spring 2000): 75–94.

Draeger, Joan. "Don Pedrito—The Great Faith Healer." *Junior Historian* 24, no. 5 (March 1964).

Gill, Mario. "Teresa Urrea, la Santa de Cabora." *Historia Mexicana* 6, no. 24 (1957): 626–644.

Gloege, Timothy E. W. "Faith Healing, Medical Regulation, and Public Religion in Progressive Era Chicago." *Religion and American Culture: A Journal of Interpretation* 23, no. 2 (2013): 185–231.

Grua, David W. "In Memory of the Chief Bigfoot Massacre: The Wounded Knee Survivors and the Politics of Memory." *Western Historical Quarterly* 46 (Spring 2015): 31–51.

Guidotti-Hernández, Nicole M. "National Appropriations: Yaqui Autonomy, the Centennial of the Mexican Revolution and the Bicentennial of the Mexican Nation." *Latin Americanist* (March 2011): 69–92.

Gutiérrez, David G. "Migration, Emergent Ethnicity, and the 'Third Space': The Shifting Politics of Nationalism in Greater Mexico." *Journal of American History* 86, no. 2 (September 1999): 481–517. Special issue, *Rethinking History and the Nation-State: Mexico and the United States as a Case Study.*

Hennessy-Fiske, Molly. "Skirting Checkpoint Often Deadly: Ranches of Brooks County Become Killing Field for Migrants." *Dallas Morning News,* July 23, 2014, 13.

Hudson, William M. "Texas's Own Saint—Don Pedrito Jaramillo." *Frontier Times* 29, no. 8 (May 1952): 222–226.

Irwin, Robert McKee. "Santa Teresa de Cabora (and Her Villainous Sister Jovita): A Shape-Shifting Icon of Mexico's Northwest Borderlands." *Bilingual Review* 29, no. 2/3 (2008): 89–100.

Johnson, Benjamin H. "The Cosmic Race in Texas: Racial Fusion, White Supremacy, and Civil Rights Politics." *Journal of American History* (September 2011): 404–419.

Lamadrid, Enrique. "El Corrido de Tomóchic: Honor, Grace, Gender, and Power in the First Ballad of the Mexican Revolution." *Journal of the Southwest* 1, no. 4 (Winter 1999): 441–460.

Larralde, Carlos. "Santa Teresa: A Chicana Myth." *Grito del Sol: Chicano Quarterly* 3, no. 2 (1978): 5–114.

López Terrada, Maria Luz. "Medical Pluralism in the Iberian Kingdoms: The Control of Extra-academic Practitioners in Valencia." In *Medical History* 29, supplement (2009): 7–25.

Macklin, Barbara June, and N. Ross Crumrine. "Three North Mexican Folk Saint Movements." *Comparative Studies in Society and History* 15, no. 1 (January 1973): 89–105.

Madley, Benjamin. "Reexamining the American Genocide Debate: Meaning, Historiography, and New Methods." *American Historical Review* 120, no. 1 (February 2015): 98–139.

Molina, Natalia. "The Long Arc of Dispossession: Racial Capitalism and Contested

Notions of Citizenship in the U.S.-Mexican Borderlands in the Early Twentieth Century." *Western Historical Quarterly* 45 (Winter 2014): 431–447.

Nathan, Debbie. "The Best Laid Plan." *Texas Monthly* (February 2013). http://www.texasmonthly.com/articles/the-best-laid-plan/.

Nava, Alex. "Teresa Urrea: Mexican Mystic, Healer, and Apocalyptic Revolutionary." *Journal of the American Academy of Religion* 73, no. 2 (June 2005): 497–519.

Offenburger, Andrew. "When the West Turned South: Making Home Lands in Revolutionary Sonora." *Western Historical Quarterly* 45 (Autumn 2014): 299–319.

Price, Robin. "Spanish Medicine in the Golden Age." *Journal of the Royal Society of Medicine* 72 (November 1979): 864–865.

Prothero, Stephen. "From Spiritualism to Theosposy: 'Uplifting' a Democratic Tradition." *Religion and American Culture: A Journal of Interpretation* 3, no. 2 (Summer 1993): 197–216.

Putnam, Frank Bishop. "Teresa Urrea, 'the Saint of Cabora.'" *Southern California Quarterly* 45 (1963): 245–264.

Ramirez, Javier. "Mexican Cinema in *el Otro Lado*: A Case Study of the Exhibition of *Angelitos Negros* in San Antonio, Texas." Paper presented at the Borderlands and Latino Studies Fall Mini-Conference at the Newberry Library, Chicago, November 9, 2013.

Reavis, Dick. "The Saint of Falfurrias." *Texas Monthly* (January 1982): 98–103.

Rodriguez, Gloria L., and Richard Rodriguez. "Teresa Urrea: Her Life as It Affected the Mexican-U.S. Frontier." *El Grito* 5 (1972): 48–68.

Romano, Octavio Ignacio V. "Charismatic Medicine, Folk-Healing, and Folk-Sainthood." Pt. 1. *American Anthropologist* 67, no. 5 (October 1965): 1151–1173.

Sanders, Nichole. "Gender and Consumption in Porfirian Mexico: Images of Women in Advertising, *El Imparcial*, 1897–1910." *Frontiers: A Journal of Women Studies* 38, no. 1 (2017): 1–30.

Schellhous, E. J., MD. "Important Letter," *Carrier Dove* (July 1892): 223.

———. "Teresa Urrea, the Healing Medium of Cabora." *Carrier Dove* 7, no. 16 (August 1890).

Shapiro, David. "Lessons from Benjamin Rush." *Connecticut Medicine* 77, no. 6 (June 2013): 361–364.

Stubblefield, Lennie E. "Don Pedrito: Benefactor of Mankind." *Cattleman* (August 1988).

Taylor, William B. "The Virgin of Guadalupe in New Spain: An Inquiry into the Social History of Marian Devotion." *American Ethnologist* 14, no. 1 (February 1987): 9–33.

Torchia, Marion M. "Tuberculosis among American Negroes: Medical Research on a Racial Disease, 1830–1950." *Journal of the History of Medicine and Allied Sciences* 32 (1977): 252–279.

Torres-Raines, Rosario. "The Mexican Origin of Rituals, Ceremonies, and Celebrations in South Texas." *South Texas Studies* 7 (1996): 131–163.

Turner, Victor. "Ritual as Communication and Potency: An Ndembu Case Study." *Southern Anthropological Society Proceedings* 9 (1975): 58–81.

Wolf, Eric R. "The Virgin of Guadalupe: A Mexican National Symbol." *Journal of American Folklore* 71, no. 279 (January–March 1958): 34–39.

Wollenberg, Charles. "Working on El Traque: The Pacific Electric Strike of 1903." *Pacific Historical Review* 42, no. 3 (August 1973): 358–369.

Zabludovsky, Karla. "Hunting Humans: The Americans Taking Immigration Into Their Own Hands." *Newsweek*, July 23, 2014. http://www.newsweek.com/2014 /08/01/hunting-humans-americans-go-war-migrants-260642.html.

Zapata, Joel. "Women's Grassroots Revitalization of South El Paso: La Mujer Obrera's Challenge to Gentrification and Urban Neglect." *Río Bravo* 23, no. 1 (Spring 2014): 24–67.

Zefron, Lori J. "The History of Laying-on Hands in Nursing." *Nursing Forum* 14 (October 1975): 350–363.

Theses and Dissertations

Barreda, Roberto Corella. "Teresa Urrea: Dios Contra el Gobierno, Narrativa Histórica." Master's thesis, El Colegio de Sonora, 2005.

Bowman, Timothy. "Blood Oranges: Citriculture, Colonialism, and the Making of Anglo-American Identity in the Lower Río Grande Valley Borderlands During the Twentieth Century." PhD diss., Southern Methodist University, 2011.

Castro, Tiffany. "Teresa Urrea: Folk Saint of Porfirian Mexico." Senior thesis, University of California, Santa Barbara.

Delgado, Jessica. "A Saint of Many Myths: Teresa Urrea, Woman and Icon in Exile." Master's thesis, University of California, Santa Cruz, 1999.

Garza, Refugio S. "En el Nombre de Dios y Don Pedrito Jaramillo." Master's thesis, Texas College of Arts and Industry, Kingsville (later Texas A&M–Kingsville), 1952.

Godsey, Maria Yolanda. "Discursos y Representaciones de Teresa Urrea." Master's thesis, Texas A&M University–Kingsville, 2002.

Hendrickson, Brett. "Healing Borders: Transcultural Expressions of Mexican-American Folk Healing." PhD diss., Arizona State University, 2010.

Hernández-Berrones, Jethro. "Revolutionary Medicine: Homeopathy and the Regulation of the Medical Profession in Mexico, 1853–1942." PhD diss., University of California, San Francisco, 2014.

Martin, Désirée. "Bordered Saints: Unorthodox Sanctity Along the Border in Mexican and Chicana/o Literature." PhD diss., Duke University, 2004.

Mazzaferri, Anthony J. "Public Health and Social Revolution in Mexico: 1877–1930." PhD diss., Kent State University, 1968.

Morgan, Brandon. "Columbus, New Mexico, and Palomas, Chihuahua: Transnational Landscapes of Violence, 1888–1930." PhD diss., University of New Mexico, 2013.

Ribb, Richard Henry. "José Tomás Canales and the Texas Rangers: Myth, Identity, and Power in South Texas, 1900–1920." PhD diss., University of Texas at Austin, 2001.

Romano, Octavio. "Don Pedrito Jaramillo: The Emergence of a Mexican-American Folk Saint." PhD diss., University of California, Berkeley, 1964.

Sánchez, Aaron E. "From Pocholandia to Aztlán: Belonging, Homeland, Politics, and Citizenship in U.S.-Mexican Thought, Texas 1910–1979." PhD diss., Southern Methodist University, 2012.

Schraeder, Lia Theresa. "The Spirits of the Times: The Mexican Spiritist Movement from Reform to Revolution." PhD diss., University of California, Davis, 2009.

Urrea, Barbara. "Voice, Gender, and Collaboration in the 'Autobiographies' of Teresa Urrea and Georgia O'Keeffe." Master's thesis, Arizona State University, 1993.

Vaquera, Calli Johnson. "'If 3000 Men Were Unanimous on Any Subject, You Would Know At Once They Were Not Doctors': The Slow and Difficult Path To Professionalization of Medicine in Texas." Master's thesis, University of Texas at Arlington, 2006.

Index

Note: page numbers in *italics* refer to figures.